Drug Interventions
in Criminal Justice

oks

Drug Interventions in Criminal Justice

Edited by
Anthea Hucklesby and Emma Wincup

Open University Press

Open University Press
McGraw-Hill Education
McGraw-Hill House
Shoppenhangers Road
Maidenhead
Berkshire
England
SL6 2QL

email: enquiries@openup.co.uk
world wide web: www.openup.co.uk

and
Two Penn Plaza, New York, NY 10121-2289, USA

First published 2010

A catalogue record of this book is available from the British Library

ISBN-13: 978-0-33-523581-0 (pb) 978-0-33-523580-3 (hb)
ISBN-10: 0-33-523581-6 (pb) 0-33-523580-8 (hb)

Library of Congress Cataloging-in-Publication Data
CIP data applied for

Typeset by Aptara Inc., India
Printed in the UK by Bell and Bain Ltd, Glasgow.

Fictitious names of companies, products, people, characters and/or data that may be used herein (in case studies or in examples) are not intended to represent any real individual, company, product or event.

Mixed Sources
Product group from well-managed
forests and other controlled sources
www.fsc.org Cert no. TT-COC-002769
© 1996 Forest Stewardship Council
FSC

The **McGraw·Hill** Companies

Contents

List of figures

List of tables

Notes on the contributors

Anthea Hucklesby is Reader in Criminal Justice and Deputy Director of the Centre for Criminal Justice Studies, University of Leeds.

Stuart Lister is Lecturer in Criminal Justice at the Centre for Criminal Justice Studies in the School of Law, University of Leeds.

George Mair is Professor of Criminal Justice at Liverpool John Moores University.

Gill McIvor is Professor of Criminology at the University of Stirling, Co-Director of the Scottish Centre for Crime and Justice Research and Visiting Professor at the Glasgow School of Social Work, University of Strathclyde.

Matthew Millings is Lecturer in Criminal Justice at Liverpool John Moores University.

Ian Paylor is Head of the Department of Applied Social Science at Lancaster University.

Layla Skinns is a Lecturer in the Centre for Criminological Research at the University of Sheffield.

Alex Stevens is Senior Lecturer in Criminology at the University of Kent.

Paul J. Turnbull is Co-Director of the Institute for Criminal Policy Research at King's College London.

Alison Wilson is a Senior Associate Researcher based in ASSURE at Lancaster University.

Emma Wincup is Senior Lecturer in Criminology and Criminal Justice at the University of Leeds and Deputy Director of the Centre for Criminal Justice Studies.

1 Introduction

Anthea Hucklesby and Emma Wincup

Crime remains high on the political agenda and it has become something of a truism to state that a large part of the crime problem is related to illegal drug use. In particular, the consumption of heroin, crack and cocaine is viewed as a primary contributor to a range of crimes, especially acquisitive crime which forms the greatest proportion of crime statistics. Consequently, breaking the drugs–crime link has become one of the main aims of drug policy during the past decade. Initiatives to tackle drug-related crime have proliferated and have emerged within a rapidly changing landscape of legislation, policy, and service provision. Criminal justice agencies have become key players in channelling drug users into drug treatment services.

This book focuses on the range of drug interventions now available at all stages in the criminal justice process which have been put in place to reduce drug-related offending. It comprises a series of eight chapters from eleven authors who were all actively engaged in researching these new initiatives from criminological/criminal justice perspectives. Each chapter brings together theory, policy and research (including the author's own research) to provide a thorough review and analysis of the operation, impact and effectiveness of one or more drug interventions. A further chapter is dedicated to researching drug interventions in criminal justice.

Many of the measures which are discussed in this book have been brought together under the Drug Interventions Programme (DIP) and as a result it merits more detailed discussion in a separate chapter (see Turnbull and Skinns, Chapter 4 this volume). Despite some of the measures predating the creation of DIP and others falling outside its remit, this programme is currently the main vehicle for promoting desistance from drug-related crime and has been heavily resourced. DIP links together drug and criminal justice agendas, both political priorities since Labour came into power in 1997. It epitomizes the shifting emphasis of drug policy towards achieving criminal justice rather than health-orientated goals. Nonetheless, the provision of drug treatment requires the health care infrastructure to operate and DIP is an arena in which the policies and responsibilities of several government departments come together.

Our principal aim in this introduction is to highlight some of the issues raised in the chapters which follow. In the next section we investigate academic understandings of the link, or more precisely links, between illegal drug use and criminal behaviour. We then turn our attention to the development of drug policy across the UK and its implementation. In particular, we consider the emphasis placed on partnership working, the opportunities it purports to offer and the difficulties of realizing these in practice. Finally, we consider three themes which arise throughout the subsequent chapters: the effectiveness of drug treatment provision, the importance of throughcare, and equality and diversity issues. However, before going further it is necessary to reflect briefly on terminology used in the book to describe those individuals subject to the various drug interventions offered throughout the criminal justice process.

The drug interventions which are the concern of this book are aimed at drug users whose use of drugs is judged to be problematic. Readers need to be aware that there is little agreement about what constitutes problem drug use. The government tends to view problem drug users as individuals who use Class A drugs, judged to be the most harmful and closely linked with offending, namely heroin, cocaine and crack. Indeed, most legislation relating to drug interventions uses this criterion for inclusion (for examples see Mair and Millings, and Hucklesby, Chapters 5 and 6 this volume). For criminal justice agencies, the most problematic aspect of such drug use is involvement in offending behaviour, and especially acquisitive crime which is purportedly linked to funding drug use. Given the sheer diversity of players involved in working with drug users, it is inevitable that others might adopt alternative definitions. For example, they might focus on those engaged in drug use – sometimes referred to as drug misuse – which is problematic in the sense that it has harmful consequences in terms of health. Such definitions, which may be more or less exclusive than those adopted by criminal justice agencies, tend to focus on behaviours such as drug injecting or polydrug use or patterns of consumption, for example whether use is excessive or indicative of dependence.

Drugs and crime

While few would dispute that there is a relationship between drug use and crime, both the nature and the extent of the relationship are widely debated. By and large in media and public discourse, the relationship between drug use and crime is clear and the solutions straightforward: criminal justice agencies need to take firm action against those 'addicts' who repeatedly offend to finance their 'habit' (see Taylor, 2008). In contrast, a recurring theme within academic research is the need to appreciate the complexities of the drug–crime nexus and adopt a multifaceted response. We cannot do justice here to the breadth of work which has explored the connections between drug use and crime (see Bennett and Holloway, 2007, 2009; McSweeney et al., 2007 for recent reviews). Instead we offer a brief overview of the literature.

Conceptualizing the links between drug use and crime is a complex task and, unsurprisingly, some academics have chosen to make it more manageable by restricting their analysis to particular forms of crime: for example, Goldstein (1985) concentrated on the links between drug use and violence, whereas Seddon (2000) focused on the relationship between 'non-recreational' (in essence problematic use) and 'acquisitive' crime (i.e. theft, burglary, robbery, shoplifting, fraud and deception). Given the range of behaviour encompassed by the concepts of 'crime' and 'drug use', this appears to be the most appropriate way to proceed. The typical approach adopted by those seeking to make sense of the connections between drug use and crime is to develop a typology, although there is disagreement on the number of categories within them (see, for example, Bean, 2008; Bennett and Holloway, 2007, 2009; Hough,1996; McSweeney et al., 2007; Seddon, 2000). The usual starting point is to consider whether there is a causal relationship between drug use and crime and, if so, which behaviour precedes the other. In general terms, the conclusion reached is that we should be wary of explanations that suggest that crime is an inevitable consequence of drug use or vice versa because although research studies may provide some data which support the view that drug use and crime are strongly linked, it is difficult to disentangle which behaviour is the cause, which is the effect and what is the role played by other factors. Furthermore, it is important not to rule out the possibility that crime and drug use are behaviours which occur simultaneously yet are not linked.

Critical commentary on studies which do attempt to argue for a direct causal relationship between drug use and crime have helped to shift understanding away from overly deterministic explanations in favour of those which take on board the complex nature of the relationship and the range of factors which may be related to both drug use and crime. While such explanations are in many respects not fully developed, there is a growing appreciation of the plethora of risk factors – individual, cultural, socio-economic, environmental – associated with both drug use and crime. For example, Lloyd's (1998) review of risk factors for problem drug use (defined loosely as non-experimental use) found that involvement in crime was a risk factor for problem drug use but there were many other factors relating to the family (for example, parental or sibling drug use), school (for example, exclusion), mental disorder, social deprivation and young age of onset of drug use. He concluded that these factors are highly connected and best viewed as a 'web of causation' (Lloyd, 1998: 217).

In the next section we turn our attention to the development of strategic thinking on how best to deal with drug use. In many respects, a somewhat simplistic understanding underpins policy and practice with its current emphasis on tackling drug-related crime through tasking criminal justice agencies with channelling suspects, defendants and offenders into treatment. However, there is a growing realization within strategies of the need for a more holistic approach to preventing and treating drug use.

The development of strategic thinking in the UK

Drug strategies typically operate in three spheres: prevention, treatment and enforcement (Fraser and Padel, 2002), and all current strategies across the UK, and their predecessors, include this trio of interventions. We can trace the development of a genuine strategic response to tackling drugs back to 1995 when the White Paper *Tackling Drugs Together* (Home Office, 1995) was published. Focused solely on England, it laid the foundations for successive drug strategies by putting in place structures to establish a coordinated approach, most notably through the creation of Drug Action Teams (DATs) (to be discussed in the next section). It also signalled the development of Prison Service drug strategies (see Paylor et al., Chapter 9 this volume). Other parts of the UK assumed a broadly similar approach; however, there were some distinctive aspects. For example, the first Welsh strategy (Welsh Office, 1996) chose to include alcohol in its remit and has continued to do so in successive strategies (National Assembly for Wales, 2000; Welsh Assembly Government, 2008).

The 1995 strategy was quickly followed by a more far-reaching strategy published in 1998 (President of the Council, 1998) which attempted to lay out the trajectory of drug policy for a further decade. It focused mainly on England but described itself as relevant to Scotland, Wales and Northern Ireland. Each of these three countries subsequently produced its own strategic thinking with the content being dictated by the political changes related to devolution which had taken place shortly before their preparation. For example, the newly created Scottish Parliament was granted powers to make and implement crime policies which were distinctive (see McIvor, Chapter 7 this volume) whereas the National Assembly for Wales was not.

Within *Tackling Drugs to Build a Better Britain* (President of the Council, 1998) there were early indications of what was to follow. The document recognized the need to tackle drug-related crime and anti-social behaviour, and included reducing levels of repeat offending among drug-misusing offenders as one of its four key objectives. Included in the programme of action to achieve this objective were references to using criminal justice agencies – the police and the courts – as referral agents, and an accompanying performance indicator was to 'increase the number of offenders referred to and entering treatment programmes as a result of arrest referral schemes, the court process and post-sentencing provision' (President of the Council, 1998: 19). Furthermore, a further key objective was to 'increase participation of problem drug misusers, including prisoners, in drug treatment programmes which have a positive impact on health and crime' (President of the Council, 1998: 23) and similarly the numbers of participants were to be monitored as a mechanism for scrutinizing the progress of the strategy's progress.

Before the 1998 strategy had reached the end of its 'shelf-life', an updated version was published (Home Office, 2002). Forming part of an attempt to sharpen the focus of drug policy and improve its effectiveness, the 2002 strategy was not an attempt to start 'from scratch' (Home Office, 2002: 3), but it did include a number of new developments. Most significantly, given the focus of this edited collection, it proposed a major expansion of services within the criminal justice system 'using every opportunity from arrest, to court, to sentence' to get drug-misusing offenders into treatment (Home Office, 2002: 4) alongside a stronger emphasis on Class A drugs and problem drug users who cause the greatest harm to themselves and their communities. The Drug Interventions Programme (DIP) launched in 2003 was a realization of the strategic thinking advanced in the previous year. Described in more detail in Turnbull and Skinns (Chapter 4, this volume), DIP aimed to bring together the different interventions which had proliferated to channel into treatment drug users caught up in the criminal justice process. It aims to promote continuity of 'care' and enhance the effectiveness of treatment through the provision of ongoing support relating to drug use and other problems, for example housing.

The most recent drug strategy – *Drugs: Protecting Families and Communities* (HM Government, 2008) – continues to advocate the importance of using criminal justice processes as a mechanism to refer drug users into treatment and places especial attention on those drug users perceived to cause the most harm. Like its predecessor it continues to emphasize a particular understanding of the relationship between drug use and crime. Within the strategy there is a tendency to assume that all those who use Class A drugs are problem drug users who commit crime as a direct consequence of their drug use, thus promoting abstinence from drugs will result in desistence from offending. The 2008 strategy (HM Government, 2008) does identify that former drug users need support to address problems which make it difficult for them to become reintegrated into society. Recognition of this is closely allied to broader government agendas to tackle social exclusion through addressing worklessness.

The 2008 drug strategy highlights the vital role played by the Prison and Probation services in addressing drug-related offending. Developing this further, the National Offender Management Service (NOMS) launched its own three-year drug strategy later the same year (NOMS, 2008), three years after it published the first one (NOMS, 2005). The new strategy has two main strands relating to improving the effectiveness of existing services and developing new initiatives in prison and in the community respectively. It is accompanied by an action plan which sets out the measures that will be taken by NOMS and its partnership agencies to deliver these two strands. Partnership working has been a consistent theme within drug strategies and therefore merits more detailed discussion in the section below.

Partnership working

The promotion of joint working at all levels is not peculiar to drugs policy but has been advocated to tackle crime more generally and a wider range of social policy concerns (see Carnwell and Buchanan, 2008, for examples). It forms part of the Labour government's attempt to modernize the organization and delivery of public services through continued adoption of the principles of new public managerialism (McLaughlin et al., 2001). The 1995 strategy (Home Office, 1995) paved the way with the introduction of Drug Action Teams. These multi-agency partnerships bring together key agencies from health, local authorities (social services, education, housing) and criminal justice, and since 2001 have operated with the same boundaries as local authorities. While some Drug Action Teams remain, others have ceased to exist in their own right and have merged with the Crime and Disorder Reduction Partnerships formed following the Crime and Disorder Act 1998 which have a specific statutory responsibility with regard to 'substance misuse'. The key mechanism for delivering the current drug strategy is Local Strategic Partnerships. These are non-statutory locally based partnerships which act as a single overarching coordination framework within which other partnerships can operate.

The literature on partnership working (see Carnwell and Buchanan, 2008, for a recent example) has consistently emphasized the gap between the ideals of joint working, namely coordination and integration, and the reality. Subsequent chapters in this volume concur with this view (see, for example, Turnbull and Skinns Chapter 4, Hucklesby, Chapter 6 and Paylor et al., Chapter 9), emphasizing, in particular, the tensions and conflicts which can arise when the distinct professional ideologies, culture and practices of health care providers and criminal justice agencies come together. These research findings remind us that it is foolish to assume that partnership working is a panacea for tackling complex social problems, and encouragingly the 1998 strategy (President of the Council, 1998) recognized the need to adopt a more judicious approach. It warns that 'partnership is not an end in itself, and can be an excuse for blurring responsibilities and inactivity' (President of the Council, 1998: 11). Nonetheless it advocates partnership working because it offers the potential to have a greater impact on the drugs 'problem' than the actions of disparate agencies. The latest drug strategy (HM Government, 2008) continues to emphasize partnership working.

Partnership working at a local level has been mirrored with developments at a national level. Tackling Drugs to Build a Better Britain (President of the Council, 1998) was pioneered by a 'Drugs Tsar' located in the Cabinet Office with a cross-departmental coordinating brief. Since 1998 there has been a major shift in responsibility. By the time the *Updated Drug Strategy* (Home Office, 2002) had been launched in 2002, drug policy was the responsibility of the Home Office and it is important to appreciate that the Home Office which took on this role looked considerably different from the current Home Office. The Home Office is now responsible for immigration control, security and order. Following the creation of the Ministry of Justice in 2007, it retained responsibility for policing, but other aspects of criminal justice now come under the auspices of the Ministry of Justice. The Home Office shares responsibility for drug policy with other government departments: both the Department of Health and Department for Children, Schools and Families own Public Service Agreement targets related to drugs, and others, including the Ministry of Justice, are tasked with playing a significant role in the delivery of the strategy. Government departments are supported by the work of national government agencies who are most directly involved in delivering the strategy. Of particular significance to our focus here on drug interventions is the creation of the National Treatment Agency (NTA) in 2001, a special health authority within the NHS, whose role is to improve the availability, capacity and effectiveness of drug treatment.

There is also partnership working at a regional level through the plethora of new structures which have developed during the past decade. England is now divided into nine regions, each with its own government office. Working in conjunction with other regional partners (for example, the NTA regional offices and regional offender managers), one of their roles is to provide support to local partnerships with responsibility for drug policy and to identify and share good practice (see HM Government, 2008). They have taken on the work previously undertaken by the Home Office Drug Prevention Advisory Teams in the hope that regional activity on drugs can become more closely allied to other regional government responsibilities, for example neighbourhood renewal.

It is important to emphasize that the latest drug strategy (HM Government, 2008) proposes an alternative approach to promoting partnership working. While it does not advocate the abolition of drug-specific delivery structures which have been developed, it seems to favour 'mainstreaming' the delivery of the drug strategy by ensuring that 'action to tackle substance misuse is at the core of national, regional and local planning and delivery processes in all departments and agencies that have a role to play in delivering the drug strategy' (HM Government, 2008: 38). It is too early to tell how this might play out in practice but it is possible that it signals the end of the DIP as it currently operates.

Despite the rhetoric of partnership working, DIP currently operates largely as standalone programme with little integration into the broader structures of criminal justice. This position has arisen for a two main reasons. Firstly, DIP currently has a ring-fenced funding stream. Secondly, DIP comes under the remit of the Home Office rather than the Ministry of Justice despite relying on many agencies who are managed through the Ministry of Justice for its effective implementation. The separation at a strategic level has been translated on the ground with DIP working in parallel with other criminal justice agencies such as the Probation Service, resulting in overlaps and gaps in service provision particularly in relation to wraparound issues (see Hucklesby, Chapter 6 this volume). Information exchanges and coordination have also been victims of the separation of DIP from the wider criminal justice system (Ville and Company, 2009). Recent moves to increase coordination between the sectors can be seen in the setting-up of pioneer sites of Integrated Offender Management model (see Lister and Wincup, Chapter 3, and Turnbull and Skinns, Chapter 4 this volume), although at the time of writing (autumn 2009) funding for these ceases in March 2010 leaving their future uncertain. Contemporaneously, the future of ring-fenced funding for DIP must be in doubt given the expectation that public spending will have to be reduced. This is despite a recommendation that DIP remains separately funded and some evidence that it provides value for money (Ville and Company, 2009). The danger of mainstreaming and/or removing the ring-fenced finance is that the money will be siphoned off into other services and less emphasis will be placed upon tackling drug use (Ville and Company, 2009). But it may also have benefits, most notably less duplication, increased coordination and an increased likelihood that underlying causes of drug use and offending will be tackled.

Having examined drug strategies and the structures in place to implement them we now turn our attention to several themes which arise consistently in the chapters that follow.

The effectiveness of drug treatment

Successive drug strategies are premised on the assumption that treatment works. There is an unquestioning commitment to using drug treatment as a mechanism to reduce crime rates. Every intervention requires suspects, defendants and offenders to undergo an assessment and then comply with follow-up treatment or face an alternative that many would regard as less desirable. This raises a number of issues which are discussed in this section. The first of these is whether treatment capacity is sufficient and whether it is geographically situated in the right places. There is no doubt that the availability of treatment has improved since 2001, but lack of capacity in some areas, and the extended waiting times which result, limit access to treatment (Luty, 2002; Marsden et al., 2009).

The second related point is whether the available treatment is appropriate. There is a tendency for treatment services to concentrate on opiate users while services for other users – including those who use crack, cocaine and stimulants – are generally much more limited. Even within opiate services, the range of treatment is often restricted to methadone or other substitute prescribing, resulting in some users complaining about a lack of diversity of treatment (see, for example, Hucklesby et al., 2007). Arguably, the domination of substitute prescribing in drug treatment services has arisen partly because of the criminal justice agenda: it is the quickest and easiest way to meet short-term targets related to reductions in offending because, in theory at least, it deals with the need to commit crime to fund drug use (Coid et al., 2000). Evidence of its ability to deal with drug use in the longer term is more limited. Indeed, some drug users talk about being 'parked on methadone' and are critical of the policy of substitute prescribing believing that it does not deal with their drug problems (see Hucklesby et al., 2007). Furthermore, some individuals consistently report that they 'top up' their methadone prescriptions with heroin (Hucklesby and Wincup, 2007a,b; Hucklesby et al., 2007). By contrast, prison treatment services concentrate on detoxification and psycho-social interventions, although there is little evidence of the latter's success in terms of reducing drug use (PricewaterhouseCoopers, 2007). Consequently there is a lack of fit between prison- and community-based services. Criminal justice interventions have also been criticized for failing to deal with the underlying causes of drug use and so-called wraparound issues such as housing, accommodation and employment (see, for example, Hucklesby et al., 2007; Ville and Company, 2009; Turnbull and Skinns, Chapter 4 this volume). This may partially reflect the location of DIP interventions within criminal justice rather than broader social policy or public health agendas.

The third issue is related to the indiscriminate nature of the drug interventions used by criminal justice agencies and the extent to which the interventions capture drug users in need of treatment who have yet to access it. Undoubtedly, problem drug users who have never accessed treatment or who have not done so recently are captured by the various drug interventions. However, they also ensnare individuals who do not regard their own use of drugs as problematic and for whom there is little evidence that their use of drugs has harmful consequences for wider society. An example would be occasional cocaine users for whom use of drugs and involvement in crime is largely coincidental (see Hucklesby et al., 2007; Hucklesby, Chapter 6 this volume). What to do with these individuals, sometimes for considerable periods of time, presents challenges for drug workers. A second group who are caught up in the DIP, when arguably they may not need to be, are individuals who are already receiving treatment. The extent of 'recycling' of individuals within DIP is not clear. If the link between drug use and crime is as strong as suggested by some then levels of recycling would be expected to be high especially among those offenders who fail to complete DIP. Currently, measuring the extent of individuals re-entering DIP is difficult because it is impossible to access the necessary data owing to only anonymized data being made available (see Hucklesby and Wincup, Chapter 2 this volume). Measuring the extent of 'recycling' is important because it is likely to distort outcomes and overestimate the effectiveness and value for money of the DIP.

The introduction of the 'tough choices' agenda emphasizes the place that coercion plays in the DIP which is the fourth issue (see Skodbo et al., 2007). At each stage of DIP, suspects, defendants and offenders are given the 'choice' whether to engage with treatment. The choice is not a free one as the alternative is something undesirable such as being remanded in custody. While critics have often suggested that coercing people into treatment makes treatment less likely to be successful, there is now an array of evidence to suggest that coerced treatment is at least as effective as treatment entered into voluntarily (see Stevens, Chapter 8 this volume). Another, arguably more pertinent, issue is whether individuals should be coerced into treatment at all, particularly when they have yet to be found guilty of committing an offence. There is certainly a rights-based argument that individual should be able to use drugs if they so wish provided that they do so in ways which are not harmful to others. The Welfare Reform Act 2009 (Schedule A1) which allows for benefit claimants to be questioned and interviewed about their drug use and in some circumstances drug tested. Claimants whose drug use in deemed to impact upon their availability to work are required to be assessed and abide by a rehabilitation plan which may involve drug treatment if claimants consent. Benefits can be withdrawn for up to 26 weeks if claimants fail to comply with any of the provisions relating to drugs contained in the Act.

Treatment is a finite resource. Even though the availability of treatment has increased in the past decade it is not clear what the impact of the expansion of criminal justice 'clients' has had on drug treatment services. There is some evidence to suggest that DIP has had a positive impact on treatment provision and waiting times (Ville and Company, 2009).

However, questions are still raised about whether waiting times are similar for individuals wanting to enter treatment from outside the criminal justice process and those entering it from within; whether the treatment experience has changed because of the criminal justice focus and, if so, how; and whether closer alignments to criminal justice agencies deters individuals from seeking treatment of their own accord. It is possible that at least some drug users view the criminal justice process as the only way to get into treatment, potentially resulting in individuals committing offences to access treatment services.

Probably the most important issue is whether treatment works both in the short term and in the long term. The 2008 drug strategy acknowledges that there are gaps in the evidence base in relation to treatment and there is considerable potential to develop more effective forms of treatment (HM Government, 2008). Marsden et al. (2009) note that evidence relating to the effectiveness of treatment is limited. Only a small number of studies have been undertaken and methodological problems characterize them all. For example, Marsden et al. (2009) had no control group and looked only at outcomes while individuals were in treatment and not afterwards. Research tends to suggest that treatment for users of heroin or cocaine is more effective in terms of reducing drug use than treatment of users of both drugs (Gossop et al., 2003; Williamson et al., 2006; Marsden et al., 2009); but these are outcomes for all individuals entering treatment not just those who access it through the criminal justice system. It may be that the latter group differ in important respects from drug users as a whole. A related issue is how to measure the success of treatment. Drug use is a relapsing condition so engagement with treatment for six or twelve weeks, or even longer, does not necessarily mean that individuals are 'cured' (see Hucklesby and Wincup, Chapter 2 this volume). A drawback of most studies looking at treatment outcomes is that they only measure outcomes in the short term, usually when individuals are still in treatment. Longitudinal studies of drug users are rare.

The importance of throughcare

This brings us to the issue of throughcare. The provision of throughcare is one of the most challenging aspects of dealing with offenders (see Hucklesby and Hagley-Dickinson, 2007). The latest NOMS Drug Strategy (2008) includes strengthening the continuity of case management between the community and custody as one of its broad objectives (NOMS, 2008: 4), and effective throughcare is highlighted as one of the three key elements of the strategy as it pertains to prisons (NOMS, 2008: 10). The strategy discusses some of the ways in which improved case management might be achieved, including: strengthening links between agencies; improving information flow; engaging with families; increased levels of supervision, monitoring and surveillance; and improved preparations for release. However, it also views throughcare narrowly, focusing on the continuity of services between prison and the community. In part this is understandable because particular problems have been identified with prisoners who often return to drug use and crime after release and the prevalence of drug-related deaths of ex-prisoners (see Paylor et al., Chapter 9 this volume). Yet it appears to ignore the needs of individuals who receive treatment in the community who may face similar problems when support is withdrawn. Indeed, the lack of exit strategies, particularly in the early stages of the criminal justice process, has been identified as a particular gap in DIP (for example, see Hucklesby, Chapter 6 this volume).

DIP as a multi-agency partnership is viewed as the main vehicle for the provision of throughcare. Effective throughcare requires that services and support are provided to all drug-using offenders to ensure that, once drug use has been stabilized or abstinence achieved, they do not relapse into their old lifestyles. DIP is a step in the right direction but gaps in provision have been identified, especially in relation to the provision of housing and other support essential for sustaining long-term abstinence (see Ville and Company, 2009). There appears to be little acknowledgement that the actions of criminal justice agencies themselves may make it difficult for individuals to both abstain from drug use and desist from crime (see Lister and Wincup, Chapter 3 this volume, for a discussion of the potential harmful consequences of street policing). Fractures in partnership working and information sharing also limit the capabilities of DIP to provide effective throughcare arrangements (see Ville and Company, 2009; Turnbull and Skinns, Chapter 4 this volume). In sum, there is little evidence that integrated packages of support are provided to drug users consistently, and this raises questions about equality in relation to service provision. These questions are discussed further in the section below.

Equality and diversity issues

Equality issues are raised by the operation of DIP. Key questions relate to whether it provides consistent services to all members of all communities. The provision of drug services to suspects, defendants and offenders differs geographically. Intensive and non-intensive DIP areas receive different levels of funding, and service provision varies between them (see, for example, Ville and Company, 2009; and, in relation to drug testing, Mair and Millings, Chapter 5 this volume). Further differences exist in the way in which DIP is managed and between the services provided by DATs and DIP areas (see, Ville and Company, 2009; Turnbull and Skinns,

Chapter 4 this volume). These result in individuals having different experiences of DIP, and different compliance models and breach policies being adopted (see Hucklesby, Chapter 6 this volume, and Turnbull and Skinns, Chapter 4 this volume).

Public bodies, including criminal justice agencies, are already required to consider issues of equality and diversity which arise from their work in relation to race, disability and gender. These were introduced in the Race Relations (Amendment) Act 2000, Disability Discrimination Act 2005 and the Equality Act 2006, respectively. The Equality Bill 2009 will create a new equality duty which will require public bodies to consider the needs of diverse groups in the community when designing and delivering public services. It creates a single duty which encompasses race, disability and gender but also introduces new considerations, for example age and socio-economic status. Evidence in relation to the potentially different impact of drug strategies generally and DIP particularly is limited. However, evidence in relation to the criminal justice process does consistently point to differential treatment on the grounds of gender and ethnicity and this raises questions about whether female and minority ethnic suspects, defendants and offenders have equal access to drug services. A recent study undertaken by the Centre for Ethnicity and Health at the University of Central Lancashire (Mir et al., 2007) raised a number of issues which limited the capacity of DIP to work with individuals from minority ethnic groups, including language barriers and negative attitudes towards drug treatment services. Additionally, access to DIP services may vary for different ethnic groups. For example, the evaluation of Restriction on Bail (RoB) suggested that black defendants were less likely to be granted bail with RoB conditions attached than were white defendants (see Hucklesby, Chapter 6 this volume). Evidence also suggested that barriers exist which prevent members of black and minority ethnic groups from accessing drug treatment more generally (National Treatment Agency and the Centre for Ethnicity and Health, 2003). Currently, around 12 per cent of treatment 'clients' are from minority ethnic groups, with fewer than 3 per cent coming from any one minority ethnic group, but these figures are not broken down specifically for DIP (Department of Health and National Treatment Agency, 2008). Workers from minority ethnic groups currently make up a small proportion of DIP workers (Home Office, 2007a). In terms of women, in 2006 over one-quarter of individuals in contact with DIP were women (Home Office, 2007a), but, as far as we are aware, there is no research on their experiences of the programme. Female sex workers – a specific target group for DIP – have received particular attention not because of their gender-specific needs but because of the high prevalence of drug use among this group (Home Office, 2007b).

The Home Office recognizes the importance of providing services specifically aimed at minority ethnic groups and women and of increasing their engagement with DIP partly because of duties recently introduced by legalisation. For example, it has published a Race, Equality and Diversity Action Plan (Home Office, 2007a), but there is little evidence so far that the rhetoric of providing comparable services for all individuals has been translated into practice.

The structure of the book

The remainder of this book is divided into eight chapters. In Chapter 2, Anthea Hucklesby and Emma Wincup discuss some of the key challenges pertinent to researching drug interventions in criminal justice. The remainder of the chapters loosely follow the criminal justice process from beginning to end, discussing the measures which are in place to channel drug users into treatment at each stage. In Chapter 3, Stuart Lister and Emma Wincup map the different purposes which policing problem drug users serve and explore how they translate into day-to-day street encounters between police and problem drug users. The chapter also considers the role played by the police in promoting access to drug interventions and elucidates how policing can both encourage and undermine their effectiveness. In Chapter 4, Paul Turnbull and Layla Skinns chart the development of the Drug Interventions Programme and explore the main findings of the evaluation of Criminal Justice Interventions Teams. In Chapter 5, George Mair and Matthew Millings examine the development of drug testing in police stations and arrest referral schemes, drawing upon the literature and on their evaluation of the Merseyside Arrest Referral Scheme between 2000 and 2002 (Mair et al., 2002). The focus of the next two chapters is on courts. In Chapter 6, Anthea Hucklesby draws on the findings of Home Office funded evaluation of the pilots to discuss issues raised by using the remand process to put defendants in contact with drug services. Gill McIvor examines the introduction and expansion of drug courts in Chapter 7, describing the key features of their structure and operation and locating the more recent development of drug courts in the UK in an international context. Chapters 8 and 9 deal with the punishment of drug offenders. In Chapter 8, Alex Stevens examines the development of Drug Treatment and Testing Orders and the Drug Rehabilitation Requirement, comparing them to available sentences internationally. He also discusses evidence relating to quasi-compulsory drug treatment (QCT), with a specific emphasis on the links between coercion, motivation and outcome, drawing on the findings of his QCT Europe study. The final chapter, by Ian Paylor, Anthea Hucklesby and Alison Wilson, provides an overview of drug use in prison, including the scale of the problem, prison drug policy and the various measures which have been put in place to tackle the problem.

References

Bean, P. (2008) *Drugs and Crime*, 3rd edition. Cullompton: Willan Publishing.

Bennett, T. (2009) 'The causal connection between drug misuse and crime', *British Journal of Criminology*, 49(2): 513–32.

Bennett, T. and Holloway, K. (2007) *Drug–Crime Connections*. Cambridge: Cambridge University Press.

Carnwell, R. and Buchanan, J. (2008) *Effective Practice in Health, Social Care and Criminal Justice*, 2nd edition. Buckingham: Open University Press.

Coid, J., Carvell, A., Kittler, Z., Heally, A. and Henderson, J. (2000) *Opiates, Criminal Behaviour and Methadone Treatment*. London: Home Office.

Department of Health and National Treatment Agency (2008) *Statistics from the National Drug Treatment Monitoring System (NDTMS) 1st April 2007–31st March 2008*. London: Department of Health and National Treatment Agency.

Fraser, P. and Padel, U. (2002) Editorial, *Criminal Justice Matters*, 47: 3.

Goldstein, P. (1985) 'The drugs/violence nexus: a tripartite conceptual framework', *Journal of Drug Issues*, Fall: 493–506.

Gossop, M., Marsden, J., Stewart, D. and Kidd, T. (2003) 'The National Treatment Outcome Research Study (NTORS): 4–5 year follow-up results', *Addiction*, 98(3): 291–303.

HM Government (2008) *Drugs: Protecting Families and Communities. The 2008 Drug Strategy*. London: HM Government.

Home Office (1995) *Tackling Drugs Together: A Strategy for England 1995–1998*. London: HMSO.

Home Office (2002) *Updated Drug Strategy 2002*. London: Home Office.

Home Office (2007a) *Drug Interventions Programme: Race, Equality and Diversity Action Plan*. London: Home Office.

Home Office (2007b) *Good Practice Guide to Increase the Engagement of Adults involved in Prostitution within the Drug Interventions Programme*. London: Home Office.

Hough, M. (1996) *Drug Misusers and the Criminal Justice System: A Review of the Literature*. London: Home Office.

Hucklesby, A., Eastwood, C., Seddon, T. and Spriggs, A. (2007) *The Evaluation of the Restriction on Bail Pilot: Final Report*, RDS On-line Report 06/07. London: Home Office.

Hucklesby, A. and Hagley-Dickinson, L. (eds) (2007) *Prisoner Resettlement: Policy and Practice*. Cullompton: Willan Publishing.

Hucklesby, A. and Wincup, E. (2007a) *The Pyramid Project: Final Report to Depaul Trust and Nacro* (unpublished).

Hucklesby, A. and Wincup, E. (2007b) *The ROTA Project: Final Report to Citizens Advice, Legal Services Commission and HM Prison Service* (unpublished).

Lloyd, C. (1998) 'Risk factors for drug problem drug use: identifying vulnerable groups', *Drugs: Education, Prevention and Policy*, 5(3): 217–32.

Luty, J. (2002) 'Geographical variations in substance misuse service waiting times and methadone treatment of opiate dependence in England and Wales', *Psychiatric Bulletin*, 26: 447–8.

Mair, G., Millings, M. and Palmer, C. (2002) *Arrest Referral on Merseyside: An Evaluation*. Liverpool: LJMU Centre for Criminal Justice.

Marsden, J., Eastwood, B., Bradbury, C., Dale-Perera, A., Farrell, M., Hammond, P., Knight, J., Ranhawa, K. and Wright, C. (2009) 'Effectiveness of community treatments for heroin and crack cocaine addiction in England: a prospective, in-treatment cohort study', *The Lancet Online* (accessed 2 October 2009).

McLaughlin, E., Muncie, J. and Hughes, G. (2001) 'The permanent revolution: New Labour, new public management and the modernization of criminal justice', *Criminal Justice*, 1(3): 301–18.

McSweeney, T., Hough, M. and Turnbull, P. (2007) 'Drugs and crime: exploring the links', in M. Simpson, T. Shildrick and R. MacDonald (eds) *Drugs in Britain: Supply, Consumption and Control*. Basingstoke: Palgrave Macmillan.

Mir, Y., Davies, K. and Collins, C. (2007) *What we Learnt from Engaging with Black and Minority Ethnic Communities*. London: Home Office.

National Assembly for Wales (2000) *Tackling Substance Misuse in Wales: A Partnership Approach*. Cardiff: National Assembly for Wales.

National Offender Management Service (NOMS) (2005) *Strategy for the Management and Treatment of Problematic Drug Users within the Correctional Services*. London: Home Office.

National Offender Management Service (NOMS) (2008) *The National Offender Management Service Drug Strategy 2008–2011*. London: Ministry of Justice.

National Treatment Agency and the Centre for Ethnicity and Health (2003) *Black and Minority Ethnic Communities in England: A Review of the Literature on Drug Use and Related Service Provision*. London: National Treatment Agency.

President of the Council (1998) *Tackling Drugs to Build a Better Britain*, Cm 3945. London: The Stationery Office.

PricewaterhouseCoopers (2008) *Review of Prison-Based Drug Treatment Funding. Report to the Department of Health and Ministry of Justice*. London: Ministry of Justice.

Seddon T. (2000) 'Explaining the drug–crime link: theoretical, policy and research issues', *Journal of Social Policy*, 29(1): 95–107.

Skodbo, S., Brown, G., Deacon, S., Cooper, A., Hall, A., Millar, T., Smith, J. and Whitham, K. (2007) *The Drug Interventions Programme (DIP): Addressing Drug Use and Offending through 'Tough Choices'*, Research Report 2. London: Home Office.

Taylor, S. (2008) 'Outside the outsiders: media representations of drug use', *Probation Journal*, 55(4): 369–87.

Ville and Company (2009) *Moving up a Gear – the Next Steps for DIP. Executive Summary*. London: Home Office.

Welsh Office (1996) *Forward Together: A Strategy to Combat Drug and Alcohol Misuse in Wales*. Cardiff: Welsh Office.

Welsh Assembly Government (2008) *Working Together to Reduce Harm: The Substance Misuse Strategy for Wales 2008–2018*. Cardiff: Welsh Assembly Government.

Williamson, A., Darke, S., Ross, J. and Teeson, M. (2006) 'The effect of persistence of cocaine use on 12-month outcomes for the treatment of heroin dependence', *Drug and Alcohol Dependence*, 81(3): 293–300.

2 Researching drug interventions in criminal justice

Anthea Hucklesby and Emma Wincup

Introduction

In recent years there have been unprecedented opportunities to research drug use. Under Labour there has been a shift – in rhetoric if not always in practice – towards evidence-based policy. The 1998 drug strategy stated that evidence was one of its six underlying principles and it needed to be based upon 'accurate, independent research, approached in a level-headed, analytical fashion' (President of the Council, 1998: 11). It also made explicit that implementation of the strategy should be accompanied by rigorous and objective assessment of its effectiveness to aid its development, and that research and information were key components of this process. Given the rapidly changing policy context which followed on from the launch of this strategy, evaluations were often required to inform decisions about whether to 'roll out' new initiatives which tended to be introduced initially in 'pilot areas'. A number of government departments made considerable funding available for evaluations of the plethora of new interventions designed to reduce crime rates through the provision of treatment opportunities at all stages of the criminal justice process. These evaluations required researchers to pay attention to both processes and outcomes and involved data collection across a number of sites (see Turnbull and Skinns, Chapter 4 and Hucklesby, Chapter 6 this volume, for examples of studies funded by the Home Office; and McIvor, Chapter 7 this volume, for one funded by the Scottish Executive). Alongside this, small-scale evaluations of locally based interventions have been commissioned (see Mair and Millings, Chapter 5 this volume, for an example) and a variety of funding bodies, including research councils and charitable organizations, have funded studies related to drugs and crime. The Joseph Rowntree Foundation deserves a special mention because its Drug and Alcohol Programme, launched shortly after the publication of the 2002 Updated Drug Strategy (Home Office, 2002), incorporated studies of policing (see Lister and Wincup, Chapter 3 this volume, for an example of a study funded by the programme).

Finally, researchers have been able to secure funding from international bodies who have sought to develop a comparative approach to tackling a social problem which transgresses national boundaries: for example, the study described in Stevens, Chapter 8 this volume, was funded by the European Commission (see also http://www.kent.ac.uk/eiss/projects/qcteurope/index.html).

We, like other contributors to this volume, have been able to take advantage of the enhanced opportunities for conducting research on drugs and crime, and elsewhere in this volume we have presented our findings. This chapter draws on our experiences of exploring the range of drug interventions offered by criminal justice agencies and institutions as diverse as the police, courts, probation and prisons in England. It is also shaped by our reflections on conducting research on drug use more generally, which has included studies of women, young people, current and former prisoners, residents of approved premises and homeless people. The discussion is divided into four main sections which capture the key challenges pertinent to researching drug interventions in criminal justice. The first focuses on the difficulties of obtaining access both to drug users and to data held by organizations relating to their drug use, and on the special complications which arise when drug users are participants in the criminal justice process. In the next section, ethical dilemmas faced by researchers are explored. While issues relating to access and ethics have been separated out to add clarity to the discussion, it is important not to lose sight of how closely intertwined they are in practice: for instance, drug agencies might justify their unwillingness to grant researchers access to data on ethical grounds. The third section explores the range of risks faced by researchers interested in drug interventions and criminal justice and how they might best be managed. The final section considers the challenges of measuring drug use, and in particular against the backdrop of evaluating the effectiveness of drug interventions in criminal justice.

Accessing data

Within the methodological literature a distinction is often made between 'physical' and 'social' access (see, for example, Noaks and Wincup, 2004). The former refers to the process of obtaining initial access to the data one requires ('getting in'), whereas the latter term describes the process of establishing a research role, building rapport with participants and securing their trust ('getting along'). Negotiating physical access for the purposes of researching drug interventions in criminal justice rests upon securing the support of agencies at a number of different levels – national, regional and local – and from a range of criminal justice and drug treatment organizations. For example, researchers based in England wishing to access data about drug treatment may have to negotiate with the National Treatment Agency (NTA), Drug Action Teams and/or treatment providers which might include NHS and voluntary and private sector providers. Which organizations are relevant depends upon local circumstances with a plethora of different arrangements across the country. In all cases, researchers become dependent upon 'gatekeepers' – 'those individuals . . . that have the power to grant or withhold access to people or situations for the purpose of research' (Burgess, 1984: 48) – to facilitate the collection of data. Locating the appropriate gatekeeper within an organization and securing their support may itself be a significant task.

Access requirements will depend upon the project, but they might, for instance, involve making organizational data available, providing introductions to potential interviewees or allowing researchers to observe meetings. Some of the greatest difficulties faced by researchers have related to the first example and obtaining the necessary data about treatment outcomes has been particularly problematic because of concerns about client confidentiality. Such anxieties are greater in this field than in others because most drug agencies view themselves as health care agencies and thus adhere to the high level of confidentiality associated with doctor/patient relationships (see General Medical Council, 2009). The General Medical Council requires the informed consent of individuals before any data can be made available for research purposes. Often this is not possible because researchers begin their research after an initiative has been operating for a period of time. In our experience, project managers rarely, if ever, have the forethought to collect individuals' consent for data to be used for research purposes from the start of an initiative even when they are aware that an evaluation will be taking place. Consequently it proves impossible to obtain retrospective data.

Gatekeepers from across the drugs field have often been unwilling to allow researchers access to files on individual 'clients' or electronic databases or have refused to provide data required by researchers in a non-aggregated form. This has hampered attempts to evaluate drug interventions because data relating to specific individuals are necessary to link interventions with outcomes in order to measure both general and cost effectiveness. For example, during the evaluation of Restriction on Bail (RoB) (see Hucklesby, Chapter 6 this volume) data relating to treatment were unavailable in two out of the three areas. The evaluation team were informed that they could not have access to basic individual-level data such as whether 'clients' attended any appointments, how long they were in contact with the agency or the type of treatment provided (i.e. substitute prescription, residential, and so on) despite assurances about confidentiality and secure data storage, as well as pressure from Home

Office research managers to provide the data. Individualized data relating to treatment history and whether individuals were already in treatment when interventions began were also required to evaluate drug interventions but were not made available. This research experience is unlikely to be unique. Consequently, what happens during drug treatment remains a 'black box', with little if any data being made available for research purposes.

Securing access to the necessary data is unpredictable, with some organizations providing data whereas others refuse. This inconsistent approach makes it extremely difficult for researchers to plan their research strategies. For example, if researchers knew that they could not obtain access to treatment information, they could instead include questions about what treatment individuals received in interviews. This would provide some data to work with, although they would probably not be as reliable as data collated from treatment agencies. The range of service providers in the drugs field also results in variations in the types of data collected and the systems used to store them, making the research task harder. The collection of data by the NTA increases consistency across areas but the data are collected for monitoring purposes rather than for research and so lack the detail required by many researchers. Usually the data are provided to researchers only in aggregate form, with the NTA carrying out the analysis. This means that researchers are unable to check the validity and reliability of the data and cannot link these data with criminal justice data. Furthermore, treatment data are collated locally, so that if individuals have moved area, data about their past treatment histories is likely to be inaccurate. For example, there were discrepancies between data relating to past treatment histories from interviewees, the local database compiled by RoB workers and the NTA in the RoB evaluation, some of which appeared to be because defendants had been in treatment somewhere other than where they currently resided (Hucklesby et al., 2007).

Traditionally, 'client' appointments with participants in the initiatives being evaluated have provided an opportunity for researchers to gain access to potential interviewees. Commonly, researchers schedule interviews at the same time as statutory appointments to increase the chances of individuals attending. For this to operate successfully, agencies need to provide information about when appointments are taking place, thereby acknowledging that individuals are their 'clients'. Agencies often liaise with potential interviewees and provide interviewing facilities and this is extremely useful because it minimizes both the time spent arranging interviews and health and safety risks. However, during at least one evaluation such arrangements did not take place across all of the research sites because some treatment agencies refused to provide assistance, suggesting that it would compromise confidentiality if they acknowledged that named individuals were clients (Hucklesby et al., 2007). Instead, the evaluation team had to wait for defendants in court buildings, interviewing them there or in nearby cafés when their court hearings were over. While the public setting minimizes the degree of risk experienced by researchers, the lack of privacy potentially compromised the quality of the interview data. Often, interviews did not take place because court dates had been changed, defendants failed to appear or appeared when researchers were interviewing others, or defendants needed to speak with other professionals such as legal advisers and probation staff. Using court buildings as the forum to gain consent from individuals to be interviewed also has obvious disadvantages. It also runs the risk of failing to make contact with some of the most chaotic drug-using offenders.

The second major set of difficulties relates to interviewing drug users. When inviting drug users to participate in interviews about drug interventions, refusal rates may be high because they have concerns about whether the research is truly independent and are unsure about whether to believe the promise of confidentiality offered by researchers. This is likely to be especially difficult when drug users are caught up in the criminal justice process, and even more so given the increased emphasis in recent years placed upon taking appropriate enforcement action when conditions (for example, relating to bail or licences) and orders are breached (Hedderman and Hough, 2004; Padfield and Maruna, 2006; Hucklesby et al., 2007) or when drug tests are positive (Edgar and O'Donnell, 1998). Simply agreeing to talk to researchers may be viewed as an admission of drug use by individuals and they may be fearful of the consequence of this for example, prisoners may have concerns about being subject to more frequent drug testing in prisons. At the same time, it is also important to appreciate that drug users caught up in the criminal justice process may feel compelled to participate despite the best attempts of researchers to make them aware of their right to refuse. We will return to this ethical dilemma in the next section but for now note that this may mean that interviewers are provided with incomplete or inaccurate accounts because drug users are unwilling to disclose information which could put them in a vulnerable position. They may, for instance, be reluctant to talk openly about their ongoing drug use. This is one of many reasons why the accounts of drug-using offenders should be interpreted with particular care. While we need to be wary about making sweeping generalizations given the diversity of this group, it is possible to highlight some of the difficulties that researchers might face.

The first difficulty relates to drug use itself. An easily reached conclusion among those with no experience of interviewing drug users is that recent consumption of drugs impacts significantly, and indeed negatively, upon the quality of the data obtained. Drawing upon our own experiences, we find it difficult to support this view generally. Often it is not readily apparent that an individual has used drugs recently, particularly if they are a regular user. In our view, individuals who are beginning to withdraw from drugs are the most challenging group to interview. Such individuals may find it increasingly difficult to concentrate and be disinclined to answer questions, either fully or at all, at a time when they are preoccupied with their next 'fix'. On a small number of occasions when faced with such circumstances we have stopped the interview, either at our suggestion or the interviewee's request, because it would be unethical to continue. Sometimes we have been able to complete the interview at a later stage. On a few occasions individuals have been unwell or fallen asleep during interviews. In these circumstances interviews were terminated.

The second consideration relates to the frequency with which drug-using offenders are subject to questions about their drug use, offending and life in general. While research interviews are distinct from the other contexts in which such individuals are asked questions (for example, during assessments for drug treatment), for those subject to continual questioning about their behaviour the boundaries may become blurred and they may only be willing to engage with interviewers on a superficial level, providing the bare minimum of detail needed to answer the question. This creates particular difficulties for those who hope to obtain rich and detailed qualitative data via unstructured or semi-structured interviews. It can be hard to establish the necessary rapport if interviewees treat the research interview as a formal situation akin to a police interview or medical assessment rather than more informally as a 'conversation with a purpose' (Burgess, 1982). Similarly, individuals may be targeted for interviews by several teams of researchers. For example, interviews for the evaluations of the Drug Interventions Programme (DIP) and RoB were taking place simultaneously in the same courts (Hucklesby et al., 2007; Turnbull and Skinns, Chapter 4 this volume). Every effort was made to ensure that individuals were not interviewed by both teams, involving liaison between the research teams which was time consuming and not infallible. Certainly, defendants knew about both evaluations and at one point were known to be aware that the incentive payments offered by one evaluation were more than those offered by the other. With so much research activity it was also inevitable that some individuals would be interviewed for more than one evaluation. Similarly, it is possible that individuals may be invited to participate in research at different points in their journey through the criminal justice process. Under such circumstances 'research fatigue' may set in.

A further challenge for researchers working in the drugs field is keeping abreast of the range of terms used by drug users to describe the practices associated with drug use, other drug users, drugs themselves and equipment.

Learning the 'lingo' or street names is part of the occupational socialization of novice researchers but is an ongoing task as new drugs enter the market. There is also considerable regional variation, particularly when referring to specific drugs. In our experience, researchers need sufficient knowledge to be credible and to avoid appearing very naive, but it can also be productive to treat interviewees as 'experts' and offer them the opportunity to explain unfamiliar terms. For researchers who choose to collect qualitative data, an important consideration is how best to present the data gathered. Typically this involves the presentation of relatively short verbatim quotes. However, these may not be fully understood by readers of the publications in which the research findings are presented. A useful strategy in this instance is to provide a glossary. For example, Taylor's (1993) monograph based on her ethnographic research with women drug users in Glasgow includes an appendix with explanations of words and phrases used by the women; both drug terminology and more general terms peculiar to Glasgow and/or Scotland.

Up to this point we have proposed that securing the support of criminal justice and drug treatment agencies is essential when researching drug interventions in criminal justice. This is true, but it does raise issues about how other people perceive the research and the researchers. Hodgson et al. (2006) discuss the problems which can arise when undertaking research on criminal justice drug interventions. They pose the classic methodological question, 'whose side are we on?', and describe how researchers have to tread a difficult path between being viewed as an authority figure, potentially alienating suspects/defendants and offenders, and being viewed with suspicion by people in authority for talking to those in their 'care' thus hampering access. Several groups of researchers have described having difficulties being accepted into police custody suites initially and how this impacted negatively on accessing suspects (see Hodgson et al., 2006; Mair and Millings, Chapter 5 this volume). Appearances can also be important in the acceptance process, and dress can be significant (see Adams, 2000, for a discussion of this in relation to research on suspects). The RoB evaluation had to walk a tightrope between being accepted in court, requiring researchers to wear suits, and not appearing as authority figures when trying to obtain defendants' consent to be interviewed (Hucklesby et al., 2007).

Studies which rely solely on criminal justice or drug agencies to access interviewees run the risk of missing out on a population of interest, namely those drug-using offenders who are unwilling to participate in drug interventions, have breached their conditions or order or whose engagement is short-lived. Consequently, some of the most interesting groups and those that have 'failed' may be excluded, leading to an unrepresentative sample. For example, Stevens et al.'s (2008) exploration of early exit from treatment found that three (potentially overlapping) groups of drug users were less likely to remain in treatment beyond 30 days: young people, homeless people (defined as those of no fixed abode) and those not currently injecting. Consequently, those most likely to remain in treatment were the traditional client group for drug services: opiate users in their late twenties and thirties. Drug users channelled into treatment via criminal justice processes were more likely to drop out between assessment and treatment entry. Research into arrest referral schemes suggests that hard-to-reach groups in terms of project engagement include minority ethnic groups, crack users and older users (Sondhi et al., 2002). Some evaluations have attempted to interview individuals who had breached conditions or orders, but this has generally proved very difficult (see, for example, Hucklesby et al., 2007). Other evaluations have interviewed only offenders who continued on programmes or orders (for example, Turnbull et al., 2000). This has meant that pertinent questions about why individuals drop out of treatment are left unanswered. Tracking down this group is time consuming and often does not succeed. For example, individuals may be in police custody or prison, or deliberately seeking to avoid contact because there is a warrant out for their arrest. They may also be of no fixed abode and have little or no contact with mainstream agencies. Creative thinking is necessary to make contact with such groups. For instance, they may need to be accessed via other agencies which might offer them support, for example services for homeless people such as day centres or night shelters. Alongside this, snowball sampling can be used, asking participants to identify others (see, for example, Stevens et al., 2008). A further strategy is to attend court on dates when defendants are scheduled to appear, but experience from the RoB evaluation suggests that they often fail to appear or are in custody (Hucklesby et al., 2007). Attempting to set up systems with the police or the courts for the research team to be alerted once an individual reappeared did not generally work, but re-entry onto the scheme did present an opportunity to contact breached individuals (see Hucklesby et al., 2007).

One oft-proposed solution to difficulties of securing access to drug users is to offer potential participants an incentive. Such incentives might take the form of cash (see, for example, Wincup et al., 2003) or a non-cash alternative such as shopping vouchers (see, for example, Hucklesby et al., 2007). The latter are frequently viewed as more acceptable, particularly by government departments, because of fears that drug users might use cash payments to purchase drugs, and of the media outcry if the practice was to become widely known. However, some researchers within the drugs field have expressed concern about making such moral judgements about the behaviour of drug users (see Noaks and Wincup, 2004, for a brief overview of this debate) and, as others have noted (for example, Seddon, 2005), the media have been similarly disparaging about the practice of giving shopping vouchers to offenders. There are, of course, some contexts in which offering incentives is not possible, for example when conducting research in prisons. Where incentives are used, it is important that they are properly accounted for by asking interviewees to sign receipts to maintain the integrity of the research and the researchers.

The use of incentives is widely perceived as standard practice among drug researchers. Indeed, McKeganey (2001) has warned that the culture of expectation it creates is in itself problematic. Despite it being so customary, it is the subject of considerable debate. There are strong arguments for the use of incentives. Adopting what Seddon (2005) refers to as a 'business' perspective, incentives reduce refusal rates, therefore saving valuable research time. At the same time, their use raises a number of ethical issues, principally to do with the extent to which it compromises the ability of individuals to consent freely, and is not universally viewed as ethically acceptable by ethical review committees. For some, incentives serve to 'buy' stories and information. We return to a discussion of the practice of using incentives in the following section.

Ethical challenges

Researchers from varied disciplines are involved in researching drug interventions, each drawing upon their discipline's code of ethics or more generic guidance such as the Social Research Association's ethical guidelines (Social Research Association, 2003). While in many respects they are similar, each describing the professional standards that researchers should adhere to in order to ensure that they produce research which is high quality and methodologically sound while fulfilling their obligations to those involved in the research as colleagues, sponsors and participants, there are important differences. Limited space precludes a discussion of these and this section draws, in particular, on our experiences as criminologists whose starting point when conducting research is the British Society of Criminology ethical code (British Society of Criminology, 2006).

As noted earlier in this chapter, drug users may have some concerns about promises of confidentiality offered by researchers. It is important, however, not to make promises of total confidentiality in an attempt to reassure potential participants. This is especially inappropriate for a number of reasons when individuals are drug-using offenders. They may disclose that they pose a risk to others but in our experience it is more likely that they will reveal that they pose a risk to themselves. Determining when it is appropriate to treat information provided in the context of a research interview as non-confidential is far from easy because it needs to be balanced with other considerations. The current British Society of Criminology ethical code suggests that researchers should make every effort to respect the rights of those they study, their interests, sensitivities and privacy. Researchers therefore need to decide what is most appropriate following careful consideration of the situation. For example, they may feel that the best course of action if a drug user states they are engaged in 'risky' behaviours such as sharing needles is to provide information about local needle exchange schemes, but if the interviewee states or implies they are being repeatedly subject to violence or threats of it then they might adopt a more direct approach and share their concerns with an appropriate individual, for example the gatekeeper. Limits to confidentiality need to be conveyed to potential participants at the outset so they can make an informed decision about whether to participate.

Obtaining informed consent is fraught with difficulties when researching offenders. First, as previously discussed, despite reassurances that they have a choice not to, individuals may feel compelled to participate because they are involuntary participants in a criminal process which is essentially coercive, and fear the consequences if they decline. In our experience, gatekeepers do not always make it clear to defendants/offenders that they have the right to refuse. Second, levels of literacy are generally low among defendants/offenders (McMahon et al., 2004), which places a greater responsibility upon researchers to make the necessary information available in an accessible way both orally and in writing. Furthermore, there may be other relevant considerations. For example, mental health problems, which are more prevalent among drug users than among the general public (Hussain Rassool, 2001; Rethink and Turning Point, 2004), may impact upon the ability of individuals to make an informed decision regarding consent. In extreme cases, consent may also need to be sought from an additional person. More generally, individuals may perceive that there is something to be gained by agreeing to be interviewed, such as assistance with accessing treatment or that it may be viewed positively by probation or prison staff. While this may make them eager participants, there is also the possibility that they offer socially desirable responses, providing the answers they believe interviewers wish to hear.

Obtaining consent occurs at the outset but it should be viewed as a process rather than as a one-off event and participants made aware that they can withdraw, either fully or partially (for example, by refusing to answer a question), at any point. This is especially relevant to research with drug-using offenders because individuals will be asked questions which they may regard as intrusive. Additionally, they may feel unable to continue with an interview because they feel unwell. Given their involvement within the criminal justice process, it is particularly important that researchers emphasize that stopping will not have adverse consequences.

Research of this type also raises issues about what it is appropriate for researchers to say during interviews, most pertinently in terms of giving advice and information. We have already suggested that interviewers might direct interviewees to local needle exchanges but this assumes that they have sufficient knowledge, which may not be the case if the evaluation is a large-scale national one. Providing the necessary training is one solution, but this approach raises issues about the role of interviewers and potentially blurs the dividing line between researchers and workers. In our view, a better approach is that researchers urge interviewees to seek assistance from their drugs or criminal justice worker, thereby safeguarding their integrity as independent researchers.

It is becoming increasingly common for researchers to be required to submit an application for ethical review prior to collecting data, and in some instances prior to commencing the research study. For criminologists working in academic institutions, this normally involves submitting the necessary documents to a committee operating at departmental, faculty or university level. There are, however, exceptions, and criminologists seeking to collect data which requires contact with NHS patients (for example, prisoners receiving health care services) or vulnerable people (for example, young offenders) may need to gain ethical approval from an external NHS or social services committee. The process of ethical review can vary considerably but may involve committees specifying what can and cannot be done. In an article exploring drug users' motivations for participating in research, McKeganey (2001) notes that ethical review committees tend to home in on the issue of payment when faced with proposals from researchers.

While there is a danger that offering large sums of money might encourage people to participate in studies when they would prefer not to, essentially rendering their consent involuntary, the small sums of money (or non-cash alternative) typically offered are unlikely to persuade those who do not want to participate to do so. It is also important to appreciate that the motivations of individual drug users for participating in research are multi-dimensional. Fry and Dwyer's (2001) study of injecting drug users found that while almost half stated that economic gain was one of the main reasons for participation, other reasons given related to citizenship (for example, to help find solutions to drug problems), altruism, personal satisfaction and drug user activism (for instance, to improve drug services).

There is no doubt that the offer of cash or an alternative influences decisions to participate, but it is misleading to see it as merely a mechanism to bolster response rates. Payment might also be viewed as fee for a service, in other words the provision of drug users' time, knowledge and experience. Discussing the use of incentive payments for a study of homelessness, Wardhaugh (2000) argues that it is ethical practice to pay socially and economically vulnerable participants for their time and that payment brings them further into 'our' world with its emphasis on the dignity of employment and economic reward for labour. Her caveat is that researchers should seek to obtain the informed consent of participants prior to discussing payment. Incentives also often cover out-of-pocket expenses such as transport costs which arise through participation in interviews.

Managing risk

We have already noted that researchers are often required to outline how they will ensure that their research practices are ethically sound. Similarly, researchers are increasingly asked to specify the risks associated with research, make judgements about their significance and put in place strategies for minimizing risk. Risk in this context is often broadly defined and refers to risks associated with personal safety; theft, loss or damage to property; physical and emotional health and well-being, plus legal risks. It can also encompass ethical risks. All of these types of risk are relevant to researching drug interventions in criminal justice. The issue merits greater attention than we can dedicate to it within one chapter, but in the remainder of the section we draw attention to some of the most significant risks. Interested readers should consult the small but growing literature on risk and criminological research specifically (for example, Wincup, 2009) and the Social Research Association's *Code of Practice for the Safety of Researchers* (Social Research Association, 2001).

The nature of possible risks will largely depend upon the research design. For example, there are relatively few risks to personal safety associated with a project involving the collection of statistical data from drug treatment providers. But in projects of this type, data protection issues are at the fore. Researchers need to ensure that they transport and store data in line with the requirements of data protection legislation and new protocols which have been recently introduced (for example, the Ministry of Justice policy statement on data security and use of IT equipment by contractors/consultants and agency staff employed by the Ministry of Justice), taking appropriate care if using laptops and memory sticks or using encryption software. The risks are compounded when the research involves direct contact with drug-using offenders. In some respects, researchers interested in those already caught up in the criminal justice process may be better informed than other researchers about potential risks to personal safety because such individuals should have been subject to risk assessments. However, it is questionable how often such information is made available to researchers. Interviews sometimes take place on an organization's premises where safe working practices should have been adopted and appropriate security measures put in place (for example, provision of alarms). Even if such measures are in place, risk is not eradicated and researchers need to take measures to protect themselves and their property, for example taking only essential items to research interviews and not revealing personal information such as addresses. Procedures should also be put in place to ensure that line managers or fellow researchers are aware of the whereabouts of researchers undertaking fieldwork.

Risks to health and well-being are particularly pertinent when researching drug users, especially injecting drug users, and training may be necessary to promote awareness of the risks and how best to protect oneself from harm. Researchers need to be aware of the possibility of contracting blood-borne viruses, particularly hepatitis B and C which are more infectious than others such as HIV. They need to take appropriate measures to protect themselves, for example using hand sanitizing gel. Their line managers also need to appreciate that interviewing drug-using offenders can be physically exhausting, emotionally draining and stressful. Providing opportunities to discuss the research experience and, where possible, allowing time between interviews can assist researchers in coping with the demands it places upon them.

In the context of social research, legal risks are normally associated with ensuring compliance with data protection legislation or the potential for the research to have an adverse impact on the reputation of the researchers, university or a third party (for example, the funder). However, legal risks are potentially more varied for researchers interested in both drugs and offending. There is the possibility that researchers become accessories to crime and, despite calls for legal protection, this is not automatically provided to researchers (Taylor, 1993). A number of researchers in the drugs field have described how they have come perilously close to being subject to police attention (Taylor, 1993), and others have described their strategies for avoiding police questioning about their knowledge of drug dealing (Fountain, 1993). These risks are heightened when researchers are conducting ethnographies of drug use. A more likely risk for those researching drug interventions in criminal justice is that of becoming party to knowledge about ongoing drug use and offending.

One of the dangers attached to the greater emphasis on assessing and managing risk in relation to research is that it gives the impression that all risks can be identified and therefore eradicated or at least reduced. Researchers need to appreciate the unpredictability of the research context. For example, one unanticipated risk when interviewing young homeless people about their substance use was that it attracted the attention of drug dealers who were suspicious of the researchers, motives (see Noaks and Wincup, 2004: Chapter 9).

Measuring drug use

A major focus of recent drugs research has been to evaluate government initiatives to tackle drug use by suspects, defendants and offenders. Driven by an expressed desire that policy should be evidence based, evaluation teams have been commissioned to establish 'what works'. Posing this question opens up a debate about how success should be defined and measured, a thorny issue given the multiple aims of drug interventions and their potential impact on health generally, and drug use specifically, and offending behaviour. Reducing offending through tackling drug use is an important yet relatively recent aim of drug services. Attempts to re-duce drug use have always had other aims, the most important of which relate to health issues such as reducing the number of drug-related deaths and the incidence and spread of blood-borne viruses, including HIV and hepatitis. While health and criminal justice aims may sometimes coincide, they sometimes may not. For example, offenders may continue to inject drugs at pre-intervention levels, funding this through offending, but do so in a way which minimizes the chances of contracting blood-borne viruses by obtaining clean 'works'. This fulfils a health aim but not a criminal jus-tice one. Initiatives to tackle drug use also differ in terms of whether they take an abstinence-based or harm reduction approach. Criminal justice initiatives, especially in prisons, are often linked to abstinence-based ap-proaches mainly because of the issues surrounding criminal justice agen-cies being seen to condone illegal drug use (see Paylor et al., Chapter 9 this volume). By and large, health aims are more likely than criminal justice aims to be linked to harm reduction goals. The complexity and number of possible aims of drug interventions mean that in order for an evaluation to be undertaken, initiatives need clear aims, and the relative priority of each of those aims must also be outlined.

Evaluators may feel under pressure to produce definitive statements about the effectiveness of treatment because the DIP is premised on the basis that reductions in drug use will result in falls in levels of offend-ing. This requires drug-related offenders to be identified, after which it is often assumed that all drug use by them is linked with offending and all offending is linked to drug use (Reuter and Stevens, 2008). The need to appreciate the complex relationship between drug use and crime has been debated at length, most recently by Bennett and Holloway (2009). The extensive literature, which we explored briefly in the introduction to this volume, warns against the search for causality and overdetermi-nation of the link between drug use and crime. Consequently, even the findings of the most methodologically sophisticated research study, for example those utilizing the 'gold standard' randomized controlled trials as their research design, should be interpreted carefully. Evaluators need to be especially mindful of the challenges of measuring changes in the frequency, severity or nature of offending which have been discussed at length elsewhere (Lloyd et al., 1994; Mair, 1997).

The recent policy climate has tended to favour the collection of quantitative data, glossing over the potential contribution that qualitative data can offer to understanding and responding to drug use. While qualitative data cannot offer the definitive statements often favoured by those who commission evaluations, it can help researchers to understand offenders' interpretations of the relationship between their drug use and offending and their experiences of drug treatment, As Rhodes (2000) argues, qualitative data play multiple roles, including the development of effective interventions and policy responses. He argues that they can also inform the collection of quantitative data and complement and question quantitative findings. Evaluations which gather both types of data are therefore more likely to be give meaningful answers to questions about the success or not of drug interventions with offenders. However, answers are likely to be far removed from the clear-cut statements of effectiveness favoured by many policy makers.

Having discussed some of the broad themes relating to measuring the impact of interventions on drug use and crime, the remainder of this section explores the more technical issues. Measuring the subtleties of changing patterns of drug use is a challenge which is resource intensive, requiring careful recording of individuals' drug use over time. The most rigorous methodology for doing this is longitudinal research whereby individuals would be interviewed prior to and after interventions at the very least and preferably on other occasions as well. The National Treatment Outcome Research Study is the best known example of this (see http://www.dtors.org.uk/NTORS.aspx). Some studies have taken this approach, interviewing offenders on more than one occasion (for example, see Turnbull et al., 2000; Turnbull and Skinns, Chapter 4 this volume), but attrition rates between the different phases of the research are often high, resulting in sample sizes being relatively small. Following up offenders after their sentence has been completed is costly, time consuming and difficult, especially when drug users are likely to lead chaotic lives (see Burrows et al., 2001; Farrall and Calverley, 2006; Wincup and Hucklesby, 2007).

Another approach to measuring changes in drug use is to ask individuals about their drug use prior to the intervention retrospectively, either during or after the intervention, at the same time as asking them about current drug use. This approach has drawbacks, most notably how reliably individuals can recall their drug use after a period of time. We have already noted that asking individuals about their drug use in criminal justice settings may also militate against their being truthful because they fear the consequences. Other ways to enhance the reliability of offenders' accounts are to check their drug use on more than one occasion during interviews and, if interviewing them on a second occasion, going over previous drug use again. We have found the second of these is particularly important when trying to measure drug use in prison, as some prisoners have failed to disclose their drug use during their sentence until after they are released.

A further method for measuring changes in drug use is to use drug test results. In theory, these validate scientifically whether individuals are using certain drugs. Drug test results can be used on an individual or aggregate level. For example, the Prison Service uses the percentage of prisoners testing positive as a Key Performance Target and regularly cites it as a measure of the success for its drug policy (see HM Prison Service, 2008; NOMS, 2008). However, there are a number of reasons why the accuracy of this method of measuring drug use can be questioned. First, drug tests are not available for all illegal drugs and, when they are, they are not always used. Opiates, cocaine and cannabis are the drugs most widely tested for within the criminal justice system. Second, tests only measure drug use at one point in time. This has a number of consequences: some regular drug users will be missed because they happened not to be using at the time the test was carried out. This may be a particular issue if a testing regime is predictable so that individuals can tailor their drug use to fit around it. For example, little or no drugs testing happens in prisons at weekends so prisoners taking drugs on Friday know that they have a better chance of testing negative on Monday. By contrast, individuals who rarely use drugs may test positive because they happen to have used drugs just before they were tested. For example, they may have used cocaine for the first time in weeks on the night they were arrested. Third, different drugs are detected for varying lengths of time. Opiates and cocaine stay in the body for shorter periods of time than cannabis, which is likely to skew test results. Fourth, while considerable efforts have been made to prevent the avoidance of positive tests and some tests are more foolproof than others, prisoners particularly continue to report that it is possible to avoid testing positive through a variety of means, including the substitution and adulteration of urine samples (see Ministry of Justice, 2008). Fifth, use of some legal and prescribed drugs mask the use of illegal drugs and render results invalid. Sixth, tests do not show the amount of drugs used and therefore are unable to measure changes in drug use (Turnbull et al., 2000). This has particular implications for individuals who manage to reduce their drug use but not stop it completely: they may feel that it is not worth the effort because they continue to test positive and face the consequences of this. The accuracy of the tests is also doubtful in the sense that they have high cut-off levels so that individuals can potentially continue to use while testing negative. Finally, tests are open to human error and contamination. All these factors mean that the reliability of test results needs to be questioned. However, test results provide a validation of individuals' accounts of their drug use and are a useful source of data when triangulated with other sources. Yet, their value is limited also because they do not provide indications of levels of pre-intervention drug use, nor does testing continue after interventions have been completed. Qualitative approaches are likely to be the only method available to collect these types of data.

It is difficult to get a picture of changes in drug use over time or to compare research findings or changes in drug use for interventions at different stages of the criminal justice process. A major problem is the lack of consistency in the way in which research data are collected (see Holloway et al., 2005, for examples). One area of divergent practice is in the periods of time considered. For example, studies measure prior drug use over different timescales: over a lifetime (Wilkinson et al., 2003), over the year before the intervention or sentence commenced (Liriano and Ramsey, 2003; Holloway and Bennett, 2004); over a month or four weeks prior to the intervention or sentence (Turnbull et al., 2000; Wilkinson et al., 2003; Hucklesby et al., 2007). The latter approach has advantages in that it assesses drug use immediately prior to the intervention but has the disadvantage of not picking up drug use if it ceased before this even if individuals are still in the early stages of treatment. This latter point may be one explanation for the contradictory findings in relation to whether prisoners commence using certain types of drugs in prison (see Paylor et al., Chapter 9 this volume). There is also evidence that drug use peaks just before interventions commence, so using this period as a baseline might overestimate the impact of interventions (Gossop et al., 2006). Taking account of longer periods of time may mean that drug use is included which is no longer ongoing, leading to overestimates of drug use and skewing research findings. Similar issues arise when drug use is assessed during or at the end of interventions. For example, studies of prison drug use tend to ask about all drug use in prison and take no account of the length of time that prisoners have been incarcerated or of changes which might have taken place during their time in custody. Follow-up periods after interventions vary also. For example, Strang et al. (2000) followed up their sample after six months, Matrix Research & Consultancy and Nacro (2004) used a four- and eight-month period whereas Hutchinson et al. (2000) followed up individuals after one year. The difficulties with following up offenders after sentences have been completed often compounds these variations, resulting in individuals being interviewed over widely differing timescales (see, for example, Wincup and Hucklesby, 2007, in relation to ex-prisoners).

A second area of divergent practice in terms of measurement is how to assess the quantity of drugs being used. A common way of doing this is to measure frequency of use, but again, categories vary between studies (see, for example, Bullock, 2003; Hucklesby et al., 2007; Turnbull and Skinns, Chapter 4 this volume). Some studies ask about actual quantities, but this takes no account of differences in purity over time or between places. Other studies have tried to assess quantity in terms of monetary value of the drugs used. This is not satisfactory as a measure of quantity because prices vary over time and place. Furthermore, some drug users may not purchase drugs directly, for example prostitutes may receive them in exchange for selling sex. However, monetary value does provide an indication of whether individuals are likely to be able to fund their drug use through legitimate means or whether they are likely to resort to illegal methods. Reductions in expenditure on drugs may be used as an indication of success in terms of criminal justice goals (see Hucklesby et al., 2007; Turnbull and Skinns, Chapter 4 this volume).

A comprehensive approach to assessing the extent of drug use is to ascertain the types of drug used, the frequency of use, the amount of drugs typically consumed and the cost of drugs per week or per day. This presents further challenges in terms of the measurement and categorization of drug use. Since a high proportion of drug users who come into contact with the Drug Interventions Programme are polydrug users, it can result in lengthy assessment or interviews. However, such an approach enables a full picture of pattern of drug use to be ascertained. Drug users may then be grouped into categories for analysis (see Bullock, 2003, and Hucklesby et al., 2007, for examples). The search for ideal types involves compromises, and outliers always exist. Whatever methods are adopted, they mean little in terms of being able to compare research findings unless there is some agreement between researchers about the measures which are used and over what periods of time.

There are also definitional inconsistencies. Many studies use terms (such as problem drug users, dependent and recreational drug use) whose definitions are contested and vary between studies. For example, Holloway and Bennett (2004) refer to high rate users, whom they define as using an illicit drug on at least 15 out of the last 30 days. This is a lower threshold than that used in other studies which cite daily or near daily use as comprising their highest category of users (for example, Bullock, 2003; Hucklesby et al., 2007). Other studies rely on individuals' own definitions of their drug use, particularly in terms of dependence (for example, Lister and Wincup, Chapter 3 this volume).

A further area where there is a lack of agreement and transparency is in relation to assessing what can be defined as a successful treatment episode. Very few studies give details of what treatment has been received during the intervention (most likely, as discussed earlier in this chapter, because of a lack of availability of the information). It may be that some individuals subject to interventions actually get very little assistance whereas others get some intensive help. The studies do not tend to disaggregate their findings along these lines. Even if they did, it raises questions about how long individuals have to be in treatment before it can be said to be successfully completed. As with desistance from offending, it may be that drug users can never be viewed as absolute desisters because there is always the possibility of relapse (Maruna, 2001). The National Treatment Agency tends to use a measure of 12 weeks in treatment. This was used as constituting a successful treatment episode in one of our studies (Hucklesby et al., 2007) despite scant evidence that this is the optimum time. Twelve weeks is somewhat arbitrary in the sense that individuals differ and some will require longer and others shorter periods of time for treatment to be deemed successful. A further issue arose in the RoB research in relation to how to deal with defendants who were already in treatment when they were made subject to the intervention. In these circumstances nothing changed for most of the defendants – for example, they did not receive any additional treatment – which raises questions about whether it is credible to include their treatment outcomes within the research findings as if they were a result of the intervention. In such circumstances, it is almost impossible to know whether the intervention contributed to the outcomes, and if it did, to what extent. Similarly, if individuals are subject to more than one intervention at any one time or a series of interventions as they pass through the criminal justice process it is impossible to disaggregate the impact of each element. Given that recent initiatives under DIP have attempted to plug gaps and bring in a case management approach, identifying the particular elements which were successful may not be crucial. It may be that the cumulative impact of DIP on drug use is what matters. However, this approach may result in an ineffective intervention being funded when the money could be utilized elsewhere.

Measurement issues are compounded when data are gathered by others. Often researchers rely on monitoring data which are collected for purposes other than the research. Certainly, case files are kept for other purposes. Consequently, crucial data may be missing or not completed consistently. There may be misunderstandings about the data requirements and data may be incorrectly or inconsistently recorded. Such problems are commonplace and can add to the sensitivities of project staff who feel burdened, and sometimes threatened, by the research process. Project staff often feel that the requirements of research, and particularly recording of data, take them away from their 'proper' work of spending time with clients. For these reasons, negotiating the buy-in of project staff on the ground is an important element of carrying out research on drug interventions. One important way of doing this is to disseminate research findings and recommendations down to all the staff on the project. In our experience, this rarely happens, with management personnel preferring instead to keep findings at their level.

Conclusion

This chapter has explored some of the issues which arise when researching and evaluating drug interventions and drug use more generally. One hurdle to undertaking this task is that published research reports tend to include only limited descriptions of the research methodology so that it is not always transparent how the research was undertaken, what measures were used and how definitions were arrived at. They also tend to be sanitized accounts so it is not possible to obtain an insight into what practices were followed to ensure that the physical, emotional, ethical and legal risks were kept to a minimum and how any difficulties encountered were resolved. This might be because many of the reports are published by official sources such as the Home Office and Ministry of Justice, where space precludes a lengthy methodological discussion. It may also arise because of a perceived need to uphold the integrity of the research by keeping any methodological shortcomings, challenges or compromises hidden. The situation is compounded because final reports of some of the most important evaluations of drug interventions have not been published. The combined effect is to prevent the sharing of experiences and to stifle open dialogue about the issues and problems which arise with this type of research. It also militates against consistency of approach, particularly in relation to the measurement of drug use, which reduces the comparability of findings and prevents the accumulation of evidence about how, why and for whom interventions succeed or fail.

Researchers face major methodological challenges when researching drug use and criminal justice separately, and bringing the two together results in further challenges particularly in terms of access and ethical issues. One particular area of concern is access to treatment data. Interventions are premised on the assumption that receiving treatment will reduce drug use and therefore offending, but the barriers to accessing treatment data prevent any consideration of the nature of the treatment received or whether it is linked to reductions in drug use or offending. While the confidentiality of medical data is important, questions need to be asked about how treatment generally, and particular forms of treatment more specifically, are to be evaluated when access to data is denied. Indeed, the recent review of funding for prison-based drug treatment services raises considerable issues about the lack of evidence of success for some of the more prevalent treatment options within the prison system (PricewaterhouseCoopers, 2008). Accessing official data more generally has become more difficult since the research discussed in this book was completed. This is due to increasing awareness of data security in light of several events involving the loss of personal data by government departments and researchers, which has resulted in increased requirements being adhered to before data are released. Researchers will have to demonstrate increasingly that data security is a priority and that measures are in place to minimize the chances of loss.

The research activity in the area of drug interventions in the criminal justice system is to be welcomed and there is no doubt that it has added to our knowledge of drug use, its treatment and its relationship with offending. Furthermore, the research has been strengthened by being undertaken by individuals from a variety of backgrounds, sometimes working together in interdisciplinary teams, providing a range of perspectives and expertise. However, much of the research has been in the form of evaluations funded by government to establish whether particular interventions 'work'. This has narrowed the focus of drugs research, partly because this is where the funding has been available and, to a degree, because it has kept many drugs researchers tied up over a period of years. One of the findings from the evaluations has been the limited knowledge base which exists in relation to many aspects of drug use and the need for them to be supported by different forms of research using a wider range of research designs and methodologies, including longitudinal research.

The future for drugs research is uncertain. One of the major sources of funding during the past decade has been the Home Office but there have been few opportunities to tender for projects on drug interventions in criminal justice during the past two to three years. The 2008 drug strategy (HM Government, 2008a) suggested that more funding might become available, particularly for studies relating to drug treatment. It stated that the government would 'seek to develop a strategic research programme over the next ten years that draws on enhanced partnership working between government, academia and the wider international research community in order to further develop our evidence base and support the delivery of our new drug strategy' (HM Government, 2008a: 56). In the first instance, it envisages that the government would commission a review of the existing research which would identify priority areas for research. Improving the evidence base relating to drugs is included as a strategic objective in the action plan which accompanies the drug strategy (HM Government, 2008b). The action plan also promises a cross-government research plan which is aligned to developing international evidence. However, at the time of writing (autumn 2009) the plan has not been published. It seems credible to suggest that pressures to reduce public expenditure may make it difficult to proceed with the programme of research and pilot programmes envisaged by the drug strategy. The unintended benefit of the lack of government funding is that it is likely to free up experienced drug researchers to undertake a wider range of research drawing on a broader set of methodologies thus enriching the evidence base relating to drug use and potentially questioning some of the assumptions upon which government policy is currently based.

References

Adams, C. (2000) 'Suspect data: arresting research', in R. King and E. Wincup (eds) *Doing Research on Crime and Justice*. Oxford: Oxford University Press.

Bennett, T. and Holloway, K. (2009) 'The causal connection between drug misuse and crime', *British Journal of Criminology*, 49(4): 513–31.

British Society of Criminology (2006) *Code of Ethics for Researchers in the Field of Criminology*. London: British Society of Criminology.

Bullock, T. (2003) 'Changing levels of drug use before, during and after imprisonment', in M. Ramsay (ed.) *Prisoners' Drug Use and Treatment: Seven Research Studies*, Home Office Research Study 267. London: Home Office.

Burgess, R. (1982) 'The unstructured interview as a conversation', in R. Burgess (ed.) *Field Research: A Sourcebook and Field Manual*. London: Allen & Unwin.

Burgess, R. (1984) *In the Field: An Introduction to Field Research*. London: Allen & Unwin.

Burrows, J., Clarke, A., Davison, T., Tarling, R. and Webb, S. (2001) *The Nature and Effectiveness of Drugs Throughcare for Released Prisoners*, Research Findings 109. London: Home Office.

Edgar, K. and O'Donnell, I. (1998) *Mandatory Drug Testing in Prisons: The Relationship between MDT and the Level and Nature of Drug Misuse*, Home Office Research Study 189. London: Home Office.

Farrall, S. and Calverley, A. (2006) *Understanding Desistance for Crime: Theoretical Directions in Resettlement and Rehabilitation*. Buckingham: Open University Press.

Fountain, J. (1993) 'Dealing with data', in D. Hobbs and T. May (eds) *Interpreting the Field: Accounts of Ethnography*. Oxford: Clarendon Press.

Fry, C. and Dwyer, R. (2001) 'For love or money? An exploratory study of why injecting drug users participate in research', *Addiction*, 96(9): 1319–25.

General Medical Council (2009) *Patient Confidentiality*. http://www.gmc-uk.org/guidance/current/library/confidentiality.asp#1 (accessed 15 September 2009).

Gossop, M., Trakada, K., Stewart, D. and Witton, J. (2006) *Levels of Conviction flowing Drug Treatment: Linking Data from the National Treatment Outcome Research Study and the Offenders Index*, Home Office Findings 275. London: Home Office.

Hedderman, C. and Hough, M. (2004) 'Getting tough or being effective: what matters?', in G. Mair (ed.) *What Matters in Probation*. Cullompton: Willan Publishing.

HM Government (2008a) *Drugs: Protecting Families and Communities. The 2008 Drug Strategy.* London: HM Government.

HM Government (2008b) *Drugs: Protecting Families and Communities' Action Plan 2008–2011.* London: HM Government.

HM Prison Service (2008) *Annual Report and Accounts 2007–2008*, HC 860. London: The Stationery Office.

Holloway, K. and Bennett, T. (2004) *The Results of the First Two Years of the NEW-ADAM Programme*, Home Office Online Report 19/04. London: Home Office.

Holloway, K., Bennett, T. and Farrington, D. (2005) *The Effectiveness of Criminal Justice and Treatment Programmes in Reducing Drug-Related Crime: A Systematic Review*, Home Office Online Report 26/05. London: Home Office.

Home Office (2002) *Updated Drug Strategy 2002.* London: Home Office.

Hodgson, P., Parker, A. and Seddon, T. (2006) 'Doing drugs research in the criminal justice system: some notes from the field', *Addiction Research and Theory*, 14(3): 253–64.

Hucklesby, A., Eastwood. C., Seddon, T. and Spriggs, A. (2007) *The Evaluation of Restriction on Bail Pilots: Final Report*, RDS On-line Report 06/07. London: Home Office.

Hussain Rassool, G. (ed.)(2001) *Dual Diagnosis: Substance Misuse and Psychiatric Disorders.* Oxford: Blackwell Publishing.

Hutchinson, S., Taylor, A., Gruer, L., Barr, C. Mills, C., Elliott, L., Goldberg, D., Scott, R. and Gilchrist, G. (2000) 'One-year follow-up of opiate injectors treated with oral methadone in a GP-centred programme', *Addiction*, 95(7): 1055–68.

Liriano, S. and Ramsay, M. (2003) 'Prisoners' drug use before prison and the links with crime', in M. Ramsay (ed.) *Prisoners' Drug Use and Treatment: Seven Research Studies*, Home Office Research Study 267. London: Home Office.

Lloyd, C., Mair, G. and Hough, M. (1994) *Explaining Reconviction Rates: A Critical Analysis*, Home Office Research Study 136. London: Home Office.

Mair, G. (ed.) (1997) *Evaluating the Effectiveness of Community Penalties.* Aldershot: Avebury.

Maruna, S. (2001) *Making Good: How Ex-convicts Reform and Rebuild their Lives.* Washington, DC: American Psychological Association Books.

Matrix Research & Consultancy and Nacro (2004) *Evaluation of Drug Testing in the Criminal Justice System*, Home Office Research Study 286. London: Home Office.

McKeganey, N. (2001) 'To pay or not to pay: respondents' motivations for participating in research', *Addiction*, 96(9): 1337–8.

McMahon, G., Hall, A., Hayward, G., Hudson, C., Roberts, C., Fernandez, R. and Burnett, R. (2004) *Basic Skills Programmes in the Probation Service: Evaluation of the Basic Skills Pathfinder*, Home Office Online Report 14/04. London: Home Office.

Ministry of Justice (2008) *Disrupting the Supply of Illicit Drugs into Prisons: A Report for the Director General of National Offender Management Service by D. Blakey*. London: Ministry of Justice.

National Offender Management Service (NOMS) (2008) *The National Offender Management Service Drug Strategy 2008–2011*. London: Ministry of Justice.

Noaks, L. and Wincup, E. (2004) *Criminological Research: Understanding Qualitative Approaches*. London: Sage.

Padfield, N. and Maruna, S. (2006) 'The revolving door at the prison gate: exploring the dramatic increase in recalls to prison', *Criminology and Criminal Justice*, 6(3): 329–52.

President of the Council (1998) *Tackling Drugs to Build a Better Britain: The Government's Ten-Year Strategy for Tackling Drugs Misuse*, Cm 3945. London: The Stationery Office.

PricewaterhouseCoopers (2008) *Review of Prison-Based Drug Treatment Funding*, Report to the Department of Health and Ministry of Justice. London: Ministry of Justice.

Rethink and Turning Point (2004) *Dual Diagnosis Toolkit: Substance Misuse and Mental Health – A Practical Guide for Professionals and Practitioners*. London: Rethink and Turning Point.

Reuter, P. and Stevens, A. (2008) 'Assessing UK drug policy from a crime control perspective', *Criminology and Criminal Justice*, 8(4): 461–82.

Rhodes, T. (2000) 'The role of qualitative research', in J, Fountain (ed.) *Understanding and Responding to Drug Use: The Role of Qualitative Research*. Lisbon: European Monitoring Centre for Drugs and Drug Addiction.

Seddon, T. (2005) 'Paying drug users to take part in research: justice, human rights and business perspectives on the use of incentive payments', *Addiction Research and Theory*, 13(2): 101–9.

Social Research Association (2001) *Code of Practice for the Safety of Researchers*. London: Social Research Association.

Social Research Association (2003) *Ethical Guidelines: December 2003*. London: Social Research Association.

Sondhi, A., O'Shea, J. and Williams, T. (2002) *Arrest Referral: Emerging Findings from the National Monitoring and Evaluation Programme*, Drug Prevention Advisory Service Paper 18. London: Home Office.

Stevens, A., Radcliffe, P., Sanders, M. and Hunt, N. (2008) 'Early exit: estimating and explaining early exit from drug treatment', *Harm Reduction Journal*, 5: 13.

Strang, J., Marsden, J., Cummins, M., Farrell, M., Finch, E., Gossop, M., Stewart, D. and Welch, S. (2000) 'Randomised trial of supervised injectable versus oral methadone maintenance: report of feasibility and 6-month outcome', *Addiction*, 95(11): 1631–45.

Taylor, A. (1993) *Women Drug Users: An Ethnography of a Female Injecting Community*. Oxford: Clarendon Press.

Turnbull, P., McSweeney, T., Webster, R., Edmunds, M. and Hough, M. (2000) *Drugs Treatment and Testing Orders: Final Evaluation Report*, Home Office Research Study 212. London: Home Office.

Wardhaugh, J. (2000) 'Down and outers: fieldwork amongst street homeless people', in R. King and E. Wincup (eds) *Doing Research on Crime and Justice*. Oxford: Oxford University Press.

Wilkinson, C., Hucklesby, A., Pearson, Y., Butler, E., Hill, A. and Hodkinson, S. (2003) 'Management of drug-using prisoners in Leicestershire', in M. Ramsay (ed.) *Prisoners' Drug Use and Treatment: Seven Research Studies*, Home Office Research Study 267. London: Home Office.

Wincup, E. (2009) 'Researching crime and criminal justice', in C. Hale, K. Hayward. A. Wahidin and E. Wincup (eds) *Criminology*, 2nd edition. Oxford: Oxford University Press.

Wincup, E., Buckland, G. and Bayliss, R. (2003) *Youth Homelessness and Substance Use: Report to the Drugs and Alcohol Unit*, Home Office Research Study 258. London: Home Office.

Wincup, E. and Hucklesby, A. (2007) 'Researching and evaluating resettlement', in A. Hucklesby and L. Hagley-Dickinson (eds) *Prisoner Resettlement: Policy and Practice*. Cullompton: Willan Publishing.

3 Policing problem drug users

Stuart Lister and Emma Wincup

Introduction

Recent estimates suggest that there are approximately 329,000 problem drug users (defined as users of opiates and/or crack cocaine) in England (Hay et al., 2008), many of whom are frequent offenders, typically committing crimes such as fraud, burglary, robbery and shoplifting to fund their drug consumption (Gordon et al., 2006). As a consequence, such individuals frequently encounter the police in adversarial circumstances, whether initiated by the police, private security guards or the public. Many problem drug users are highly visible to the police, spending lengthy periods of time in public places where police patrols are most intensively deployed. This chapter maps the different purposes which policing problem drug users serves and explores how they translate into day-to-day street encounters between police and problem drug users. Most importantly, given the focus of this volume, it considers the role played by the police in promoting access to drug interventions and elucidates how policing can both encourage and undermine their effectiveness.

Despite the frequency with which police encounter problem drug users, these interactions have rarely received research attention. Instead, criminologists have concentrated on the policing of drugs, ranging from explorations of low-level (or street-level) drug law enforcement (for example, Collison, 1995; Murji, 1998; Aitken et al., 2002; Dixon and Maher, 2002), through to considerations of high-level international efforts to curtail the supply of illegal drugs (see South, 2007) and, in between, actions to disrupt middle-level drug markets (for example, Hobbs and Pearson, 2001, 2003). More is known about the realities of policing cannabis users. Commissioned by the Joseph Rowntree Foundation as part of its Drug and Alcohol Programme, two studies focused on the policing of cannabis, first as a Class B drug (May et al., 2002), and subsequently, following its reclassification in 2004,[1] as a Class C drug (May et al., 2007). Together they chart the shift in policy and practice away from arresting drug users for most possession offences towards the use of street warnings.

This chapter therefore relies heavily on the findings of a recent study of the street policing of problem drug users. Commissioned by the Joseph

Rowntree Foundation, the research set out to explore the nature, processes and outcomes of routine interactions between problem drug users and the police. The study[2] was conducted over an 18-month period in three police forces in England and Wales and employed a mixed-method research design (see Lister et al., 2008, for a full account of the aims of the research and the methodology). Interviews were conducted with 45 police officers and 62 problem drug users. Interviews alongside focus groups were also used to capture the experiences of 22 (non-police) security-orientated personnel, including private security guards, council-employed street and neighbourhood wardens, and CCTV operators. Over 100 hours were also spent directly observing street policing personnel at different times of the day across a range of contexts.

As discussed in the introduction to this volume, problem drug use is a fluid and contested concept. For the purposes of the study it was loosely defined as individuals using opiates and/or crack cocaine. Attempts to impose a more rigid definition were resisted because exploring different definitions of the concept and how these shape policing responses was a fundamental research question. The term 'policing' also merits further discussion as the range of activities it captures, where it takes place and by whom are not readily apparent. Although 'policing' refers to a set of practices undertaken by a wide array of institutional actors (for example, public police, private security, council wardens), this chapter concentrates on the role of the public police operating in openly accessible street settings. It is important to clarify the range of personnel from the public police involved in policing problem drug users. While there was considerable variation between the three sites, it was possible to identify some broad trends. First, policing this group was not the preserve of specialist drug teams. Only one force had a dedicated drugs team and its remit was to take enforcement action against dealers of Class A drugs rather than drug users. While some specialist teams were heavily involved in policing problem drug users, they were interested in them for reasons other than their drug use; for example, because they were known persistent offenders. Second, a range of teams shared responsibility for policing problem drug users, including criminal investigation teams, responsive teams and neighbourhood teams: the latter typically comprising police community support officers (PCSOs) working alongside police constables.

Mapping out the policy terrain

The study took place against a backdrop of considerable policy development. The drug strategy *Tackling Drugs to Build a Better Britain* (President of the Council, 1998), was nearing the end of its ten-year term. Within this strategy, the police were identified as key players, particularly in relation to two of the four overarching aims: communities (reducing crime and anti-social behaviour) and availability (action on supply), but also in relation to young people (education and prevention) and treatment (improving access and participation). In terms of day-to-day street policing, forces were asked to focus resources on the detection of drug-related crime and to refer offenders to treatment, where appropriate, at the same time as reducing levels of street dealing and the availability of drugs in communities.

An updated strategy launched in 2002 (Home Office, 2002) included a tougher focus on Class A drugs (i.e. those judged to be the most harmful to an individual and society) such as heroin and cocaine and expanded the number of points in the criminal justice process at which offenders could be directed towards treatment. It also stated that a priority was to work with 'the 250,000 Class A drug users with the most severe problems who account for 99 per cent of the costs of drug abuse in England and Wales and do most harm to themselves, their families and communities' (Home Office, 2002: 2). In an attempt to coordinate the range of opportunities to refer offenders to treatment from the point of arrest through to release from prison, the Drug Interventions Programme (DIP) was launched in 2003. The police have become one of the key partner agencies in delivering this programme, and in some areas have taken on a leading role (see Turnbull and Skinns, Chapter 4 this volume). As of June 2009, 23 of the 43 police forces in England and Wales are eligible to test those arrested for or charged with 'trigger' offences (i.e. those deemed to be drug-related such as acquisitive crime; see Mair and Millings, Chapter 5 this volume) and a further seven are able to test on charge only (Home Office, 2009; National Treatment Agency, 2009). Testing allows the police to identify users of heroin, crack and cocaine and refer them to DIP. Consequently the police play a key role in terms of channelling, and in many respects coercing, drug users caught up in the criminal justice process into treatment. Since the implementation of sections 22–27 of the Criminal Justice Act 2003, the police (with the authorization of the Crown Prosecution Service) have also been able to attach a DIP rehabilitative condition to a caution for adults (i.e. those over 18). This disposal is an alternative to prosecution for first-time and low-level offenders. It requires offenders to engage with drug treatment services, or potentially face being charged and possibly prosecuted for the initial offence (see Home Office, 2008, for a description of the eligibility criteria, the 'menu' of conditions available and compliance).

Towards the end of the fieldwork phase, a consultation for a new strategy was published (HM Government, 2007). Subsequently launched in 2008, the current drug strategy, *Drugs: Protecting Families and Communities*

(HM Government, 2008), places emphasis on restricting the supply of illegal drugs and reducing the demand for them. Local police forces therefore have the dual role of channelling drug users into treatment while simultaneously tackling local drug markets and supply networks. Like its 2002 predecessor, the new drug strategy emphasizes targeting the most prolific drug-using offenders, but identifies more explicitly the requirement for the police to work in partnership with other agencies in this respect. In keeping with the special emphasis the strategy places on protecting communities alongside families, it also outlines the need for the police to work *with* communities to address their concerns about drugs.

Although the strategy maps out the broad trajectory of government policy on drugs, it is important to recognize that policing policy does not always closely align with the vision of the drug strategy because it is shaped by its own discrete set of strategic drivers. For example, contrary to the strong enforcement rhetoric of successive national drug strategies, the relative absence of 'drugs' within the Police Performance Assessment Framework (until recently the primary means by which the government measured the performance of local police forces) has, in effect, relegated the priority given to drug offences by local police managers (Chatterton, 2008; Royal Society of Arts 2007). Although the 1995 White Paper *Tackling Drugs Together* (HM Government, 1995) did aspire to create strategic alignment between the policy domains of drugs and policing, requiring police and their partners to produce local anti-drugs strategies outlining local plans to meet national objectives for tackling drugs (Newburn and Elliot, 1998), there remains no overarching and coherent policy on policing problem drug users. Consequently, over the past decade, the strategic response of the police towards this group has tended to be shaped by a variety of governmental agendas and policy initiatives which have influenced the organization, focus and delivery of local policing. Furthermore, the police are also subject to a bewildering array of competing demands for service which they must try to meet within limited resources. Consequently, in the necessary process of prioritization, police practices do not always accord with drugs policy. For instance, following the downgrading in the controlled status of cannabis, the 2002 *Updated Drug Strategy* suggested that police forces should increase enforcement activity towards Class A drug offences; yet in the three sites studied by May and colleagues (2007), owing to resource constraints no such operational shift occurred.

Foremost among demands for service has been the political emphasis placed on the reduction of 'volume crime', a shorthand referent for burglary, personal robbery and high incidence forms of vehicle crime. Subsequently, government pressure brought to bear on local police managers through the use of statutory performance indicators and Public Service Agreement targets has resulted in those problem drug users who regularly commit acquisitive crime being increasingly prioritized by the police (Neyroud and Disley, 2007). This development, coupled with the lower priority accorded to drug offences, has led Parker (2006: 6) to suggest that in terms of operational focus 'there has been a switch from policing drugs to policing drug users who are also acquisitive offenders'. To this end, there has been an increase in the frequency of proactive surveillance patrols directed towards 'known' offenders which aim to disrupt and deter their criminal activities. In accordance with this objective, police have become increasingly involved in offender-focused, multi-agency supervision schemes, such as the Prolific and other Priority Offender (PPO) programme, which monitor closely the whereabouts and behaviours of identified offenders.

Introduced in September 2004, the PPO programme was a policy response to increasing recognition that a very small proportion of highly recidivist offenders were responsible for a disproportionately large amount of crime (Dawson and Cuppleditch, 2007). It therefore reflects an 'intelligence-led' approach towards reducing reoffending, in which police activity is orientated towards the 'criminal' rather than the 'crime'. Although not aimed specifically at problem drug users, the national evaluation of the programme found that its 'clients' were 'more likely to misuse "hard" drugs, more likely to misuse a variety of drug types, more likely to be fully occupied by the pursuit and misuse of drugs; and their offending was more likely to be judged as being linked to their drug misuse' (Dawson, 2007: 6). Multi-agency work within the PPO programme coalesces around the following interrelated strands: prevent and deter; catch and control; and rehabilitate and resettle. Employing what has been termed a 'carrot and stick approach' (Bateman, 2005), it offers support to offenders to help them resettle and desist from offending; for example, for drug users the 'carrot' is priority access to drug treatment. The 'stick' for those who do not engage with the tiers of support available to them is close multi-agency monitoring, thus reifying the threat of swift enforcement action for those not complying with any post-release licence conditions (for example, to desist from using controlled drugs). Subsequently, the DIP and PPO programme have been aligned 'to establish an even tighter *grip* on those drug misusers that commit the highest amount of crime' (NOMS, 2009: 2, emphasis added).

Building on the alignment of the DIP and PPO programme, a more expansive and coordinated form of offender supervision known as Integrated Offender Management (IOM) was launched in July 2008 across six 'pioneer' sites. IOM broadly adopts the same model of intervention as the PPO programme but extends the coverage to a wider cohort of offenders by targeting for supervision those released from short-term prison sentences (i.e. less than 12 months) who are not subject to statutory supervision by other criminal justice agencies. It therefore offers a way of extending the reach of 'community supervision' while deepening and rationalizing the nature of joint working among police, probation, drug treatment agencies, social housing providers, electronic monitoring companies, employment agencies and 'third sector' voluntary organizations. For example, one element of the IOM scheme is unannounced home visits from the police for those under supervision. Sometimes referred to as 'disruption visits', this form of proactive surveillance aims to ensure compliance with the scheme by reminding 'clients' of the pervasive reach of police powers. It is clearly the intention of government to roll out nationally the IOM approach (see Home Office/Ministry of Justice, 2009), thereby increasing the likelihood of problem drug users being routinely subjected to police monitoring and intervention.

Over the same period the convergence of the anti-social behaviour and drugs agendas has brought a wide range of (often drug-related) low-level and socially problematic behaviours to the forefront of public policy concerns. As a result, some problem drug users have increasingly attracted policing attention for engaging in street activities intimately linked to social and economic exclusion, in particular rough sleeping, begging, street drinking and prostitution (Johnsen and Fitzpatrick, 2007). Strongly influenced by Wilson and Kelling's 'broken windows' theory of neighbourhood decline (1982), the anti-social behaviour agenda promotes authoritative intervention against those individuals and groups whose behaviour or presence might be construed as likely to adversely affect public sensibilities over 'place well-being' and 'neighbourhood safety' (Innes and Jones, 2006). Subsequently, perceptions of security and order have become a key driver of police activity, reflected in the growth of 'reassurance-based' policing strategies which claim to enhance levels of police visibility and respond to the priorities of local communities. As a result, the police, often working jointly with their local authority partners in Crime and Disorder Reduction Partnerships, have been increasingly tasked, both from above by government-imposed directives and performance targets, and below by the demands of residents' groups and local businesses, with 'cleaning up the streets' and therein tackling visible forms of drug-related impropriety.

Since 1998, successive pieces of legislation have given police and councils a raft of novel enforcement powers and administrative tools to combat 'anti-social behaviour' in its various guises, including drug use and dealing itself (see Crawford, 2009, for a summary). Many of these enforcement tools are spatially based and preventative in orientation, mostly either prohibiting certain behaviours or excluding 'undesirable' persons from specific locations. For example, introduced by Section one of the Crime and Disorder Act 1998, Anti-Social Behaviour Orders (ASBOs) have been widely used to exclude from specified public spaces those who have caused, or were likely to cause, harassment, alarm or distress to others. Importantly, these widely drawn civil sanctions can now be tied to coerced drug treatment. Under section 20 of the Drugs Act 2005, where an adult's drug use is related to the behaviour under review, a drugs 'intervention order' can be attached to an ASBO requiring recipients to access treatment (for example, drug counselling). At the same time there has been a dramatic expansion in the range of low-level offences for which police officers, along with PCSOs and other persons accredited by the chief constable of a local force, can issue a Penalty Notice for Disorder (PND) (an 'on-the-spot' summary fine of either £50 or £80). Initially introduced by Section one of the Criminal Justice and Police Act 2001, PNDs can now be issued for various offences, including those of theft (up to the value of £100), criminal damage (up to the value of £300) and possession of cannabis. Such powers tend to be highly discretionary, providing the police with a greater and more flexible range of enforcement options when responding to problem drug users than before. For instance, rather than seeking to gain evidence of a person's drug use (for example, possession of Class A drugs), the police can take action against problem drug users though these more diverse methods and sanctions. Yet the PND scheme has drawn sharp criticism for the lack of procedural safeguards governing their use, which in effect allows patrolling police operating with great discretion to dispense punishment to those whose legal culpability has not been established by a court of law (see Young, 2008).

The implementation of these policy shifts has been facilitated by a series of interrelated changes within policing. First, there has been a sizeable increase in the operational capacity of the police. Since 2000, across the 43 local police forces in England and Wales, the number of available police officers has increased by almost 20,000 to over 141,000 (approximately 16 per cent) (Mulchandani and Sigurdsson, 2009). Furthermore, since the introduction of the Police Reform Act 2002 over 16,500 PCSOs have been recruited to increase the visible presence of the police in local neighbourhoods. Operating with a limited range of powers, PCSOs mostly focus on fostering community relations, providing reassurance and tackling low-level anti-social behaviour. Powers available to them in specified circumstances include the power to disperse groups in designated areas, to detain persons for thirty minutes, to stop and search, to seize alcohol and to issue Penalty Notices for Disorder. Second, a large proportion of local police resources have been restructured into over 3,600 Neighbourhood Policing Teams (NPTs). Operating to a 'citizen-focused' agenda, these locally devolved units were established to provide proactive and problem-solving responses to local problems of order (Home Office, 2004). NPTs comprise dedicated teams of police officers and PCSOs, the intention being to enhance knowledge of and ownership of local problems, including the activities of local offenders. They also, therefore, have an important intelligence-gathering function, for example undertaking surveillance both of suspected or 'known' offenders and of crime and disorder 'hotspots'. Third, the national roll-out of the National Intelligence Model, a tool for gathering and analysing information, has resulted in police patrols being deployed in a more targeted manner, for instance towards those individuals and groups which intelligence reports indicate are actively involved in offending (Tilley, 2008). Fourth, the Crime and Disorder Act 1998 has placed a statutory duty on police and other local agencies to work in partnership to address public concerns over crime and disorder. As a consequence, police have far greater access to the wealth of personal information held by partner agencies (for example, local authorities, probation) on problem drug users. They are also able to facilitate and encourage local authorities and other social housing providers to use the full range of resources and powers available to them to deal with problem drug users in ways that lie beyond the criminal justice process (Lee and South, 2008).

Policing problem drug users: understanding its objectives

Broadly stated, the study found that the overarching objective of the police towards problem drug users was concerned with controlling their everyday activities in order to manage the risks and potential harms they presented to local communities. As we have described above, the lens of coercive police intervention was selectively focused on specific groups of drug users who were designated to be a 'problem' by the police, albeit operating within partnership frameworks. In this regard, the 'problem' was rarely articulated in terms of their actual drug use but, instead, it related to the harms that their drug use potentially caused to others, whether through committing acquisitive crime or by engaging in behaviour perceived to be anti-social. Consequently, the primary objective of the public police was concerned less with drug law enforcement and far more with protecting the public from a 'risky' population perceived to be a threat to local order and security. Pursuing this objective resulted in prioritizing preventative approaches to police work in which anticipatory forms of engagement with problem drug users were pursued as a means of containing the broad array of harms arising from their drug-related behaviours. It therefore accorded with what has been described elsewhere as a 'community damage limitation' approach wherein police goals are multifaceted and overlapping, for instance focusing on reducing levels of crime but also negating the public's fear of crime (Lee, 1996). In seeking to manage these risks, it is important to recognize the limitations of policing ambitions: policing did provide a pathway into drug treatment, but fulfilling this procedural outcome was less the priority of street policing than managing the public harms associated with problem drug use.

In pursuing their objective of controlling problem drug users, police utilized assorted processes of surveillance, identification, categorization and exclusion. As Ericson and Haggerty (1997) have described, the collection and distribution of knowledge about suspect populations is central to this task. In this regard, neighbourhood policing resources were routinely deployed by police managers to undertake surveillance of public and quasi-public places where problem drug users were known to congregate, either to use drugs or, more likely, to engage in other forms of anti-social behaviour (for example street drinking, begging, rough sleeping). Once located and categorized as a 'problem', drug users were frequently questioned before being moved on and thus subject of a temporary form of exclusion. Such surveillance patrols enabled the police to map so-called crime and disorder hotspots and manage them while simultaneously providing further intelligence to inform future patrol work. They also provided a means by which the police could control wider tracts of territory (i.e. sometimes referred to as *their* 'ground'). Indeed, temporarily 'moving people on' did not apply merely to highly localized 'criminogenic' places, but was often a default response that led to 'risky individuals' being instructed by police to move beyond the boundaries of a specific residential area, commercial centre or area of administrative jurisdiction (for example, a police division). In this regard, police objectives could be short-term and highly personalized, ensuring that spatial displacement of problem drug users into the 'territory of another' was routinely pursued as an appropriate, albeit informal, policy objective in its own right.

Information collected from surveillance patrols also fed into databases profiling the identities and offending histories of local problem drug users. The construction of these databases enabled knowledge of this population to be collated and disseminated throughout locally based police teams, usually at daily tasking meetings. Information was also frequently collected from individuals who were unknown to the police but attracted their suspicion: sometimes individuals were stopped and interrogated in the street for looking 'out of place' (for example, being of dishevelled appearance), at other times for being 'in the wrong place' (for example, in known open drug markets). This use of discretion was heavily informed by police cultural perceptions of criminality and 'respectability'. Equally, judgements about who was 'out of place' were informed by interpretations about the nature of specific locations and desirable agency within them (see also Herbert, 1997). It became apparent during observations that police officers applied different behavioural thresholds to different places and policed them accordingly. Once identified, 'known' individuals and those accompanying them were, to varying degrees, monitored as they went about their daily activities and subjected to regular low-level uses of police authority, for example being stopped and searched, asked to account for their presence in public places, checked against police databases, or generally questioned. Sometimes these encounters were in response to a specific crime, but mostly they served broader, more regulatory ambitions which are described below.

First, these encounters enabled police to assess the well-being, general outlook and dispositional attitudes of problem drug users, thus refining their knowledge base of whom among this population presented the greatest risk of engaging in behaviour that warranted closer and ongoing police attention. Second, they provided the police with opportunity to try to gain information which could be used as intelligence to help detect past, or prevent future, crimes. In particular, divisional 'jobbing' detectives, whose role is focused mostly on investigating crime incidents, reported that they often treated problem drug users in an instrumental manner. For example, one of our police interviewees described entering into 'bargaining agreements' with problem drug users, whereby in exchange for information it was tacitly understood that he would in the future, for instance, 'turn a blind eye' rather than execute an arrest warrant against them (see also Collison, 1995: 180; Hobbs, 1989: 203). As such, the crime-related information held by problem drug users, although they might not be aware of its utility, potentially acted as a resource they could draw upon to cultivate more amicable (or at least less repressive) relations with police. Third, they informed problem drug users that their presence and behaviour were being continually monitored and scrutinized. Police-initiated encounters with problem drug users therefore were a form of 'communicative surveillance' that served as a visible and tangible reminder of the proximal threat of police intervention. Fourth, and related, the low-level use of authority within these encounters served as an instrumental means of imposing discipline on a 'deviant' population. The ambition here was to encourage recipients to regulate their own behaviour so they avoided receiving unwanted police attention, for example by keeping away from specific areas. In other words, the regularity of low-level police interventions sought in part to motivate, through coercive actions, drug users to amend their behavioural routines, but also more broadly to change their lifestyle. However, this had negative implications for the provision of drug interventions, which we will now explore.

Street encounters with problem drug users: implications for drug interventions

One of the main aims of the research was to advance understanding of the nature, processes and outcomes of the day-to-day street policing of problem drug users. Elsewhere (Lister et al., 2008) we have attempted to characterize the range of encounters between problem drug users and policing personnel (focusing on the public police), concluding that most were informal, unplanned and preventative in orientation. As we have noted above, the majority of encounters were future-orientated, being prompted by a concern for what a problem drug user *might do* rather than what they *had done*. Such proactive policing methods, particularly when employed repeatedly, were often judged by recipients to be unwarranted and thus generated much hostility and antagonism. Moreover, many of our interviewees also perceived that the exercise of discretionary authority in street contexts, whether formal through stop and search or informal through cursory questioning, was often intentionally oppressive if not punitive. This finding was perhaps unsurprising as accounts of the culture of patrolling police officers have repeatedly identified the way it promotes the negative labelling of certain groups (i.e. 'the dross') and sustains intolerant, authoritative and discriminatory attitudes towards such groups (for example, Van Maanen, 1973; Choongh, 1997; Reiner, 2000; Foster, 2003). Our study found that, within the police value-system, problem drug users were one such group. As a consequence, the nature of their encounters with police had implications for the extent to which this group accessed drug treatment. These implications will be explored in the remainder of this section.

It is important to appreciate that only a small minority of the encounters described above resulted in a problem drug user being directed towards drug treatment. As we have stressed already, few encounters were initiated in response to an actual offence which might trigger a referral to the Drug Interventions Programme. Even when an offence had been committed, the usual processes of arrest, caution and charge could be circumvented if summary justice was dispensed (see Young, 2008, for a discussion of the shift towards summary justice). During the study period, such disposals were becoming increasingly popular because they appeared to offer a timely and cost-effective way to divert those who committed low-level offences away from the criminal justice process. However, for problem drug users, summary justice disposals such as issuing PNDs had the effect of removing an opportunity to access the Drug Interventions Programme and thus be provided with timely access to drug treatment. In recognition of this oversight, the Ministry of Justice has recently issued further guidance clarifying the inappropriateness of such sanctions for 'substance misusers' who have committed retail theft or criminal damage (Ministry of Justice, 2009). Where (and if) a person apprehended for an offence has been identified by police as a problem drug user, then the guidance proposes that alternative penalties should be considered which facilitate access to drug treatment. First, it suggests that police officers should consider the possibility of offering a conditional caution. Second, it advises that allowing the courts to sentence an offender might be more appropriate. While the new guidance fails to specify the meaning of 'substance misuser', it does remind officers that they have the power to test an individual for drug use once they have been charged with committing one of the specified offences (for example, theft) or if an inspector suspects the offence is drug related. Much therefore hinges upon whether an individual officer suspects someone to be a problem drug user based upon factors such as their appearance, intelligence reports, evidence of drug paraphernalia or prior knowledge. This subjective assessment is likely to lead to inconsistent practices. In addition, the change in policy potentially allows offenders who 'misuse substances' to receive higher tariff penalties than those who do not, justified upon the grounds that it affords them an opportunity to access treatment.

While it is fair to conclude that referring offenders to drug treatment was not a routine element of street policing, there were some exceptions. Some of the problem drug users interviewed did relay stories of individual police officers encouraging them to end their drug-using careers or putting them in touch with support agencies. This less conflictual face of police work tended to emerge only where more pro-social relationships between individual police and drug users had been allowed to forge over time. They can, however, best be viewed as fairly isolated examples. Where drug users were referred to treatment services, referral tended to be carried out by officers working within specialist teams which targeted particular groups of offenders (for example, persistent offenders) or those engaged in behaviours perceived to be problematic (for example, street homelessness or begging). Moreover, such referrals to drug and other support agencies mostly took place against a backdrop of law enforcement and were motivated as much by a concern with tackling priority crimes or 'cleaning up' the streets as by a desire to promote the well-being of individual drug users or public health more generally.

At one of the three sites, for example, a pre-arrest drug team had been established comprising two police officers and a worker from a local drugs agency. With funding from the local drug action team, they targeted problem drug users engaged in 'high volume' crime who were not being channelled into treatment through other criminal justice routes, either at the pre-trial stage (see Hucklesby, Chapter 6 this volume) or through sentences issued by the courts (see Stevens, Chapter 8 this volume). While seeking treatment was voluntary as it was not linked to statutory criminal justice processes, in practice offenders had little choice but to comply because unwillingness to be referred to treatment providers risked escalating the degree of police scrutiny that they were subjected to. The scheme was innovative in many respects, not least because of the novel partnership established between the police and a drug agency. Relationships between the police and drug agencies can be fraught with difficulties. The latter have often been reluctant to develop a close association with the former for fear that it may deter potential clients from accessing their services. Information sharing, or more precisely the perceived unwillingness of drug agencies to share information about their clients, constitutes a further barrier. There is also the potential for a clash of professional ideologies and working cultures given the focus of the police on enforcement and the harm reduction approach typically deployed by drug agencies (Seddon, 2007).

Given the regularity of contact between problem drug users and the police, the constructive potential of their encounters could be exploited to serve a purpose beyond regulation and control. There is a long-established tradition of taking advantage of the police custody suite setting to refer individuals to sources of support (Mair and Millings, Chapter 5 this volume), which could be mirrored in street contexts by patrolling officers. At its most basic this referral function involves moving people and information between relevant service providers, for example providing contact details of specific agencies that can offer support or, taking a more active stance, referring individuals directly to such agencies (see Crawford et al., 2005 for a discussion of the linking and referral function of front-line police staff). As problem drug users typically face multiple problems (McSweeney et al., 2004; Kemp et al., 2006), police personnel would need to be aware of the opportunities and capacities of a range of local support agencies that could offer problem drug users help with housing, employment or health-related matters. It may be that more pressing issues, for example homelessness or poor mental health, need to be tackled before it is appropriate to explore the possibility of entering drug treatment. More radically, it might involve police personnel offering basic on-the-spot advice, although it is foreseeable that this option would require them to undergo considerable training, while raising questions about the appropriate limitations of the police role. A major obstacle, however, is that problem drug users tend to be sceptical about the nature of police offers of assistance and therefore often seek to keep their contact with police to a minimum to avoid the threat of receiving what they perceive to be hassle.

While, as we have noted earlier in this chapter, policing was largely a prospective activity, it was influenced by knowledge of past behaviours. Consequently, those with histories of problem drug use and offending often found themselves defined continually with reference to their previous problematic behaviours (rather than any current attempts to desist from drug use and offending), and were thus subjected to ongoing police intervention. This labelling process often had a demoralizing effect on those who experienced it and undermined their attempts to establish an identity unrelated to offending and drug use. In particular, the study uncovered considerable resentment towards the police among those who felt they were continually being stopped or searched, often in highly visible public places. Despite the regulations governing the use of stop and search powers outlining provisions to minimize embarrassment to those against whom the power is used (see Police and Criminal Evidence Act 1984, Code of Practice A, 2008), several interviewees believed the goal of those exercising it was the exact inverse. Exposing individuals to such exclusionary practices did little to foster the attempts of problem drug users to (re)integrate themselves into mainstream society. At its most extreme it could lead to problem drug users moving to areas where they were unknown to the police thus severing their links with drug treatment providers. Accessing equivalent support in a new location can be problematic and involves undergoing further assessments and the possibility of a lengthy wait for treatment. Furthermore, access to some services, especially those relating to housing, may be available only to those who can prove they have a connection with the local area to which they have moved. Alternatively, individuals may remain within an area but render themselves invisible in an attempt to escape police attention. This might involve actively disengaging with services or making it difficult for outreach services to locate some of the most vulnerable problem drug users such as rough sleepers.

In the remainder of this section we turn our attention to two specific instances from our research study where police practices impinged upon the harm reduction ethos promoted by drug treatment agencies. The first, and the most widespread problem, related to the police finding drug paraphernalia on an individual following a stop and search.

A recurring theme within many police officers' accounts was that arrest would invariably follow if a person was found in possession of Class A drugs and they had little or no discretion in this matter. In contrast, the police officers interviewed reported that finding only drug paraphernalia on an individual (for example, hypodermic needles, burnt foil, glass smoking pipes) offered an opportunity to exercise greater discretion and arrest would not be an inevitable outcome. Their differing accounts of how they would proceed reflected divergent practices both within and between police forces when officers were faced with a similar set of circumstances. While some officers might arrest an individual, justifying such an action on the grounds that it would be to the benefit of the arrestee (for example, promoting access to treatment) or to the community (for example, helping to secure the closure of a crack house), others may decide that there is little possibility of a successful prosecution and so allow the drug user either to keep the equipment or confiscate it. Taking the latter course of action can result in policing practices encroaching on harm reduction agendas and, in particular, the ambitions of needle exchange schemes to promote safe injecting practices. For example, some problem drug users described how injecting equipment had been taken from them by police and thrown in a public bin, posing a health risk to the community. Indeed, some described how the threat of confiscation and the associated embarrassment of being searched in a public place and thus exposed as a user of Class A drugs, led them to avoid carrying injecting equipment in public places. These examples demonstrate that policing activities have the potential to increase the likelihood of injecting drug users sharing their 'works' because their own are no longer available, thus exposing problem drug users to blood-borne viruses such as HIV and hepatitis.

The varying practices described above suggest a pressing need for clear guidance in relation to this fuzzy area of policing practice. National guidance is needed to promote consistency, but supplemented by local policies that offer practical solutions: for example, details of needle exchange schemes that drug users could be referred to or the provision of advice to police officers on how to dispose of needles safely. There are recent precedents for replacing the discretionary use of authority with a more prescriptive approach to drugs. Coinciding with the reclassification of cannabis in 2004, the Association of Chief Police Officers issued guidance advising officers to issue street warnings for most cannabis possession offences, arresting only when aggravating circumstances exist such as smoking in public or in the vicinity of young people. It would, however, be naive to assume that guidance inevitably leads to consistency. May et al.'s (2007) study of the impact of reclassification on the policing of cannabis possession found that across the four participating sites, street warnings were used as a way of dealing with offences of cannabis possession but they were by no means the norm and were rarely used in some areas.

The second example relates to the police using drug agencies as a place to locate certain individuals, for example offenders subject to an arrest warrant or merely those identified to be 'of interest'. Although this strategy offers a convenient way to access a typically transient population, it is questionable on both instrumental and moral grounds. First, this practice may not be the most effective means of minimizing any (health or crime) risks to the public arising from problem drug use. To encourage drug users to access, and, most importantly, to continue to access, treatment drug services need to be viewed as 'safe spaces' that are primarily concerned with the health and well-being of an individual. The presence of uniformed police officers outside or inside the premises of those agencies providing drug treatment services is likely to undermine this goal. The establishment of DIP has resulted in police officers, drug workers and other professionals being physically co-located for the purpose of developing holistic support structures for problem drug users. However, these

partnership arrangements focus on those already 'inside' the criminal justice system and operate therefore in a very different context from community drug treatment services, whose clients are likely to include some
individuals who wish to avoid encountering police.

Second, it may be ethically unsound for police interventions to be deployed in such a way that they impinge on the desires and motivations
of those wishing to access treatment in order to improve their health (see
Neyroud and Beckley, 2001, for a discussion of the extent to which ethical
principles underpin integrity in police decision making). In this context,
at one site a protocol had been drawn up between the police and drug
agencies in an attempt to manage their relationship in a mutually beneficial way. Any alleged breaching of the protocol could be reported to one
of two named police officers in the division with a specific drugs coordination brief and they would then act promptly to investigate and follow
up accordingly.

Concluding comments

Whether it is possible for relationships between police and problem drug
users to be anything other than adversarial is a moot point, but it is evident that the current state of play has damaging consequences for those
wishing to end their drug-using and criminal careers. Accordingly, the
overriding message we wish to convey in this chapter is that effective
partnership working between police and drug treatment providers is essential to ensure that street policing of problem drug users enhances, or at
least does not detract from, the best efforts of drug treatment providers to
reduce harm and promote abstinence from drugs. The challenges of joint
working are considerable given the range of players involved from the
statutory, voluntary and private sectors and their different professional
cultures, ideologies and practices.

The rapidly escalating architecture of partnership structures, multi-
agency forums and integrated case management arrangements greatly enhances the potential for the police to develop their role as gatekeepers to
drug treatment and other support agencies. The findings of the study,
however, revealed that the cultural adaptations of operational policing
personnel to this new environment lagged some way behind strategic
visions. For instance, when dealing with problem drug users, officers
tended to eschew any pretensions they might have towards delivering
a 'citizen-focused' style of policing, in which the 'service' is responsive to
the needs of 'customers' (see Home Office, 2004). Welfare concerns did not
feature much in the way that police talked about or, indeed, responded
to problem drug users: benevolent overtures advocating assistance, care

and rehabilitation were the (rare) exception, less the rule, and were driven more by a desire to manage crime and anti-social behaviour than by a concern to 'help' individual drug users. Instead, traditional law enforcement methods were mostly deployed as blunt tools of control that aimed to manage the potential criminogenic risks arising from problem drug use. Such individuals were encouraged via proactive and targeted policing 'to take care of the self' by governing their own conduct in accordance with the norms dictated by local police (Foucault, 1986 [1984]), in particular, where they could go. One potential consequence of this surveillance activity is that drug users sever ties with local support agencies, including drug treatment providers.

Importantly, and unsurprisingly, the police overwhelmingly conceptualized the risks associated with problem drug use in terms of crime, disorder and fear of crime rather than health. Specifically, their priority was largely on containing more serious crime than drug possession offences, while maintaining the 'appearance of public order on the street' (Skolnick, 1966: 87). There are three points we wish to make here regarding the role of the police in channelling drug users into drug treatment. First, it may be viewed as perverse that the police (acting on government steer) have relegated the enforcement priority given to drug offences, particularly possession, at the very moment drug treatment expenditure has become closely (albeit not exclusively) pegged to criminal justice interventions. One outcome is that problem drug users who do not engage in serious or acquisitive crime, whether to fund their drug use or otherwise, do not have the same opportunities to access drug treatment. Second, as we have described above, where drug users are seen by police as a resource to obtain important information about more serious crimes, then they may be able to use this status to circumvent court processes and, in turn, entry into drug treatment. Third, a recurring theme of police research has been the extent to which the greater part of the policing task is not concerned with 'law enforcement' but with 'order maintenance' and 'public reassurance' (Reiner, 2000), delivered, for example, through community foot patrols and attending calls from the public for assistance. By implication, processing drug users into drug treatment through formal law enforcement mechanisms is far less central to the policing task than the broader requirement to sanitize and securitize public space (see Raco, 2003). In this regard, we have drawn attention to the myriad of encounters in which the police choose to intervene against problem drug users wherein no criminal offence has taken place and there is no intention to prosecute.

Finally, while this chapter has focused on the role of the public police, specifically in promoting criminal-justice-based drug treatment interventions, we should not overlook the activities of private policing operatives who are functionally detached from the government's drive to channel drug-using offenders into drug treatment. As we noted in the introduction to this chapter, the policing of problem drug users is not the sole preserve of the public police. In particular, private security personnel working in the private and quasi-private domains, for example of retail stores, shopping precincts, and licensed bars and clubs, also frequently encounter problem drug users in adversarial circumstances. Yet the ambitions of the private security sector are guided by the pursuit of profit, not the bureaucratic requirements of local partnership frameworks (South, 1988). In this regard, a central finding from research on private security personnel is their tendency to deal with 'transgressors' in an informal, parochial and exclusionary manner which circumvents recourse to the criminal justice process (Shearing and Stenning, 1981; Wakefield, 2003; Button, 2007). For instance, in their work on nightclub 'bouncers' Hobbs et al. (2003) found that it was in the commercial interests of pub and club owners to instruct 'their' security personnel not to contact the police when someone was found on their premises in possession of controlled drugs, but rather to simply exclude them from the premises. Similarly, retail store guards may opt to exclude an apprehended 'shoplifter' rather than contact the police because liaising with the police is time consuming and potentially escalates the level of conflict with those apprehended (Crawford et al., 2005). Such research raises critical questions over the extent to which public and private networks of policing are 'joined up' in their responses to problem drug users.

Notes

1. Cannabis was reclassified again in 2009 and is now defined as a Class B drug under the 1971 Misuse of Drugs Act.
2. Toby Seddon of the University of Manchester was the third grantholder.

References

Aitken, C., Moore, D., Higgs, P., Kelsall, J. and Kerger, M. (2002) 'The impact of a police crackdown on a street drug scene: evidence from the street', *International Journal of Drug Policy*, 13(3): 193–202.

Bateman, M. (2005) 'The Wolverhampton Prolific and Other Priority Offenders' Programme', *British Journal of Nursing*, 14(17): 924–8.

Button, M. (2007) *Security Officers and Policing: Powers, Cultures and Control in the Governance of Private Space*. Aldershot: Ashgate Press.

Chatterton, M. (2008) *Losing the Detectives: Views from the Frontline*. Leatherhead: Police Federation. http://www.polfed.org/Losing_The_Detectives_complete_report_jan08.pdf.

Choongh, S. (1997) *Policing as Social Discipline*. Oxford: Clarendon Press.

Collison, M. (1995) *Police, Drugs and Community*. London: Free Association Books.

Crawford, A. (2009) 'Governing through anti-social behaviour: regulatory challenges to criminal justice', *British Journal of Criminology*, 49(6): 810–31.

Crawford, A., Lister, S., Blackburn, S. and Burnett, J. (2005) *Plural Policing: The Mixed Economy of Visible Security Patrols*. Bristol: Policy Press.

Dawson, P. (2007) *The National PPO Evaluation – Research to Inform and Guide Practice*. Home Office Online Report 09/07. London: Home Office.

Dawson, P. and Cuppleditch, L. (2007) *An Impact Assessment of the Prolific and Other Priority Offender Programme*, Home Office Online Report 08/07. London: Home Office.

Dixon, D. and Maher, L. (2002) 'Anh Hai: policing, culture and social exclusion in a street heroin market', *Policing and Society*,12(2): 93–110.

Ericson, R. and Haggerty, K. (1997) *Policing the Risk Society*. Oxford: Clarendon Press.

Foster, J. (2003) 'Police cultures', in T. Newburn (ed.) *Handbook of Policing*. Cullompton: Willan Publishing.

Foucault, M. (1986 [1984]) *The History of Sexuality. Vol. 3: The Care of the Self*, trans. R. Hurley. New York: Pantheon.

Gordon, L., Tinsley, L., Godfrey, C. and Parrott, S. (2006) 'The economic and social costs of Class A drug use in England and Wales 2003/4', in N. Singleton, R. Murray and L. Tinsley (eds) *Measuring Different Aspects of Problem Drug Use: Methodological Developments*, Home Office Online Report 16/06. London: Home Office.

Hay, G., Gannon, M., MacDougall, J., Millar, T., Williams, K., Eastwood, C. and McKeganey, N. (2008) *National and Regional Estimates of the Prevalence of Opiate Use and/or Crack Cocaine Use 2006/07: A Summary of Key Findings*, Research Report 9. London: Home Office.

Herbert, S. (1997) *Policing Space: Territoriality and the Los Angeles Police Department*. Minnesota: University of Minnesota Press.

HM Government (1995) *Tackling Drugs Together: A Strategy for England 1995–1998*. London: HM Government.

HM Government (2007) *Drugs: Our Community, Your Say. A Consultation Paper*. London: HM Government.

HM Government (2008) *Drugs: Protecting Families and Communities. The 2008 Drug Strategy*. London: HM Government.

Hobbs, D. (1989) *Doing the Business: Entrepreneurship, The Working Class, and Detectives in the East End of London*. Oxford: Oxford University Press.

Hobbs, D., Hadfield, P., Lister, S. and Winlow, S. (2003) *Bouncers: Violence and Governance in the Night-Time Economy*. Oxford: Oxford University Press.

Hobbs, D. and Pearson, G. (2001) *Middle Market Drug Distribution*. London: Home Office.

Hobbs, D. and Pearson, G. (2003) 'King Pin? A case study of a middle market', *Howard Journal of Criminal Justice*, 42(4): 335–47.

Home Office (2002) *Updated Drug Strategy 2002.* London: Home Office.

Home Office (2004) *Building Communities, Beating Crime.* London: Home Office.

Home Office (2008) *Conditional Cautioning and the DIP Condition: Operational Guidance for Criminal Justice Integrated Teams and Partners.* London: Home Office.

Home Office (2009) *Guidance for the Implementation of the DIP Provisions of the Drugs Act 2005*, Annex A. London: Home Office.

Home Office/Ministry of Justice (2009) *Integrated Offender Management: Government Policy Statement.* London: Home Office/Ministry of Justice.

Innes, M. and Jones, J. (2006) *Risk, Resilience and Recovery: Security and Transforming the Prospects of Places.* York: Joseph Rowntree Foundation.

Johnsen, S. and Fitzpatrick, S. (2007) *The Impact of Enforcement on Street Users in England.* York: Joseph Rowntree Foundation.

Kemp, P., Neale, J. and Robertson, M. (2006) 'Homelessness among problem drug users: prevalence, risk factors and trigger events', *Health and Social Care in the Community*, 14(1): 319–25.

Lee, M. (1996) 'London: community damage limitation and the future of drug enforcement', in N. Dorn, J. Jepsen and E. Savona (eds) *European Drug Policies and Enforcement.* London: Macmillan.

Lee, M. and South, N. (2008) 'Drugs policing', in T. Newburn (ed.) *Handbook of Policing*, 2nd edition. Cullompton: Willan Publishing.

Lister. S., Seddon, T., Wincup, E., Barrett, S. and Traynor, P. (2008) *Street Policing of Problem Drug Users.* York: Joseph Rowntree Foundation.

May, T., Duffy, M., Warburton, H. and Hough, M. (2007) *Policing Cannabis as a Class C Drug: An Arresting Change.* York: Joseph Rowntree Foundation.

May, T., Warburton, H., Turnbull, P. and Hough, M. (2002) *Times they are A-changing: Policing of Cannabis.* York: Joseph Rowntree Foundation.

McSweeney, T., Herrington, V., Hough, M., Turnbull, P.J. and Parsons, J. (2004) *From Dependency to Work: Addressing the Multiple Needs of Offenders with Drug Problems.* Bristol: Policy Press.

Ministry of Justice (2009) *Criminal Justice and Police Act 2001 (S1-11) Penalty Notice for Disorder Police Operation Guidance: Retail Theft and Criminal Damage*, Circular 2009/04. London: Ministry of Justice.

Mulchandani, R. and Sigurdsson, J. (2009) *Police Service Strength: England and Wales*, Home Office Statistical Bulletin 13/09. London: Home Office.

Murji, K. (1998) *Policing Drugs.* Aldershot: Ashgate.

National Offender Management Service (NOMS) (2009) *The National Offender Management Service Drug Strategy.* London: Ministry of Justice.

National Treatment Agency (NTA) (2009) *Drug Testing on Arresting and Charge.* http://www.nta.nhs.uk/areas/criminal_justice/drug_testing_on_arrest_or_charge.aspx.

Newburn, T. and Elliot, J. (1998) *Police Anti-Drug Strategies: Tackling Drugs Together Three Years On*, Crime Detection and Prevention Series Paper 89. London: Home Office.

Neyroud, P. and Beckley, A. (2001) *Policing, Ethics and Human Rights*. Cullompton: Willan Publishing.

Neyroud, P. and Disley, E. (2007) 'The management, supervision and oversight of criminal investigation', in T. Newburn, T. Williamson and A. Wright (eds) *Handbook of Criminal Investigation*. Cullompton: Willan Publishing.

Parker, H. (2006) 'Keeping the lid on: policing drug-related crime', *Criminal Justice Matters*, 63: 6–38.

President of the Council (1998) *Tackling Drugs to Build a Better Britain*, Cm 3945. London: The Stationery Office.

Raco, M. (2003) 'Remaking place and securitising space: urban regeneration and the strategies, tactics and practices of policing in the UK', *Urban Studies*, 40(9):1869–87.

Reiner, R. (2000) *The Politics of the Police*, 3rd edition. Oxford: Oxford University Press.

Royal Society of Arts (2007) *Drugs – Facing Facts: The Report of the RSA Commission on Illegal Drugs, Communities and Public Policy*. London: Royal Society of Arts.

Seddon, T. (2007) 'Coerced drug treatment in the criminal justice system: conceptual, ethical and criminological issues', *Criminology and Criminal Justice*, 7(3): 269–86.

Shearing, C. and Stenning, P. (1981) 'Modern private security: its growth and implications', in M. Tonry and N. Morris (eds) *Crime and Justice: An Annual Review of Research*. Chicago: University of Chicago Press.

Skolnick, J. (1966) *Justice Without Trial: Law Enforcement in Democratic Society*. New York: Wiley.

South, N. (1988) *Policing for Profit*. London: Sage.

South, N. (2007) 'Drugs, alcohol and crime', in M. Maguire, R. Morgan and R. Reiner (eds) *The Oxford Handbook of Criminology*, 4th edition. Oxford: Oxford University Press.

Tilley, N. (2008) 'Modern approaches to policing: community, problem-orientated and intelligence-led', in T. Newburn (ed.) *Handbook of Policing*. 2nd edition. Cullompton: Willan Publishing.

Van Maanen, J. (1973) *Working the Street: A Developmental View of Police Behavior*, MIT Working Paper 681-73. Boston: Massachusetts Institute of Technology.

Wakefield, A. (2003) *Selling Security: The Private Policing of Public Space*. Cullompton: Willan Publishing.

Wilson, J. and Kelling, G. (1982) 'Broken windows', *The Atlantic Monthly*, March, pp. 29–37.

Young, R. (2008) 'Street policing after PACE: the drift to summary justice', in E. Cape and R. Young (eds) *Regulating Policing: The Police and Criminal Evidence Act 1984 Past, Present and Future*. Oxford: Hart Publishing.

4 Drug Interventions Programme: neither success nor failure?

Paul J. Turnbull and Layla Skinns

Introduction

Since the mid-1990s UK central government has pursued a policy of ensuring that those problem drug users caught up in the criminal process receive not only punishment but also treatment and social care to help them address their drug use. Commitment to, and investment in, this policy has increased over the years. By channelling problem drug users, that is, those who use heroin, crack and cocaine, into treatment, the aim is to reduce drug-driven crime (Seddon et al., 2008). Some have argued that this focus has led to the 'criminalization' of drug policy in Britain and a move away from a public health approach to drug issues (Stimson, 2000; Hunt and Stevens, 2004). However, Seddon et al. (2008) have recently suggested that the new focus of drug policy exists alongside the 'old arrangements' and needs to be 'understood' in the context of recent economic, social and cultural changes. For example, Seddon et al. describe significant changes in drug use, particularly among many young people who regularly use a range of drugs recreationally. Also, chronic use of heroin and cocaine has grown significantly during the past twenty years.

As other chapters in this volume have shown, between 1998 and 2003, the number and type of criminal-justice-based drug interventions has increased, including arrest referral, court ordered drug treatment and other diversionary approaches. The Drug Interventions Programme (DIP) was launched in 2003, although many sites were not operational until 2005. This programme aimed to bring together the criminal-justice-focused initiatives that had been rolled out over the previous five years. During its short history it has received a considerable amount of investment, although the exact amount is unclear; a figure of over £600 million in the past five years is mentioned by the National Treatment Agency for Substance Misuse (2009) and a figure of over £900 million suggested by the Home Office (drugs.homeoffice.gov.uk/drug-interventions-programme/strategy). The DIP's stated aim is to break the cycle of drug misuse and crime by making every stage in the criminal justice system an opportunity for drug-misusing offenders to engage in treatment. Some interventions operate right across England and Wales, while additional 'intensive' elements operate in those areas with the highest rates of acquisitive crime (68 Drug Action Team areas in England and three in Wales). Interventions include drug testing, Restriction on Bail, conditional cautioning and required drug assessments.

An essential objective of the programme is the delivery of 'throughcare' and 'aftercare'. Throughcare is the system which seeks to promote continuity of approach from arrest to sentence and beyond. Aftercare is the support which allows clients to access further drug treatment services as required and non-drug-specific services such as housing, employment and education (also known as wraparound services) in an attempt to ensure reintegration into the community and continuity of care. There is a strong evidential base to suggest that the impact of drug treatment can be substantial, but is best sustained by the integration or reintegration of treatment recipients into mainstream society by the provision of housing and access to education, training and jobs (McSweeney et al., 2008).

The throughcare and aftercare elements of DIP are delivered by Criminal Justice Integrated Teams (CJITs). The policy guidance suggests that CJITs allocate a case manager after a drug-misusing offender has been assessed and taken onto the CJIT caseload. The CJIT worker will then develop a care plan with the offender for the delivery of, or referral to, appropriate services. The extent and nature of a CJIT worker's involvement depend on the approach taken to case management and, to some extent, the needs with which the client presents (Skodbo et al., 2007).

This chapter draws mainly on the national evaluation study of CJITs commissioned by the Home Office (Institute Criminal Policy Research, 2007). The evaluation was carried out over a two-year period from the end of 2004. The scale and complexity of the intervention made the evaluation challenging. Many CJITs were in the early stages of service delivery when the evaluation started, with additional services and interventions being added to the DIP, including the introduction of a new monitoring system, the Drug Interventions Record (DIR). Even the name of the programme was changed in the early stages from Criminal Justice Intervention Programme (CJIP) to DIP. The study fell into three parts: a process evaluation of 20 CJITs involving interviews with over 300 staff and nearly 100 clients; an impact evaluation involving a survey of over 700 CJIT clients many of whom were interviewed at several follow-up points and were recruited from 36 CJITs; and an economic analysis of the costs and savings associated with CJITs on data derived from the client survey and activity data from 49 CJIT sites.

The authors were largely involved in the process evaluation and therefore the main focus of this chapter will be on implementation and delivery issues with a briefer examination of impact.

Processes within the CJITs

In theory, the DIP brings together a range of professionals from community-based drug treatment and social care providers, with representatives from criminal justice agencies such as the police, probation and prison services. These professionals sit under the umbrella of the Criminal Justice Integrated Teams (CJITs), and have responsibility for reducing drug-related crime by engaging problematic drug-using offenders in treatment and wraparound services. This overview of DIP focuses on data collected about operational staff in two phases (phase one being in the early stages of implementation – December 2004 to April 2005 – and phase two being six to nine months later) and across twenty sites.

It is difficult to define clearly how CJIT operates because there were wide variations between sites. These included how teams were managed, for example the lead service could be the police, probation, local authority or a drug service; how roles and functions were performed and by whom, for example some sites had specialist staff undertaking specific roles, others had a more generic approach; whether teams were actual or virtual, for example in some sites workers were co-located in a building, in others they could be based in different buildings across a town or city. During their early stages of development CJITs had to cope with shortages of qualified staff. The unique combination of criminal justice and drugs interventions offered by DIP made it hard to find staff with the appropriate combination of skills. Constraints on space mean that we can only provide an overview of broad trends and commonalities between sites rather than exploring in detail the variations between sites.

Case managers

A crucial element of DIP was the notion of continuous care, meaning that problematic drug users were continuously in touch with staff from the CJIT whether in police custody, prison or referred to helping agencies in the community. Therefore, the key operational role in the CJITs was the case manager (also known as care coordinator, case coordinator or key worker). Although there was information provided centrally about what the role of case manager entailed, there was little advice given about how it was to be implemented practically. Broadly speaking, case management is concerned with the longitudinal management of clients with long-term chronic, enduring or relapsing health problems and the aim is to maintain contact in order to improve health and social functioning of the client. The concept of case management was first used in the 1970s in the USA as a way of managing patients with severe mental illness on their return to the community, after long periods in hospital. This sometimes entailed securing services and support from third parties in the community.

In spite of there not being a significant tradition or evidence of success of using case management practices with drug users in the UK, they were formally introduced into the Models of Care strategy in 2002 (Keetley and Weaver, 2004). Models of Care is the national framework for the commissioning of substance misuse services for adult drug misusers. Case management was deemed appropriate for drug users owing to the multifaceted nature of their problems and the likely benefits for engaging and retaining drug users in appropriate services. In the CJITs, it was intended that a case manager would take overall responsibility for a client's needs, developing a care plan and ensuring that needs were met, monitored and reviewed. The case manager also brokered interventions with outside agencies. In practice, though, CJIT case managers did not perform all of these functions and in some areas they also took on related but separate roles, as referral workers based either at court or in police custody areas.

As found in other research (see Keetley and Weaver, 2004), CJIT case managers were drawn from various professional backgrounds. Of those who participated in the telephone survey conducted in early 2005, just over two-fifths (41 per cent) previously worked in the criminal justice field, either for the police or for the Probation or Prison Services. Twenty-eight per cent had previously worked in the drugs field and 17 per cent were from other professions such as social services, education or voluntary sector organizations (for example, women's refuges). Perhaps unsurprisingly, few had a portfolio of criminal justice, drugs and health related professional experience. These differences in professional background raise questions about consistency between case managers in terms of what they were able to deliver.

The types of workers recruited as case managers reflected the agency leading DIP at the strategic level. In thirteen of the research sites the DIP was led by the local Drug Action Team (DAT), two by the Probation Service, two by the police service and three by drug treatment services. In Peterborough and Leeds, former police officers were employed as case managers. This opens up a debate about the quality of their relationship with clients, some of whom they may have dealt with in the past as offenders.

Issues relating to the background of case managers also emerged as new DIP interventions were added. For example, the introduction and rollout of the Tough Choices programme, although built on activities already under way in police stations such as arrest referral and drug testing on arrest, introduced coercion as an ethos to what had largely been a voluntary or at most a quasi-coercive approach. Also, the introduction of work with those on Restriction on Bail and Prolific and Priority Offenders added a further dimension of monitoring and enforcement which had not been part of the DIP/CJIT working practices in most areas. These changes in approach were culturally difficult for some CJIT workers, particularly those from health and social care backgrounds, who were not comfortable with taking on the role of 'controllers'.

Initial engagement and assessment

CJIT's aim was to contact drug-using offenders and arrestees at a number of points in the criminal justice process. Home Office performance monitoring data for the nine months from May 2005 to February 2006 showed a total of just under 24,000 referrals or contacts with potential clients. Unfortunately, it was not possible to disaggregate these data into referrals (that is, those potential clients referred to CJITs by other parties such as drug services and the Probation Service) and those with whom CJIT workers made a direct initial contact. The majority of those were achieved through police custody suites (67 per cent, $n = 16,145$) and the courts (19 per cent, $n = 4,610$), with the remainder being evenly distributed among prison, probation, drug treatment services and self-referrals. Although it is to be expected that the number of referrals from police custody suites and courts would be higher than other routes because of the greater volumes of individuals passing through them, given the high numbers of probationers and prisoners with substance misuse issues there was still a relatively low level of referrals from prisons and probation. This suggests difficulties in gaining referrals via such routes. In contrast, the presence of CJIT workers in both the courts and police stations – at least during office hours – may have increased referral rates from these locations. These numbers are likely to have been boosted by the introduction of the Tough Choices initiative in April 2006 in certain 'intensive' DIP areas. This initiative meant that anyone arrested for 'trigger offences' was tested for drugs on arrest and, if they tested positive for heroin, crack or cocaine, subject to an initial assessment and referred for a mandatory assessment by the CJIT. The Home Office has published some information about the delivery and impact of Tough Choices, and from 1 April to 30 June 2006 just over 11,000 arrestees tested positive for heroin, crack or cocaine (Skodbo et al., 2007). From July to December 2005, 43 per cent of potential clients dropped out after first contact and before the CJIT assessment. This meant that just under 6,000 assessments were completed during this period. Case managers perceived that clients dropped out at this early stage because of a lack of motivation (26 per cent), as a result of renewing relationships

with old drug-using friends (22 per cent) and being imprisoned (18 per cent). Edmunds et al. (2002), in an unpublished study of those offered help by the forerunner schemes (Arrest Referral) to CJIT found that arrestees had three main groups of reasons for declining help or dropping out of the referral process. These related to: tensions arising from help being offered within an essentially punitive criminal process; the type and quality of treatment which was available; and the overwhelming pressures of a drug-using lifestyle, for example the desire to maintain friendship with other drug users. The final set of reasons was confirmed by CJIT case managers who suggested that this was the second most common reason for offenders dropping out of treatment.

When attempting to explain dropout rates, CJIT case managers focused on the client rather than any deficiency in service provision by the CJITs. However, it is possible that the time lag between initial assessment and first contact with the CJIT was too great for some. While 70 per cent of those responding to the telephone survey reported that clients would be assessed within five days of being referred to the service, there were no data available to verify these claims. Alternatively, it may have been that even five days was too long a wait for some problematic drug users. Stevens and colleagues, when considering why those seeking treatment exited within the first 30 days of contact with treatment services, found that there was little evidence that waiting times affected disengagement and that this was more often related to the type of service being offered and the type of drug user already attending the service (Stevens et al., 2007). They found that those who do not belong to the traditional drug service user groups, that is younger, homeless and non-injecting drug users, were more likely to exit treatment at this early stage because they found services off-putting and their opening hours and location inaccessible.

Since the introduction of Tough Choices, the *requirement* to attend the assessment or face a fine or even imprisonment has had an impact on the numbers having contact with DIP. Skodbo and colleagues reported that 77 per cent of the 11,000 or so who had given a positive sample on arrest attended their initial meeting with a DIP worker. Of this group, 93 per cent completed an assessment within 28 days (Skodbo et al., 2007).

Care planning and onward referral

Once potential clients were assessed they became part of the CJIT caseload and were assigned a case manager. Home Office monitoring data revealed that 32 per cent of clients left the programme between initial assessment and before being taken onto the CJIT caseload. This may have been because they dropped out, in spite of being in need of help or because they did not require any further contact with the CJIT. Either way, between

July and December 2005 just under 4,000 clients were taken onto CJIT caseloads. Since the introduction of Tough Choices, nearly 3,900 individuals were identified as needing further intervention, 83 per cent agreed to further help and of this group 88 per cent received a care plan. However, if all those who were already in contact with DIP, who did not enter custody or who were not on probation were excluded, only 35 per cent of those tested positive on arrest received a care plan within 60 days of arrest (Skodbo et al., 2007).

Once on the CJIT caseload, clients were supposed to draw up a care plan with their assigned CJIT worker, indicating the goals to be achieved and monitored. The care plan was reportedly reviewed at regular intervals, with 53 per cent of case managers reporting case reviews taking place within four weeks of clients being taken onto the CJIT caseload. Nearly all (95 per cent) reported having case review within 12 weeks. Clients were also asked if they had a care plan; not all were aware of it as a written document, but most knew what their long-term goals were and regularly discussed these with their case manager. However, the fact that the care planning process was largely client-led meant that CJIT workers had to balance client expectations with what realistically could be delivered to them. For example, clients might think they needed higher doses of substitute drugs than the prescribing doctors were willing to prescribe.

In terms of the interventions available to clients and included in care plans, CJITs were able to deliver Tier two interventions directly to clients but generally referred elsewhere for specialist interventions such as prescribing, housing, education and training. Tier two interventions included assessment, general advice and information, and specific advice on harm reduction. Yet, the partner agencies providing some of these specialist interventions were rarely involved in care planning, which may have resulted in a mismatch between care plans and available services and added to clients' unrealistic expectations.

In January 2005, performance monitoring data showed that the most common form of intervention provided to clients in twelve of the twenty sites was substitute prescribing, followed by counselling in five sites. There were no data for the remaining two sites. Similarly, when case managers were asked to assess how easy it was for their clients to get access to a range of support and interventions, those most readily available included: motivational interviewing, drop-in services and rapid prescribing. Less accessible facilities included: detoxification services, residential rehabilitation, financial support and housing provision.

Case management

We found that, on average, a case manager would have 19 'live' cases on their caseload at any one time and that clients were typically case managed for 19 weeks, with managers mostly contacting clients every two weeks although much of this also depended on client need. Case managers also reported that motivational interviewing was the activity that they most commonly engaged in during appointments with clients, followed by care planning. However, it was clear that the content of sessions was not always predetermined; case managers were generally flexible enough to deal with client needs as they arose. Sessions were generally structured to meet whatever client needs emerged on the day. They tended to last between half an hour and an hour.

The research showed a gradual development of case management across all sites in the evaluation. By the end of phase one, there was some form of case management taking place in the majority of sites, but the specific approaches varied between sites and, at times, between individual workers at the same site. After the first phase of the research, it was possible to characterize case management practices, using three ideal-types:

1. Referrers and re-engagers – CJIT team makes initial contact. The CJIT case manager creates a care plan, identifying agencies to which to refer clients. Once the client engages with services, case management responsibility passes to the primary service provider. If the client disengages, the CJIT case manager attempts to re-engage.
2. Retainers – CJIT team makes initial contact. CJIT case manager refers to other agencies, but retains case management responsibility and monitors client's progress.
3. Referrers – CJIT team makes initial contact and makes referrals to other agencies. Client's progress is not monitored.

In the second phase of the research, when case managers were asked about which of these ideal-types best described their practices, 60 per cent of those interviewed described themselves as referrers and re-engagers, whereas 40 per cent described themselves as retainers and none described themselves as referrers. While 'refer and re-engage' may have been a practical solution, given the time constraints on CJIT workers, it also relied upon the agencies to which the client had been referred notifying the CJIT worker if their client disengaged. If such reporting mechanisms were not in place then clients may have slipped through the net. In only four sites was it mentioned that there was a coordinated effort to ensure that clients were monitored from a central base, involving CJIT administrative staff. The majority of other sites had a less formal system, which involved the case managers monitoring clients as they saw fit. The onus was almost always on the case managers to monitor clients, other agencies rarely proactively reported back to the CJIT case manager on their client's progress.

In addition, it may also be the case that the organizations to which CJIT clients were referred were unwilling to be brought under the DIP umbrella or be closely associated with what some have identified as quasi-coercive approach to engaging with potential service users. Certainly, there was a similar reaction by community-based organizations such as domestic violence groups to becoming part of, or having closer links with, Community Safety Partnerships. These organizations did not want to be a part of, or associated closely, with mainstream statutory services (Skinns, 2005). Taken together, this evidence raises questions about whether the referrer and re-engager approach to case management was the most effective one. Page (2008: 46) has described the CJITs as an 'assessment and referral agency with a primary substance misuse focus' and this would seem to be an accurate description if the re-engagement element of the DIP process was not working as intended because staff were not effective at re-engaging clients. Furthermore, the findings suggest that the goal of continuous care was not met fully while clients were in the community or in terms of the referral process between organizations within the CJITs, as we discuss next.

Integration

Here we describe the issues facing the DIP sites in providing an integrated service across the criminal justice, drug treatment, social care and reintegration services that individual offenders may need access to.

> I mean the fundamental thing with DIP is I mean you're trying to
> get people to stop operating in silos as they have done tradition-
> ally ... so inevitably you do get some problems getting people to
> actually see the bigger picture ... they look at it in their own lit-
> tle world ... it's about breaking down the barriers between them
> isn't it.
>
> (DIP Project Manager, North West)

As this quotation illustrates, the multi-agency nature of the CJITs means that they have been beset by challenges and enduring issues, which have also been noted in other research on multi-agency partnerships (see, for example, Blagg et al., 1988; Sampson et al., 1988; Crawford and Jones, 1995; Crawford, 1997, 2001; Bowling, 1998; Audit Commission, 2002; Skinns, 2005). In particular, research studies on multi-agency partnerships such as the Community Safety Partnerships have illustrated that differences in working practices, occupational cultures, priorities and ideologies can undermine their operation (see, for example, Skinns, 2005). Several authors have also highlighted the particular strains on relationships that multi-agency partnerships face when involving partners from health and criminal justice sectors in the provision of services to drug-using offenders (Turnbull et al., 2000, Hunter et al., 2005). The CJITs were not immune from these agency differences. While 56 per cent of case managers, interviewed in phase two of the research, reported that agency differences did *not* impact on working relationships, 39 per cent said that they did. Interviewees in phase one questioned whether staff from criminal justice and treatment agencies had similar goals or, if not, whether the different goals were compatible. In eight sites, staff felt that there were shared goals and understandings or pointed to the diverse but complementary roles and responsibilities the various agencies had within the CJIT process. In five areas, however, interviewees thought that the criminal justice and health agendas reflected diverse ideologies about how to deal with problematic drug users, which were difficult to reconcile. For example, partner agencies placed different emphases on the role of coercion and freedom of choice when dealing with drug-using offenders. Partner agencies also varied in terms of staffing, line management and service delivery. All together this meant that some interviewees felt that they were 'culturally miles apart' from some of their colleagues in the CJIT. Interviewees also noted that organizations within the CJIT, in particular, the Probation Service, Prison Service and CARATs (see Paylor et al., Chapter 9 this volume), and courts and Crown Prosecution Service had different priorities and pressures associated with performance targets.

Indeed, these differences may have been one contributing factor to difficulties with information sharing. In phase two, 63 per cent of respondents felt that all agencies were willing to share information. Of the remaining 29 per cent who did not agree with this statement, statutory and non-statutory treatment providers were identified as having the most concerns about information sharing and were described as being most concerned about client confidentiality (88 per cent) and how the information was to be used (35 per cent). Difficulties with information sharing arose in spite of these areas having strategic protocols in place, suggesting that such protocols may not be an effective way of encouraging information sharing. Further support was found for this conclusion during the phase two telephone survey of case managers, which showed that the majority of staff were uncertain about the existence of protocols. There were even uncertainties within areas; some case managers reported that there was a protocol in place whereas others in the same site reported that there was not. None were able to identify when the protocol was signed or who had signed it.

Differences between agencies and difficulties with information sharing may also have inhibited integration and the delivery of the continuous care promised by DIP, particularly in relation to the timeliness and quality of the referral process between CJITs and CARATs and the transfer of responsibility for clients, which fostered mistrust between both groups of workers. In phase two of the research, staff suggested referrals from prison were often too late to enable CJIT workers in the community to meet with the client before they were released and to develop a package of care for them on release. This finding has been confirmed by several studies and more specifically with regard to drug service provision for black and minority ethnic prisoners (Harman and Paylor, 2005; Fountain et al., 2007). A recent qualitative longitudinal study of 40 prisoners, albeit research which did not explicitly evaluate the DIP, found that drug treatment arrangements were not always in place for those leaving prison, and, if arrangements had been made, they did not always materialize (Hartfree et al., 2008).

By contrast, in other parts of the DIP staff had established cooperative working relationships. One example of this was police custody areas. It was reported that CJIT workers had trained police officers about the nature of the DIP and their presence in the custody area meant that everyday interactions between staff had improved cooperation between agencies. Similarly, respondents to the case managers' survey in phase two of the research largely perceived DIP to have helped to integrate a range of agencies in the provision of services for drug-using offenders, but had yet to reduce duplication in how clients are processed *within* that system. Taken together, these findings suggest that by phase two of the research integrated working relationships within the CJITs were partial rather than total, and this may have inhibited continuity of care. However, whether the potential lack of continuity of care had an impact on drug use and the offending behaviour of DIP clients is difficult to assess. We will now consider self-reported changes in individual drug use and offending behaviour.

Impact and economic analysis

The entire DIP enterprise is based on the premise that by identifying those with problematic drug-using patterns and intervening to curb them, drug-related offending behaviour will be prevented. There remains some debate about the extent of the linkage between illicit drug use and crime, the direction of causality between drug use and crime, and the certainty of our knowledge about the links (see, for example, Stevens, 2007). As Seddon has pointed out, there are three main explanations of the link: drug use, leads to crime, crime leads to drug use, and both drug use and crime are related to one another (Seddon, 2000). It is important to bear these three explanatory models in mind when considering the findings from our impact analysis.

The impact and economic analysis were based on analysis of data gathered in a survey of CJIT clients. In all, 1,415 interviews were conducted with 703 CJIT clients. CJIT clients were recruited and interviewed one to three months after CJIT assessment ($n = 468$), recruited and interviewed or re-interviewed three to six months after their CJIT assessment ($n = 517$) and a third and final interview took place six to nine months after initial assessment ($n = 430$). In total, 209 clients were interviewed on all three occasions, 282 were interviewed twice and 212 only once. At all three interviews, the majority were still in contact with CJITs (89 per cent at first interview, 82 per cent at second interview and 74 per cent at third interview). As the initial recruitment of potential interviewees was undertaken by CJIT – they had to secure consent to be contacted by researchers – we have no information about response rates.

Problems in recruiting CJIT clients had an impact on the robustness of the findings. The reduced sample size had an impact on the statistical power of the original design and altered the timing of recruitment at baseline interview. The sample turned out to be rather homogeneous (i.e. it contains mainly CJIT clients who have been referred, assessed and taken onto the caseload). Nonetheless, this did not affect the ability to describe the impact of CJITs on drug use and offending behaviour in the aggregate. Delays in the recruitment of CJIT clients may have introduced a selection bias in our sample. It seems fair to assume that those who participated in this research were more likely to be those that continued to receive a service from CJITs and other treatment providers. Those who dropped out of the programme were less likely to participate in initial and follow-up interviews. Therefore these data probably represent, to some degree, those who were more successfully engaged by CJITs. This is not unusual for research dealing with this type of population.

Changes in drug use and offending

There were major changes in drug use reported by the sample between the first and subsequent follow-up interviews. The numbers using heroin dropped from 79 per cent before contact with CJIT to 46 per cent at follow-up interview. Daily or regular use of heroin (i.e. those using more than 20 days per month) dropped from 68 per cent to 12 per cent. Reported use of crack fell from 59 to 28 per cent and daily or regular use of crack fell from 24 per cent to 6 per cent. Those spending more than £1,000 per month on drugs fell by nearly 50 percentage points, from 65 per cent to 16 per cent.

Changes in offending behaviour, although showing reductions, were not as marked as changes in drug use. These changes are generally in line with the findings of other research studies which have considered the impact of the introduction of drug treatment on drug use (Gossop et al., 2003; McIntosh et al., 2007). Only 34 per cent of CJIT clients reported offending at first interview, and this reduced to 20 per cent at third interview. For those offending, the mean number of crimes committed declined from 8.4 to 2.7 crimes per month. This means that some of those in the sample who were exposed to CJIT stopped offending and those who continued to offend did so less frequently. Even those for whom the changes in the level of offending were significant, it is important to note that levels of reported crime at baseline are low compared with other samples of problematic drug users contacted within the criminal justice system (McSweeney et al., 2008). However, they are broadly similar to those entering treatment voluntarily, for example the National Treatment Outcome Research Study (Gossop, 2005).

Potential reasons for the apparent low crime rate within the dataset were considered. There were no significant differences in reported crime that could suggest the crime rate was lower than expected. There are a number of other explanations that could not be tested. First, it could be that the subjects recruited to the sample committed less crime than others who had contact with CJITs. Second, there may have been a selection bias to those who commit less crime in the month before CJIT, which is part of the contact and engagement process. For example, those who commit more serious levels of offending were imprisoned or given community sentences with a drug rehabilitation requirement and were therefore supervised by the Prison Service or Probation Service. Finally, there could have been systematic under-reporting of crime because of fear of breaches in confidentiality or not wanting to admit to offending to an interviewer. Also, even when those we interviewed no longer had contact with CJIT we found that their rates of offending and drug use were no higher than those who still had contact with CJITs.

It is conceivable that the levels of crime reported by respondents may be true, but that those who get taken onto the CJIT caseload are not representative of problematic drug users that are processed by the criminal justice system. As mentioned at the beginning of this section, it may also be that the basic assumptions underlying the DIP enterprise are, to some degree at least, misplaced. For example, problematic drug use may lead to significant increases in offending behaviour but may not provide a full explanation of why this population is involved in a criminal lifestyle (McSweeney et al., 2008). Tackling other factors such as social exclusion and social inequality may have a bigger role to play in understanding and explaining offending behaviour among problematic drug users (Seddon, 2000; Wilkinson and Pickett, 2009).

Other outcomes

There were a number of outcomes that could not be measured. The sample of CJIT clients interviewed was unevenly distributed between sites; over half the sites were unable to recruit 20 interviewees. This meant there was an insufficient sample population from each CJIT to measure differences between sites. The delays in recruitment and interviewing also had an impact on measures of mental health and social functioning. There was little change comparing baseline and follow-up data and it is suspected that this was because baseline interviews were carried out after exposure to CJIT (between one and three months).[1]

Costs of crime

Value for money has been an increasingly important measure of success for all criminal justice initiatives and it is especially relevant to DIP given the extensive funding received. Cost analysis attempts to measure the costs of the scheme against the benefits, but it is not an exact science because many costs are unavailable, resulting in assumptions being used as the basis for calculations. There is also little agreement about the benefits which arise from schemes. Government tends to focus on reductions in offending (measured by reconviction rates or self-reported offending) and, in the case of DIP reductions, reductions in drug use and drug spend, but such measures fail to capture the range of benefits which might arise from initiatives such as stable housing, improved job readiness and so on.

As described earlier, there was a significant reduction in the number and frequency of crimes committed; however, only a minority of individuals in this study (20 per cent, $n = 141$) committed a crime to which a cost could be attributed. This was due to the lack of reliable estimates relating to the unit costs of crimes at the time, in particular crimes relating to the handling of stolen goods and the use and distribution of illicit drugs. For example, over one in five of interviewees reported handling stolen goods in the month before being taken onto the CJIT caseload. This means the cost reduction presented here may underestimate the true overall figure.

On average, the average cost of crimes in the month before involvement with CJIT was approximately £2,800. This dropped to £1,050 by the time of the third interview. This shows a statistically significant change in costs ($p < 0.01$). This calculation excludes some outlying cases; one case had committed crimes in excess of £350,000 and was removed from the analysis. The average cost of the crime-reducing effect for our sample during the interview period was £5,982.

On average, for the cases in the sample, the expenditure per case was about £1,600. The cost of providing CJIT relies on the analysis of aggregate expenditure of each CJIT, a top-down average expenditure per case. The problem with this approach is that rather than illustrating the cost of services received it loads on service development and set-up costs; in addition, costs related to services other than case management are not included in the calculations, for example the cost of treatment. There was a wide variation in the average expenditure per case of providing CJIT, from just over £920 to just under £3,500. The cost of providing CJIT set against the reduction in offending produced a saving of £1,120 per case per month for those who were interviewed six to nine months following assessment. Overall, the findings suggest that effect of CJITs on the cost of crimes appears to be broadly offset by the cost of providing the service. Again further caution should be exercised when interpreting these results as the research was not able to take account of all the potential benefits. For example, the CJIT process is likely to have conferred health and social welfare benefits to those in receipt of this intervention which were not measurable.

Conclusion

The findings presented here on the DIP enterprise are more equivocal than definitive. This is for a number of reasons, some related to the design, development and implementation of DIP/CJITs, others to do with methodological problems faced by the evaluation team.

A 'whole-system' approach and continuity of care are difficult enterprises whatever the area of service delivery. It has become something of a holy grail within policy and service delivery aimed at drug users and offenders, but there are few examples of its successful application. Case managers were intended to be an instrumental part of the CJITs, enabling them to meet their goal of providing continuous care for problematic drug-using offenders in the community while they were referred to other 'helping' agencies or as they moved through the criminal justice process. The attrition rates, at least in the early period of implementation, demonstrate that case managers were not entirely successful in fulfilling this role. Clients did disengage from the CJITs and this may not have been entirely due to the client. Most case managers perceived their role as 'referrers and re-engagers', yet only a few services had structures in place to monitor disengagement from the agencies to which they had been referred. In reality, therefore, it is likely that case managers were more 'referrers' than 'referrers and re-engagers'. However, these case managers were also constrained by systemic factors. As with other kinds of multi-agency initiatives, variation between agencies, such as different ideological positions about the relative importance of voluntary or forced treatment, was likely to be a factor that affected information sharing and, more importantly, the extent of integration and cooperative working practices and, ultimately the continuity of care of clients.

Most time and effort, at least while this research was being carried out, appeared to be focused on increasing the numbers participating in DIP and in the early stages of assessment and referral of community-based drug-using offenders. Work on developing and refining case management, throughcare and aftercare, as well as targeting those leaving prisons was often neglected or was implemented only partially. This was not because the importance of this work was unrecognized but because the imperative became demonstrating activity. The two concerns here are that this may have had a lasting impact on the working practices and culture within DIP/CJITs, and that it actively worked against providing an end-to-end service. In fact, it may have encouraged the maintenance of the status quo, including a focus on immediate, short-term outcomes without much concern for the medium- or longer-term rehabilitation or integration of drug-using offenders. It may be, as so often is the case, that practices adopted early on in service delivery are difficult to change. Given that the government's latest drug strategy highlights, and some would even say prioritizes, a more rehabilitative and integrative approach to drug treatment, including those aimed at drug-using offenders, it will be interesting to see whether DIP/CJITs can respond and play their part in this challenging enterprise (HM Government, 2008).

Once CJIT clients were in contact with treatment services they made considerable changes in their drug-using patterns and offending behaviour. All measures of drug-using behaviour showed significant decreases. These included the regularity of the use of both heroin and crack and the percentage of the sample spending more than £1,000 per month on drugs. The reductions in offending behaviour, however, were less marked than those achieved in drug use. The self-reported offending rates pre-CJIT (i.e. month prior to first contact with CJIT) of those interviewed for this evaluation were lower than those reported in similar studies of problematic drug users in contact with the criminal justice system (Turnbull et al., 2000; McSweeney et al., 2007).

The lower-than-expected pre-CJIT crime rates had the greatest impact on the findings produced by the analysis of the economic data. Even though the analysis indicated there was a cost-reducing effect, with the average monthly cost of crimes estimated to fall for the sample by £2,700, this effect is not significantly different from the cost of providing the service. Overall, the cost-reducing effect of CJITs on the cost of crimes appears to be broadly offset by the cost of providing the service. However, not all crimes committed could be assigned unit costs and it was not possible to assign monetary valuations to all the potential benefits associated with CJITs. This is likely to mean that both the costs of crimes committed as well as the potential benefits of participation of CJIT were underestimated.

Contrary to the adage 'a rolling stone gathers no moss', DIP/CJIT kept gathering additional interventions as part of its portfolio of work despite being in the early stage of implementation. This meant that the teams often had to refocus their approach to service implementation and delivery, and therefore to some degree their objectives, in order to respond to a dynamic policy agenda. While it should be acknowledged that innovation and adaptation can be a useful as part of a pilot and early stages of service implementation and delivery, these are best undertaken at a local level in order to fulfil local needs or to address a gap in service delivery. However, in this instance it appeared that policy was decided centrally with little account taken of local conditions. This was quite an unsettling environment in which to aim to establish a very different way of working with drug-using offenders.

When our research was completed it was clear that while advances had been made in developing a more integrated approach to contacting, assessing, referring and providing the initial phase of drug treatment for drug-using offenders, less progress had been made in providing case management and throughcare and aftercare. There is a wide range of evidence that indicates the different elements that make up DIP/CJIT can have a positive impact on drug use and offending; however, our research failed to show that DIP/CJIT was more than the sum of its parts. It is difficult to say whether this situation has changed in the intervening years since there is little contemporary independent research evidence available. To have more chance of success of fulfilling its objectives, a focus on establishing effective case management practices and on the medium- and longer-term needs of drug-using offenders is required. Also, a focus on those whom it is more difficult to engage, for example those leaving prison, could pay higher dividends, particularly in terms of reoffending rates. Conversely, trying to provide everyone that produces a positive test result for a Class A drug in a police station with an intervention seems less likely to have an impact. Some of those with whom DIP comes into contact through this route will be casual, recreational or non-problematic users of drugs, and intervention of this type is less likely to have an influence on their offending behaviour.

At the time of writing, the integration of DIP/CJIT into a model called Integrated Offender Management (IOM) is being piloted. The aim of IOM is 'to deepen and extend joint identification and assessment, offender management and information sharing frameworks for those offenders in the community' (Home Office, 2009). The plan is to build on existing partnerships and working arrangements and to deliver multi-agency problem-solving approaches as well as offender management continuity and consistency, particularly to those offenders who have recently been released from prison from a short sentence and have no statutory supervision requirements. It is likely that this new way of working will place greater responsibility on DIP/CJIT workers to monitor, review and closely supervise their clients. As we have reported in this chapter, this element of the work of DIP proved particularly difficult to deliver. It will also pose important challenges: to the work ethos of individual CJIT workers and their practices; to existing, often fragile, partnership arrangements; and, importantly, to the relationship between worker and offender/clients. As we have seen, the level of integration needed to deliver an intervention like DIP faced significant hurdles, many of which were only partially overcome. The IOM proposals calls for a level of integration of working practices not yet experienced or delivered by criminal justice, social and care professionals working with drug-using offenders. Given the limited information available pointing to the success of DIP/CJIT, both in terms of the practices to provide integrated service delivery and case management, it seems premature to extend this approach even further at this stage.

The future of DIP/CJIT may face further challenges when the consequences of the 2008/09 economic crisis have an impact on the funds available to pay for such interventions. Any existing, future or further interventions of this type will inevitably be more closely scrutinized and those that are seen as unsuccessful will find it difficult to hold onto the levels of funding they have previously experienced. Given the high level of funding DIP/CJIT has enjoyed it is likely that it will receive particularly close attention.

Acknowledgements

We would like to acknowledge the work of colleagues Matt Hickman (University of Bristol) and Jose-Luis Fernandez (London School of Economics) in undertaking the impact analysis work reported in this chapter.

Note

1. While information on drug use and crime could be collected retrospectively for the month prior to CJIT contact, this was not possible for the (standardized) measures of mental health and social function which, by the time they were measured, may have improved as a result of CJIT.

References

Audit Commission (2002) *Community Safety Partnerships*. London: Audit Commission.

Blagg, H., Pearson, G., Sampson, A., Smith, D. and Stubbs, P. (1988) 'Inter-agency cooperation: rhetoric and reality', in T. Hope and M. Shaw (eds) *Communities and Crime Reduction*. London: HMSO.

Bowling, B. (1998) *Violent Racism*. Oxford: Clarendon Press.

Crawford, A. (1997) *The Local Governance of Crime: Appeals to Community and Partnerships*. Oxford: Oxford University Press.

Crawford, A. (2001) 'Joined-up but fragmented: contradiction, ambiguity and ambivalence at the heart of New Labour's "Third Way"', in R. Matthews and J. Pitts (eds) *Crime, Disorder and Community Safety*. London: Routledge.

Crawford, A. and Jones, M. (1995) 'Inter-agency co-operation and community-based crime prevention: some reflections on the work of Pearson and colleagues', *British Journal of Criminology*, 35(1): 17–33.

Edmunds, M., Dennis, D., Turnbull, P.J. and Hough, M. (2002) 'From pillar to post: a study of non-engagement in arrest referral and treatment services'. Unpublished paper, South Bank University, London.

Fountain, J., Roy, A., Anitha, S., Davies, K., Bashford, J. and Patel, K. (2007) *Issues Surrounding the Delivery of Prison Drug Services in England and Wales, with a focus on black and minority ethnic prisoners*. Preston: University of Central Lancashire.

Gossop, M. (2005) *Drug Misuse Treatment and Reductions in Crime: Findings from the National Treatment Outcome Research Study (NTORS)*. London: National Treatment Agency for Substance Misuse.

Gossop, M., Marsden, J., Stewart, D. and Kidd, T. (2003) 'The National Treatment Outcome Research Study (NTORS): 4–5 year follow-up results', *Addiction*, 98(3): 291–303.

Harman, K. and Paylor, I. (2005) 'An evaluation of the CARAT initiative', *Howard Journal*, 44(4): 357–73.

Hartfree, Y., Dearden, C. and Pound, E. (2008) *High Hopes: Supporting Ex-prisoners in their Lives after Prison*, Research Report 509. London: Department for Work and Pensions.

HM Government (2008) *Drugs: Protecting Families and Communities. The 2008 Drug Strategy*. London: HM Government.

Home Office (2009) *Integrated Offender Management: Government Policy Statement*. http://www.crimereduction.homeoffice.gov.uk/ppo/IOMGovernmentPolicyStatement.pdf.

Hunt, N. and Stevens, A. (2004) 'Whose harm? Harm reduction and the shift to coercion in UK drug policy', *Social Policy and Society*, 3(4): 333–42.

Hunter, G., McSweeney, T. and Turnbull, P. (2005) 'The introduction of drug arrest referral schemes in London: a partnership between drug services and the police', *International Journal of Drug Policy*, 16(5): 343–52.

Institute for Criminal Policy Research (2007) *National Evaluation of Criminal Justice Integrated Teams: Summary*. London: ICPR.

Keetley, K. and Weaver, T. (2004) 'Evaluation of the Drug Interventions Programme: literature review of case management'. Unpublished report, Centre for Research on Drugs and Health Behaviour, Imperial College, London.

McIntosh, J., Bloor, M. and Robertson, M. (2007) 'The effect of drug treatment upon the commission of acquisitive crime', *Journal of Substance Use*, 12(5): 375–84.

McSweeney, T., Stevens, A., Hunt, N. and Turnbull, P.J. (2007) 'Twisting arms or a helping hand? Assessing the impact of "coerced" and comparable "voluntary" drug treatment options', *British Journal of Criminology*, 47(3): 470–90.

McSweeney, T., Turnbull, P.J. and Hough, M. (2008) *The Treatment and Supervision of Drug-Dependent Offenders: A Review of the Literature prepared for the UK Drug Policy Commission*. London: UK Drug Policy Commission. http://www.ukdpc.org.uk/resources/RDURR_ICPR_literature_review.pdf.

National Treatment Agency for Substance Misuse (2009) *Breaking the Link: The Role of Drug Treatment in Tackling Crime*. London: National Treatment Agency.

Page, G. (2008) 'Domestic violence and mental health problems: theory, policy and practice in a Drug Intervention Programme arrest referral population'. Unpublished MPhil thesis, University of Cambridge.

Sampson, A., Stubbs, P., Smith, D., Pearson, G. and Blagg, H. (1988) 'Crime localities and the multi-agency approach', *British Journal of Criminology*, 28(4): 478–93.

Seddon, T. (2000) 'Explaining the drug–crime Link: theoretical, policy and research issues', *Journal of Social Policy*, 29(1): 95–107.

Seddon, T., Ralphs, R. and Williams, L. (2008) 'Risk security and the "Criminalization" of British drug policy', *British Journal of Criminology*, 48(6): 818–34.

Skinns, L. (2005) 'Cops, councils and crime and disorder: a critical review of three community safety partnerships'. Unpublished PhD thesis, University of Cambridge.

Skodbo, S., Brown, G., Deacon, S., Cooper, A., Hall, A., Millar, T., Smith, J. and Whitham, K. (2007) *The Drug Interventions Programme (DIP): Addressing Drug Use and Offending through 'Tough Choices'*, Research Report 2. London: Home Office.

Stevens, A. (2007) 'When two dark figures collide: evidence and discourse on drug related crime', *Critical Social Policy*, 27(1): 77–99.

Stevens, A., Radcliffe, P., Sanders, M., Hunt, N., Turnbull, P. and McSweeney, T. (2007) *Early Exit: Estimating and Explaining Early Exit from Drug Treatment. Executive Summary*. London: Department of Health and London School of Hygiene and Tropical Medicine.

Stimson, G.V. (2000) 'Blair declares war: the unhealthy state of British drug policy', *International Journal of Drug Policy*, 11(4): 259–64.

Turnbull, P.J., McSweeney, T., Webster, R., Edmunds, M. and Hough, M. (2000) *Drug Treatment and Testing Orders: Final Evaluation Report*, Home Office Research Study 212. London: Home Office.

Wilkinson, R. and Pickett, K. (2009) *The Spirit Level: Why do more equal societies almost always do better?* London: Penguin.

5 Arrest referral and drug testing

George Mair and Matthew Millings

Introduction

During the early 1990s, as the Conservative government struggled to regain the political advantage from the Labour Party, one of the policies that was deliberately pushed forward was crime control. Traditionally, the Conservatives were seen to be 'tough on crime' whereas Labour was 'soft', and by playing on these different images Conservative ministers considered that they might begin to improve their standing in political polls. In response to this, two clear initiatives emerged from the Home Office: one was based around Michael Howard's notorious 'Prison Works' claim, while the other was located around an emphasis upon the dangers of drug misuse and its relationship with offending. There had been some disquiet about drug misuse since the 1960s, but the Green Paper *Tackling Drugs Together* (Cabinet Office, 1994) was a more focused set of proposals than had been previously available, and made its concerns quite clear:

> There is acute public concern about the commission of acquisitive offences such as theft and burglary by those addicted to drugs in order to fund their habit. The extent to which this acquisitive crime is connected to drug taking is very difficult to determine with any accuracy, not least because both drug taking and crime are of their nature covert activities. But the government believes that a more focused effort on drug-related crime will help to make communities safer and to reassure the public.
>
> (Cabinet Office, 1994: 41)

The Criminal Justice and Public Order Act 1994 provided for drug testing in prisons (see Paylor et al., Chapter 9 this volume), a move that was followed several years later by providing the same power to the police to test arrestees.

Heightened political attention on the drugs–crime nexus led to a number of new initiatives that were introduced in a rather fragmentary and inconsistent way across the criminal justice process. In this chapter, we examine two of these: drug testing in police stations and arrest referral schemes. The former is to a considerable extent an American import (both the technology and the practice had developed in the USA), while the latter seems to have emerged in an informal, uncoordinated way in various police stations across England and Wales during the second half of the 1980s (Dorn, 1994). We discuss the development of these two initiatives, drawing upon the literature, including our own evaluation of the Merseyside Arrest Referral Scheme between 2000 and 2002 (Mair et al., 2002). The next part of the chapter focuses on arrest referral schemes, while the third section discusses drug testing of arrestees. In the final part we summarize the key themes that have emerged and speculate about future developments.

Arrest referral

It is difficult to pin down the beginnings of arrest referral schemes with any accuracy. According to Dorn (1994) they began to appear, without any central coordination, in the mid-1980s as an initiative in various police stations in England and Wales. This 'bottom-up' approach is not an unusual way for policies to develop. Several reasons account for the emergence of the schemes. First, the idea of partnership or multi-agency working began to impinge upon criminal justice agencies at this time. This approach was not grounded in any coherent operational rationale: it was simply seen as self-evidently a good thing. Second, partnership working was expected to lead to reductions in expenditure, which chimed with one of the key themes of the Conservative administration. Third, around the same time, what David Garland (1996: 452) has termed 'the responsibilization strategy' was beginning to take shape with its 'recurring message ... that the state alone is not, and cannot effectively be, responsible for preventing and controlling crime' (Garland 1996: 453). Thus, state agencies such as the police were encouraged to work in partnership with non-state organizations, meaning, for the most part, voluntary sector agencies. Responsibilization and partnership work were, therefore, intimately linked as a response to rising crime rates.

A great deal of Conservative policy was driven explicitly by the 'economy, efficiency, effectiveness' mantra. As with partnership work, these three objectives tended to be used in fairly unsophisticated ways (for example, economy was seen as synonymous with cutting costs), but again they can be seen to resonate with the concept of arrest referral. During the 1980s, crime rates increased, which resulted in considerable efforts being made to bring them under control. In this climate, arrest referral schemes made sense given the drugs–crime relationship that was beginning to be articulated clearly. Although arrest referral was a relatively minor player in this area originally, it is important to understand its origins as these have helped to shape its subsequent direction. It is notable, however, that arrest referral schemes were not supported wholeheartedly by the Advisory Council on the Misuse of Drugs (ACMD) in 1991:

> [R]eferral schemes may ... have a useful, if limited, role to play in encouraging drug misusers to make contact with services ... It is clear, however, that referral schemes play no part in the process of identifying drug misusers within the criminal justice system. Nor is it clear how they could do so without jeopardising their main purpose of encouraging misusers to seek help ... But it is worth noting that an incidental benefit flowing from the creation of such schemes is the development of closer links between the police and drug services.
>
> (ACMD, 1991: 13)

By the late 1990s, the Labour government was cementing the drugs–crime relationship in its ten-year strategy *Tackling Drugs to Build a Better Britain* (President of the Council, 1998) and the climate in which arrest referral schemes operated had changed. One of the performance indicators included in the strategy was to 'increase the number of offenders referred to and entering treatment programmes as a result of arrest referral schemes, the court process and post-sentencing provision' (President of the Council, 1998: 19). Arrest referral schemes proliferated because of the need to measure performance and because of large amounts of funding available under the Crime Reduction Programme.

At their most basic, arrest referral schemes (or police referral, drug referral, or welfare referral schemes as they have been variously called), involve police officers offering advice to arrestees who are considered to have drug problems. That may sound neat, simple and uncontentious but in fact raises significant issues including: whether the police are the most appropriate people to deliver advice about drugs; what kind of advice might be offered and the way in which this should be done; who should receive the advice; and whether, having recently been arrested, it is the best time for police officers and arrestees to have a discussion about drug problems.

Given the ad hoc, informal origins and development of arrest referral schemes, it is unlikely that such issues were considered in detail prior to schemes being set up: no doubt problems would have been dealt with as they emerged. The underlying principle of arrest referral schemes for problem drug users is quite simple: drug use is associated with offending, and therefore by tackling the former the latter will be reduced. Sondhi et al. (2002: 8) claim that the rationale for developing arrest referral schemes is based on three recurring themes within the research literature: strong links between drug use and offending; large numbers of problematic drug users entering the criminal justice system; and the effectiveness of treatment in achieving sustained reductions in drug use and associated offending.

In a review of the available arrest referral schemes, Edmunds et al. (1998) identified three different models. The earliest schemes were based upon an information model. This approach involved police officers providing basic information to arrestees about local drug treatment services. Arrestees were expected to make contact with treatment services themselves. The limitations of this model have been discussed above but it did permit the *idea* of referral to drug agencies at the point of arrest to penetrate police stations and custody suites, and it had no serious implications with regard to resources.

The second model can be described as a proactive model and involves independent drug workers being based in custody suites or on-call and tasked with carrying out preliminary assessments of arrestees on site and, if necessary, making arrangements for referral to a suitable treatment agency. This model appears to be an improvement on the information model as trained drug workers who are independent of the police are likely to have greater credibility and expertise in drug issues than are police officers. However, issues remain with this model, including: who is it aimed at; how are they accessed; and the kind of information provided. There is also an obvious potential for tension to exist between drug workers and the police because they have different agendas and cultures.

The third model is an incentive (or coercive) model, based around 'carrots' and 'sticks'. For arrestees, the criminal justice process is not something that they enter voluntarily. They may, therefore, be keen to take up any incentives that might be offered to minimize their stay within it. Thus, arrestees may be 'encouraged' to participate in an arrest referral scheme because they are aware that by seeking treatment a lesser sentence may be imposed. For example, magistrates may be more likely to deal leniently with someone who is currently in treatment for a drug problem. There are obvious legal issues that would have to be handled carefully if such an approach is followed.

Arrest referral in Merseyside

In this section we draw upon our research into the Merseyside Arrest Referral Scheme which took place during 2000 and 2002 (Mair et al., 2002). The study was one of a number that were used by the Home Office to pull together a national picture of arrest referral schemes (see Sondhi et al., 2002). The study focused on the implementation, organization and development of the scheme and involved observing arrest referral work in custody suites and courts, and visits to community treatment agencies.

Besides a great deal of informal talk with the various players in arrest referral (for the most part, police officers and arrest referral workers), formal interviews were carried out with 71 stakeholders (police, arrest referral workers, staff of treatment agencies, members of the scheme management group) and with 31 clients of the scheme. Data were also collected on those who were assessed. While we have chosen to focus on our own research, similar findings emerged from other studies of arrest referral (Dorn, 1994; Turnbull et al., 1996; Edmunds et al., 1999; Sondhi et al., 2002; O'Shea and Powis, 2003; Oerton et al., 2003; Hunter et al., 2005).

There was a history of arrest referral on Merseyside. First, the police had been operating an 'information-only' scheme for some years prior to the scheme we studied, but it had not been evaluated. Second, a six-month pilot project based in Birkenhead police station based upon the proactive model was set up in 1998. The evaluation of the scheme suggested that the model was feasible but that some issues needed to be resolved (Mair, 1999). These included: targeting the arrest referral worker's time more effectively; clarifying whether casework should be part of the job; organizing data collection; and improving the attrition rate. While the pilot project was helpful in informing the planning of the Merseyside scheme, two factors were not accounted for. First, the Birkenhead model was assumed to be replicable across the whole of the area; and second, organizational complications resulted from the location of the drugs agency to which arrestees were referred.

The basic design of the Merseyside arrest referral scheme was that workers would be based in each of the seven custody suites in Merseyside, where they could access arrestees who would have been alerted to their availability by the police. Subject to the consent of an arrestee, workers would carry out a brief assessment and arrange an appointment with a 'gateway' agency. There, a full assessment would be carried out and the client referred on to an appropriate agency/agencies. The assessment was multi-dimensional and arrestees might be referred to agencies who could offer them support with problems other than their drug use (for example, accommodation). The two gateway agencies were Merseyside Drugs Council for arrestees in the whole of the region except Wirral where ARCH initiatives carried out this task. These two organizations were the employers of the arrest referral workers in their respective areas (ARCH had been the agency involved in the original Birkenhead scheme).

The police officially welcomed the scheme but at the beginning they were not – at least at custody suite level – fully engaged with it. Plans to hand arrestees a form or a laminated card with details about arrest referral failed to materialize because there were problems with arrestees blocking toilets with the forms and cards could not be laminated due to the risk of self-harm. It took some months before police officers regularly informed arrestees of the presence of drugs workers in custody suites and did this in a way designed to encourage arrestees to see workers. The most appropriate way for arrest referral workers to be referred to by the police was never resolved. There were a number of concerns. First, talking about a drugs worker/counsellor might put off arrestees because they might not wish to acknowledge a drug problem; second, to mention counselling was also felt to be problematic because it was unavailable in the custody suite and might raise expectations; and finally, using the term 'arrest' when referring to staff implied that the workers were closely allied to the police rather than independent.

A custody suite is police territory. In the first months of the scheme the impression was given that drugs workers did not really belong there. This manifested itself in the way the police were rather reluctant to treat arrest referral workers as part of the personnel of the custody suite, in the way legal requirements under the Police and Criminal Evidence Act 1984 were used as reasons for denying access to cells, and in difficulties in finding suitable office space for arrest referral workers. Such problems eased off over time, and good working relationships developed. Indeed, interview data showed that the police acknowledged the abilities, skills and experience of arrest referral workers, and that both police and drugs workers recognized that good relationships had been forged between the two groups.

Police data suggested that in the 18-month period between April 2000 and September 2001 a total of 63,624 individuals were detained in six custody suites (excluding Wirral[1]). During the same period, arrest referral workers carried out 2,767 assessments (again excluding Wirral cases), four per cent of those detained. This small percentage is accounted for by a variety of factors. First, arrest referral workers did not provide 24-hour coverage of custody suites. Instead, hours of work tended to be 8.00 am to 4.00 pm or 9.30 am to 5.30 pm, although workers began to change their working hours as they realized when custody suites would be busy. Weekends, evenings and nights were, however, rarely covered, despite these being busy periods. As workers realized that covering court cells had considerable potential, spending time there also cut into coverage in custody suites. At best, one-third of any 24-hour period (not counting weekends) was covered by arrest referral workers. Second, in addition to the police simply failing to alert all those detained about the presence of arrest referral workers, they gave a number of reasons why arrestees could not be seen by workers. These included: arrestees were on a rest period; they were deemed to have psychiatric problems and waiting to see the community psychiatric nurse; they were under the influence of alcohol; they had been arrested for serious offences; and they were under 17 years old. In addition, some detainees were released fairly quickly so that an arrest referral worker might not have the time to make contact with them. Methods for accessing clients were *ad hoc*. At least initially, workers would visit custody suites from time to time to check who was detained. Sometimes the police contacted them. Some individuals did not wish to see a drugs worker as, by doing so, they were making clear that they had drug problems which might not help their case.

On Merseyside, there was considerable scope for much greater coverage by the scheme, although this would have significant resource implications. As a result, the scheme extended to magistrates' courts after about 12 months. Given the nature of court work, it was easier for arrest referral workers to be present at key times, usually between 9.00 am and 11.00 am. This stretched workers because they simply added this onto their work in the custody suites, although by this time they attended custody suites only when the suites were expected to be busy. Over time, 'cell sweeps' were adopted as the most effective way to make contact with arrestees. This involved workers visiting the charge desk area to search out potential clients. Those who were eligible for the scheme were identified through the custody log. Workers would then go round the cells asking arrestees if they wanted an appointment with the scheme. When an arrestee accepted the offer, a custody assistant was summoned and the individual assessed. Practice in the courts followed a similar pattern, with custody staff advising who might be the most appropriate clients to contact.

Despite the movement towards more rational and effective modes of practice as arrest referral developed, one key structural issue remained. With one drugs agency managing arrest referral on Wirral (ARCH) and another doing this job for the remainder of Merseyside (Merseyside Drugs Council, MDC), it is not surprising that there were persistent and inevitable tensions between the two. On the one hand, ARCH saw itself as having 'written the book' on arrest referral as it had been behind the original Birkenhead scheme. On the other hand, MDC covered the bulk of Merseyside and six custody suites and thus saw itself as more significant. While the management group for the project as a whole regularly exhorted both agencies to collaborate more closely, there were few signs that this was occurring. Different data collection forms were used by each agency, there were two sets of management and two sets of quarterly reports were submitted to the management group. In effect, two arrest referral schemes were operating on Merseyside during the research period, almost certainly not the most effective, efficient or economic use of resources.

The referral process did not operate as planned. Clients of the scheme were to be sent to either ARCH or MDC for a full assessment if they agreed, but this happened consistently only in Wirral (where the pilot project had run) and in Southport and St Helens. In the latter two areas, the 'gateway' scheme worked because the police station and the MDC office were located close together, thereby facilitating good working relationships between the arrest referral workers and the staff at the agency. In the other custody suites, workers, at times, referred clients directly to services that they felt were relevant. To work efficiently this approach depended upon workers knowing the waiting list situation at agencies (not always the case), and on occasion meant that clients were referred to agencies that were not their first choice. This almost certainly meant that they were less likely to attend appointments. Similarly, if clients were informed that they could not be referred to an agency because of a lengthy waiting list, then they tended to lose interest in any other option. Waiting lists were a problem, at least initially, with delays of up to six months reported in some areas for a script. Staff shortages for posts to work with problem drug users were also reported for most of the first year. To deal with some of these issues, arrest referral workers wanted to carry their own caseload of clients who could not access drug services immediately, in order to provide support and 'keep them warm' while waiting. The workers wanted to do this because they came from a counselling background but were unable to use their skills. In addition, they did not like to see clients 'abandoned' because of waiting lists, and, to a certain extent, they were not as busy in the suites as they had expected (although this situation changed over time). But there were some problems with the idea, including: agreeing which clients would receive such support; how long the scheme would last; and whether it would mask gaps in service.

As noted earlier, arrestees agreed to see an arrest referral worker in 2,767 cases during the 18-month research period. These cases represented 1,901 individuals, 27 per cent of whom were seen on two or more occasions by arrest referral workers. Three-quarters were male and one-quarter female. Seventy-five per cent were aged between 21 and 35. Two per cent were 17 or younger and this group caused problems as satisfactory arrangements for dealing with them had not been worked out with Youth Offending Teams. Four per cent identified themselves as black. Nearly three-quarters (72 per cent) of arrestees agreed to have an appointment made for them although many of those individuals failed to keep their appointment. Despite considerable efforts, it proved impossible to set up a database of arrest referral cases that followed through cases to first appointment and after. To a large extent, this was because of the number of agencies that were used for referrals, many of which were unfamiliar with rigorous monitoring and data collection.

An important measure of success for arrest referral schemes is whether arrestees enter and are retained in treatment. Data are sparse but an estimate suggested that 40 per cent of those referred attended their first appointment. The figure is probably inflated as it includes referrals to the bail support scheme and to prison-based drug services. Others studies suggest 55 per cent (Turnbull et al., 1996) and 22 per cent (Sondhi et al., 2002) of arrestees kept their first appointment. Consequently, high attrition rates were a feature of all arrest referral schemes (see Sondhi et al., 2002). Very little data exist on the outcomes of first appointments and how long clients remained in treatment. One important factor is how soon a first appointment can be made, and on Merseyside 15 per cent of cases had appointments six days or more after the preliminary assessment, which may be too long to sustain interest in accessing treatment.

Whatever the structural problems that the arrest referral scheme had to face on Merseyside, there is little doubt that the scheme was accessing a high-risk group of clients who had lengthy drug careers and who were not receiving treatment. Heroin was the drug of choice (72 per cent had used it in the month prior to arrest), with cocaine second (46 per cent). Three-quarters of those assessed said they used drugs on a daily basis. Around half admitted to having injected at least once. Around half had been using drugs for five years or more. The majority (69 per cent) were not currently in treatment: indeed half (47 per cent) claimed that they had never received any help for their drug use. Evidence of successful targeting can also be found in other studies: Oerton et al. (2003) for London; Edmunds et al. (1998) for Brighton, Southwark and Derby; and nationally in Sondhi et al. (2002).

While it is difficult to measure accurately reductions in drug use and offending, it is notable that all studies suggest that participation in arrest referral schemes is associated with reductions in both, as the results of the national monitoring programme show:

> Consistent with the findings from the evaluations of previous arrest referral pilots, three separate outcome studies in the current national evaluation programme all demonstrate consistent reductions in drug use and offending behaviour among problem drug-using offenders who have been engaged in arrest referral.
>
> (Sondhi et al., 2002: 44)

So, despite problems with multi-agency working, with effective targeting and adequate resourcing, with questions about how to deal with specific groups such as women, ethnic minorities and young people, whether or not alcohol problems should be included, with effective community resources being available when needed, and given the caveats that must accompany the outcome measures, it would seem that arrest referral is successful. If the problems just listed were all resolved then it would be even more successful. But perhaps the biggest limitation of arrest referral schemes is that they have stood alone. Instead, they need to be part of a fully integrated system of dealing with offenders with drug and alcohol problems that covers the criminal justice process as a whole. In the remainder of the chapter, one of the integral parts of such an approach, drug testing, is discussed.

Drug testing

It is possible to view developments in drug testing over the past ten or so years in two very different ways. The more optimistic view would understand developments as part of an ongoing progressive movement to identify and engage with those individuals whose chaotic lifestyles and involvement in criminal activity can be traced to their dependence upon drugs. To that end, the combined efforts of criminal justice agencies and drug treatment providers should be mobilized to provide coherent service delivery. In policy terms, this approach can be found within the 2002 Updated Drug Strategy's explicit commitment to expand and harmonize services within the criminal justice system, including a specific strengthening of the ties between drug testing and arrest referral, such that every opportunity is taken to channel drug-misusing offenders into treatment (Home Office, 2002a).

In contrast, for others the use of drug testing creates a series of moral and ethical dilemmas that neither advance the cause of tackling drug dependence nor make effective use of the energies of criminal justice agencies and drug treatment providers. They would argue that such issues as the demeaning forms of testing, concerns over the reliability and confidentiality of test results, and the tensions inherent in the very different cultures of criminal justice agents and those who provide drug treatment all serve to undermine the claimed advantages of drug testing. This section weaves a path between the two by drawing upon available research to document how we have come to the point where drug testing on arrest is seen as 'the building block of treatment within the criminal justice system' (Bean, 2004: 85), while acknowledging the research evidence that challenges faith in the policy.

There can be little doubt that research incorporating drug testing has made important contributions to informing a wider sense of the prevalence of drug misuse among those detained in custody (see, for example, Bennett, 2000, 2001; Home Office, 2003; Holloway et al., 2004; Matrix and Nacro, 2004). It has also contributed to initiating dialogue about how to address the problems identified. In the process of policy delivery too, drug testing has come to play an important role in informing the organization and provision of local drugs services, as well as providing the data required to resource more appropriate and finely tuned care plans (see Home Office, 2004). The need for agencies to respond to these challenges and engage in multi-agency working also allows drug testing to be viewed as a catalyst for increased cooperation between criminal justice agencies and drug treatment providers. These positive outcomes, however, have to be set against research findings that question the impact of drug testing, as this section of the chapter shows.

Introduced originally in 2003 as a three-year programme to develop and integrate measures for directing adult drug-using offenders out of crime and into treatment, the Drug Interventions Programme (DIP, see Turnbull and Skinns, Chapter 4 this volume) continues to be a crucial element of the government's strategy for tackling drug misuse (Home Office, 2007b). The programme is founded on the principle of increased cooperation between criminal justice agencies and drug treatment providers to reduce drug-related crime by engaging with problematic drug users, particularly those who misuse Class A drugs, and moving them into appropriate treatment and support. Drug testing on arrest marks the start of this process by identifying problematic drug-misusing offenders. Those who test positive for a specified Class A drug are required to attend two assessments of their drug use with a 'suitably qualified person' (in the vast majority of cases a Criminal Justice Interventions Team (CJIT) worker who will possess or be working towards the relevant Drug and Alcohol National Occupational Standards (DANOS) competences).

The close working relationship between criminal justice agencies (particularly the police) and drug treatment providers can in part be explained by a series of research studies that have highlighted (through drug testing) the numbers of people passing through custody suites who are using drugs (Bennett, 2000, 2001). Although interview-based research helped to establish the strength of the relationship between drug dependence and involvement in criminal activity (see, for example, Hammersley et al., 1989), drug testing, initially through the results of the New English and Welsh Arrestee Drug Abuse Monitoring programme (NEW-ADAM), has offered a new clarity to gauging the scale of drug misuse among arrestee populations.

As recently as 1995, the government acknowledged that there was no reliable statistical measure of the extent of drug-related crime. Hard data were required so that progress towards the government's aims to tackle drug-related offending could be measured. By the time of the second major drug strategy in 1998, research had already been conducted into the feasibility of implementing a programme of interviewing and drug testing offenders similar to that used in the USA (Bennett, 1995). Published in April 1998, the White Paper *Tackling Drugs to Build a Better Britain* set out an extensive ten-year strategy for tackling drug misuse. Alongside the reorganization and resourcing of drug treatment services, the strategy set out a series of objectives with measurable targets that would be used to evaluate the policy's impact (President of the Council, 1998). The role of drug testing was to measure progress towards the achievement of the goals.

Launched in July 1999 after three years of developmental work devising and testing the research methodology, the NEW-ADAM programme conducted random surveys of arrestees held in police custody suites in 16 locations in England and Wales (Bennett, 2000). Eight sites were visited each year and then revisited every two years (eight in one year and eight in the next), thereby providing both cross-sectional and trend data on issues including the prevalence of drug misuse, criminal behaviour, living arrangements, health, and experiences of treatment (Bennett, 2001). Visits would usually last 30 days during which time all available arrestees taken into custody were eligible to take part. The main methods of data collection were structured interviews and collection of urine specimens. The urinalysis provided an objective indicator of drug use among the arrestee population (Bennett, 2001).

Across the four sites of London (South Norwood), Liverpool, Nottingham and Sunderland and based on the 506 people who consented to urine testing (out of a total of 2,971 arrestees who were processed), 69 per cent tested positive for one or more illegal drugs and 36 per cent tested positive for two or more substances (Bennett, 2000: 27). Almost half of arrestees (49 per cent) tested positive for cannabis, with 29 per cent and 20 per cent testing positive for opiates (including heroin) and cocaine (including crack), respectively. The longitudinal nature of the research allowed Bennett to assess the rate and extent of changes in the prevalence of drug use over the period 1997 to 1999. The similar design to the American ADAM programme enabled cross-sectional observations to be made with results of the urinalysis. This indicated that the prevalence rates of positive tests were higher in England than in the USA for four of the six drug types (marijuana, opiates, methadone and amphetamines). By contrast, the proportion of positive tests for cocaine was significantly higher in the USA than in England but there was no significant difference in test results for benzodiazepines between the two countries (Bennett, 2000).

The results of the NEW-ADAM programme offered much more than merely outlining the extent of drug taking among arrestee populations. Given that the drug strategy had established tightly defined targets (for example, the three percentage point reduction in the proportion of arrestees testing positive for heroin and opiates), the results could be used to monitor government policy. Bennett (2000) was also able to claim that data helped to provide additional evidence on the nature of the relationship between drug use and crime. For example, the research demonstrates that drug users had higher levels of illegal income and higher rates of self-reported crime than non-users. Almost half of those interviewed believed that their drug use impacted upon their offending, allowing Bennett

(2000) to argue persuasively that drug use (especially heroin and crack/cocaine use) is associated with higher levels of both prevalence (the proportion of the population involved) and incidence (the rate of offending of those involved) of offending. Therefore, the data substantiated previously held beliefs of an association between drug misuse and criminal behaviour. The scope of the research (combining drug testing with self-report questionnaires) also helped to establish the types of criminal activities that arrestees were involved in as well as specific user characteristics. In this way the research data can be seen to supplement prevalence estimates derived from other sources such as national household surveys or the British Crime Survey, which may fail to engage the populations captured by Bennett's (2001) research (for a full discussion of the NEW-ADAM programme of research, see Bennett and Holloway, 2007).

There are, however, a number of methodological and ethical/legal issues surrounding the use of drug testing generally that the experience of the NEW-ADAM research does make more salient. In what follows, we examine these two sets of concerns and then move on to discuss the operational issues that are likely to impact upon the future of drug testing.

The methods of drug testing

First, drug testing alone can fail on occasion to give a sufficiently detailed profile of the type or amount of drugs that those being tested actually use. For example, licit drugs such as codeine, pholcodine (found in some cough syrups) and even poppy-seed bagels can cross-react with urine or oral swab samples to produce a set of positive results (Bean, 2004). Urine tests (as used in the NEW-ADAM research) are also limited by the period of detectability of the test, with estimates indicating that amphetamines are detectable up to 2 days after use; opiates, methadone and benzodiazepines detectable for up to 3 days, and cannabinoid metabolites detectable for up to 3 days from single use, up to 10 days with daily use, and up to 27 days from chronic use (Bennett, 2000). Problems were minimized in the NEW-ADAM research because the researchers used both urine analysis and self-report questionnaires as well as collected information over a variety of periods. However, drug testing programmes are rarely supported by such qualitative input. The usefulness of this strategy is fundamentally challenged by comparisons of self-report studies and testing which demonstrate that testing underestimates the prevalence of drug use (see Edgar and O'Donnell, 1998).

Table 5.1 summarizes the pros and cons of the main types of drug testing available.

The ease of undertaking tests belies the care that must be taken especially because the staff taking the test may not be fully trained. A lack

Table 5.1 The advantages and disadvantages of various methods of drug testing

Type of test	Advantages	Disadvantages	Overall
Sweat patch A small patch placed on the offender's arm for between 10 and 14 days identifies drugs through perspiration	Largely non-intrusive (even though an arm may have to be shaved), with the patches easy to apply and able to clearly evidence tampering	Variations in the amount of sweat produced from one offender to another; the risk of accidental removal is high; once the patch has been contaminated as a result of drug use, the offender can continue to use with little evidence produced	Low cost, but results can take time as the patch has to be sent away for analysis
Saliva test Using swabs oral fluids are tested	The technique is neither demeaning or intrusive	Possible concerns over cross-reactivity with over-the-counter medicines; limited 'window of opportunity' for detecting drugs in one's system; lack of clarity over cut-off points	Low cost, non-intrusive, the method of choice for DIP
Blood test Rare form of drug testing where blood is drawn from the offender under specialist supervision	Unlike saliva tests there is a general agreement on the cut-off levels	Extremely invasive; tests have to be taken in hospital; any clinicians present required to attend court at a later date; expensive; issues around the disposal of the sample	Logistical concerns around the need for specialist facilities, speed and reliability of results compromise its attractiveness
Hair test Samples of hair can be used to provide details of the history of drug use over the previous six months	Provides extensive details about the amount and type of drugs used; tamper resistant	Laboratory conditions to avoid contamination; can be a week before substance misuse will show in a sample; expensive at around £75 per test	An expensive and logistically taxing method that does offer long-term detail
Eye test Certain substances will produce significant changes in the eye's reaction to light	Non-intrusive; easy to administer; gives immediate results; detects most substances	To be successful, tests require each person to have established their own baseline levels to be set against when suspicion of drug use is aroused	If the technology is improved likely to be the flagship of the future
Urine test Samples are taken from individuals with tests revealing the levels of drug in the sample	Inexpensive; accuracy levels of between 97% and 98%	Procedures must be sufficiently foolproof and carried out by trained personnel to minimize erroneous decisions and lessen the considerable possibility of legal challenges. The test also has difficulty in recognizing multiple drug use	In spite of certain disadvantages urine testing remains the most favoured method of drug testing

Source: Bean, 2004: 100–6.

of care in following procedure may result in the integrity of the test and the accuracy of the results being compromised. Errors can occur with the equipment and deliberate forms of tampering and manipulation are possible. The labelling and processing of samples can see simple administrative oversights generate erroneous results. With all forms of testing, errors are likely and it is not uncommon to hear of the creation of false positives (when a test result shows positive for a given drug when that drug is actually absent or present below the designated cut-off level) or false negatives (when the test result indicates a negative result for a given drug yet that drug is present in the sample). Within the current guidance for the DIP, (which uses the Cozart RapiScan oral swab) there is recognition that cut-off levels may be such that offenders who admit to taking drugs may not test positive. The current levels of cut-off are justified in accordance with 'international scientific opinion [and] following advice from forensic toxicology experts', and are set at the lowest level possible to detect people who abuse drugs while excluding those who may innocently come into contact with illicit drugs (Home Office, 2007b: 17). The ambiguity that ensues arguably undermines the legitimacy and competence of the agencies responsible for delivering drug testing.

One of the findings to emerge from the research by Powell et al. (2007) into offenders' attitudes towards Drug Treatment and Testing Orders (DTTOs) was that both interviewees and workers preferred mouth swabs to urine samples. Mouth swabs are harder to cheat, easier to provide a sample for and the results were more readily available. The move, during the life course of the research project, from urine to oral swab testing resolved some of the reported problems of manipulation by enabling the collection of samples to be observed (Powell et al., 2007). However, it is still possible for interviewees to continue using drugs on the days they know they will not be tested and return negative drug test results (Powell et al., 2007). The researchers concluded that only frequent random drug testing would act as a deterrent and uphold the integrity of the policy.

Ethical and legal issues raised by testing

A second set of issues relates to the ethical and legal dilemmas raised by drug testing. In the case of the NEW-ADAM research, the use of urine analysis can reveal highly personal information about individuals such as pregnancy, epilepsy or diabetes and therefore could be considered to be highly intrusive (Bean, 2004). The physical action of passing urine can be a highly demeaning experience, and while the NEW-ADAM studies appear to have considered such matters the same cannot always be said for drug testing provision more generally. The Prison Service, for example, specifies that two officers need to be present when urine is taken. What is done with the specimen (for example, if it is to be kept and how it is to be disposed of) also sets in motion a set of questions around the defining and marking of the boundaries of non-disclosure that need to pay close attention to offenders' right to privacy and dignity (Barton and Quinn, 2002). Such concerns have been swept aside by the government as its priority is to identify offenders who require treatment and to deter their drug misuse while under criminal justice supervision (Home Office, 2003). The Criminal Justice and Court Services Act 2000 gave the police the power to drug test detainees in police custody so that individuals aged 18 or over who had been charged with or convicted of a 'trigger offence' (these include property crime, robbery and specified Class A drug offences) are tested for specified Class A drugs. Alongside this, courts were given the power to order drug testing of offenders under the supervision of the Probation Service.

Increasingly, the traditional idea that accessing treatment should be voluntary has been supplanted by a more coercive approach (see Stevens, Chapter 8 this volume). Drawing on American research which showed that treatment could be successful (see Bean, 2004; Bean and Nemitz, 2004; Longshore et al., 2004), concerns about who should or should not receive help, and whether people could successfully reduce their drug misuse if they were coerced into treatment were set to one side. While the research could occasionally be vague in defining how treatment actually functioned and with whom, the 'treatment works' discourse began to see 'control' eclipse 'care' as the model of treatment and judicial control gradually replace civil commitment (see Bean, 2004; Carver, 2004). To this end, the rolling out of pilot projects introducing drug testing provision and linking them in with arrest referral schemes was part of an extensive programme of reform that changed the infrastructure designed to tackle drugs and crime in England as outlined in the 2002 Updated Drug Strategy. In March 2002 the Street Crime Initiative was introduced by the end of that year, *Tackling Crack: A National Plan* was launched; and in the following April the Criminal Justice Interventions Programme (CJIP, soon changed to the Drug Interventions Programme) became operational (Matrix and Nacro, 2004). All were geared towards getting substance misusers into treatment.

The new provisions for drug testing contained in the Criminal Justice and Court Services Act 2000 were subjected to an evaluation commissioned by the Home Office (Matrix and Nacro, 2004). Based on research in nine pilot areas, where, by the end of October 2003, 17,586 on-charge tests had been undertaken on 11,276 individuals, the results were clear:

> As an intervention, drug testing in police stations is demonstrated to be capable of being implemented. There are some compliance

issues but these should be relatively straightforward to address via more systematic monitoring, audit and analysis of action taken locally. The test result does appear to provide the criminal justice system with a relatively firm evidence base for Class A drug use amongst detainees (compared with relying upon self-reported information alone).

(Matrix and Nacro, 2004: xv)

Testing resulted in greater use of arrest referral. The evaluation revealed an increase in offers and acceptance of offers to see arrest referral workers after drug tests compared with before tests (Matrix and Nacro, 2004). Testing on charge identified problem users and led to the majority of these individuals being referred to treatment agencies. However, the non-compulsory nature of the referral meant that many failed to keep their appointments (a major problem for arrest referral schemes, as noted above). In order to eliminate this problem and give credibility to the testing on arrest, the Drug Interventions Programme (DIP) was launched (see Turnbull and Skinns, Chapter 4 this volume).

The DIP saw drug testing on charge extend to a total of 68 Drug Action Team areas, covering more than 100 Basic Command Units (Home Office, 2007a). These 'intensive' areas were targeted specifically because they had the greatest number of heavy drug users who were also prolific offenders. The expansion of testing programmes sought to identify these individuals and to 'encourage' them to attend assessments by adding a sanction for failure to attend. The Drugs Act 2005 permitted a drug test to be carried out post-arrest rather than post-charge and specified the conditions that had to be met before testing could take place. The individual had to be 18 or over, in police custody, and arrested for a trigger offence or for an offence where a police officer of inspector rank or above suspected Class A drug use was a causal or contributory factor. As soon as detention has been approved by a custody officer, a swab is placed under the tongue of the arrestee for a few minutes until the indicator turns blue. The specially trained officer then places the swab in a test tube, taking care not to contaminate the sample. The end of the swab is shaken loose, mixed with the buffer solution to remove any debris, and the now clean fluid sample drip fed into the cartridge that is then inserted into the Cozart RapiScan testing system (Cozart, 2008). After a few minutes the system produces either a positive or a negative result. Printouts containing the test result are kept in the detainee's custody record, attached to documentation prepared for court; a copy is given to the offender (Matrix and Nacro, 2004).

Previously (under the Criminal Justice and Court Services Act 2000), individuals who tested positive were asked whether they *wished* to see a drugs worker based in the custody suite and to access treatment (Home

Office, 2007a). The Drugs Act 2005 introduced powers for the police to *require* adults who had tested positive for a specified Class A drug (heroin, cocaine) to attend a drug assessment. The assessment, conducted while individuals are detained, is a brief triage assessment enabling drugs workers to establish an individual's dependence on, or propensity to use, specified Class A drugs, to identify any immediate needs, and to give harm minimization advice (Home Office, 2007b). The Act also gave the police powers to require individuals to attend a follow-up assessment to allow drugs workers a second opportunity to build on issues identified in the initial assessment. This goes some way towards filling the gaps in previous arrest referral schemes identified earlier in this chapter.

In theory, arrestees are requested to give a sample for testing and cannot be forced to do so. However, under sections 63B and 63C of the Police and Criminal Evidence Act 1984, refusal to provide a sample without good cause is an offence which could result, on summary conviction, in imprisonment for up to three months or a fine of up to £2,500, or both (Home Office, 2007a: 12). Moreover, section 19 of the Criminal Justice Act 2003 amended the Bail Act 1976 to provide a Restriction on Bail for adults who have tested positive for specified Class A drugs. Refusal to undergo an assessment and failure to agree to participate in any follow-up recommended by the assessor can lead to bail decisions being reversed (see Hucklesby, Chapter 6 this volume).

The increasingly coercive nature of police powers to direct individuals into treatment focuses on two issues: the highly active role the police play in channelling into treatment those who have not been charged with an offence; and the amount of information that can be disclosed within increasingly populous multi-agency partnerships. By the time of the Drugs Act 2008, the police role in directing individuals from custody suites into drug treatment had become even more clear-cut through the commitment to increase to 2,000 the number of conditional cautions being issued (Home Office, 2008a: 1):

> DIP aims to use every contact a drug-misusing offender has with the criminal justice system to move them out of crime and into treatment. Conditional cautioning may not be appropriate for highly problematic drug-misusing offenders who are more likely to be prosecuted and then engage in treatment through other DIP interventions. . . It does however provide an opportunity for intervention with first time or low level offenders as an alternative to prosecution; being able to make a real contribution to preventing the escalation of their drug related offending to more problematic levels. A conditional caution with a DIP condition can be particularly effective with first time offenders and drug users who have

not yet realized or acknowledged the possible consequences of
their continued drug use.

(Home Office, 2008b: 8)

Further, one of the objectives of increasing the use of conditional cautions is to 'engage drug misusers in treatment who are not yet known to
drug services or criminal justice agencies' (Home Office, 2008b: 8). While
this objective can be seen as an understandable desire to tackle drug use
before it becomes serious and entrenched, it can also be seen as problematic and wasteful of resources insofar as it involves risk prediction and
the possibility of false positives. The diversity of powers available under
the auspices of DIP (either directly or by extension through conditional
cautioning) leads to increases in the number of people eligible to be directed into drug treatment through the criminal justice system and a drift
towards a risk-based model of working. It can also create ambiguity regarding the legal status of individuals and their introduction to, and immer-
sion within, drug treatment services. Nowhere is this more troubling than
when those required to attend and stay for the duration of both the initial
and follow-up assessment and who fail to do so without good cause, are
considered to have committed an offence and may face criminal sanctions
(Home Office, 2007a).

The Drug Intervention Record (DIR) records all the information about
what happens to individuals who are in contact with the DIP. It provides
details of compliance, the advice offered, care plans, or any activities undertaken. DIRs represent part of the increasing interchange of data between the police, criminal justice intervention teams, Crown Prosecution
Service and courts, which raises ethical concerns over levels of disclosure.
Bean (2004) has also argued that there is a danger of stigmatizing individuals who have tested positive which could negatively affect the way
individuals are dealt with by agencies within the system. This issue is even
more pertinent now that drug test histories can be used for intelligence
purposes. There is also some concern that, despite official guidance notes
to the contrary, individuals' drug test history may be used to prove drug
misuse in support, for example, of an application for an Anti-Social Behaviour Order (Home Office, 2007b: 19). The emergence of the ethics of
disclosure amid the growth of multi-agency working, especially when it
is cross-sector, renders organizational claims to areas such as domains of
expertise and standard operating procedures open to challenge (Barton
and Quinn, 2002: 35), a set of issues we move to explore briefly now.

Operational issues and the future of drug testing

The DIP is now at the core of government efforts to tackle drug misuse. It
can be seen as a shining example of evidence-based policy as various pilot

Table 5.2 Advantages of drug testing for various stakeholders

Stakeholders	Positive impact of drug testing policies
Drug Action Teams and primary care trusts	Enhanced ability to tailor treatment plans, identify what drugs are being used and help identify treatment capacity
Police	Help ascertain recent drug use of arrestees and improve general levels of understanding of drug treatment programmes and their availability
Probation	Can enhance the assessment process for pre-sentence reports leading to more appropriate sentences for offenders who might not otherwise discuss their drug use
Sentencers	More effective sentencing as a result of improved pre-sentence reports
Prison officer sentence planners	Help inform sentence planning by identifying those offenders who require drug treatment while in custody and need appropriate support on release
Arrest referral schemes	Better targeting of those for whom arrest referral services may be appropriate, increased integration of schemes within the custody suite environment especially in intensive DIP areas
Local partnerships	The implementation process of drug testing can help forge effective partnerships links and relationships, with closer ties to criminal justice agencies securing more funding and stability
Detainees	Can provide a route into treatment which may not otherwise have been sought, and can be a significant incentive to reduce drug misuse

Source: Derived from Home Office, 2002b, 2003, 2004.

projects were refined as a result of evaluations of their success. The research evidence, however, can be read negatively as well as positively. On the positive side, the increasingly close links and good working relationships between criminal justice agencies and drug treatment providers has led to a series of benefits for both parties as a direct consequence of on-charge drug testing. Table 5.2 sets out the positive consequences for the various agencies and individuals involved in drug testing.

While all of the outcomes in Table 5.2 indicate the positives that can be derived from the operation of drug testing provisions, the research, particularly with regard to the experience of operating Drug Treatment and Testing Orders, also highlights the need for caution (see in particular Turnbull et al., 2000, and Powell et al., 2007). The increasing levels of joint working between health and criminal justice agencies can lead to greater overlap, creating a series of dilemmas in the process (Barton, 1999). There are inevitable tensions between the demands of a health discourse and those of the criminal justice system. The criminal justice system is more concerned with control and management of large groups of offenders than with the well-being of individuals (Barton and Quinn, 2002). The move towards a 'risk management model', for example, increasingly views an arrestee as part of a larger group, rather than as an individual, leading to a potential clash of criminal justice and health ideologies. The DIP's collectivizing narratives and the clinical nature of either passing or failing drug tests encourages the drift into policy language that is designed to control and manage behaviour of groups of offenders. The guidance notes for those implementing DIP state that 'it is likely that a number of those persons arrested but not charged with an offence will be involved in crime . . . it is therefore a reasonable and proportionate measure [to coerce individuals to attend treatment] on the grounds of crime reduction and public protection' (Home Office, 2007b: 10). In sharp contrast, the philosophy of the holistic nature of care and treatment adopted by health agencies prefers an individualistic approach (Barton and Quinn, 2002).

Evidence of the playing out of these differences can be found in the evaluation of drug treatment and testing orders (Turnbull et al., 2000). The researchers found ideological clashes and differing working practices, with 'nurses feeling uncomfortable that their clinical independence was threatened' and tensions because of 'different working cultures and expectations' (Turnbull et al., 2000: 56). The increased harmonization of criminal justice and drug service working under the auspices of the DIP means that these differences in working styles, traditions and values have to be confronted and overcome. Whether one partner or paradigm secures dominance, or there is a real coming together in partnership, will inevitably shape the enthusiasm for, and delivery of drug testing in the future.

In addition, as the process map in Figure 5.1 indicates, the drug testing and assessment process is complex enough to cause procedural difficulties, and it is quite possible that more rather than fewer arrestees will be drawn into its ambit in the future.

Conclusion

Arrest referral and drug testing of arrestees are significant developments in themselves, but bringing the two together offers considerable added value. Each initiative needs the other to make it more effective. With regard to arrest referral, drug testing means that those seen by arrest referral workers have been clearly identified as drug users and there is objective evidence of the kinds of drugs used. Drug testing without arrest referral is only a data collection exercise (although the value of this should not be underestimated), but with the presence of drug workers in the custody suite those testing positive can be plugged immediately into an assessment and

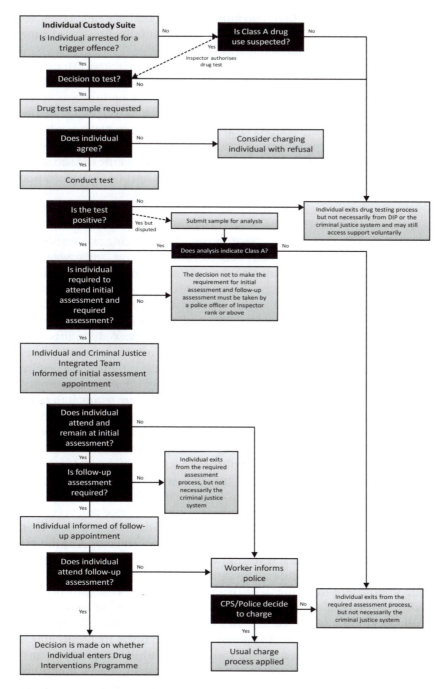

Figure 5.1 Drug testing process map.
Source: Adapted from Home Office, 2007c

referral process. Although the two initiatives emerged separately, common sense and the general direction of policy made it only a matter of time before the two were brought together.

But while arrest referral and drug testing are greater together than they are separately, some key issues remain. First, partnership working between police officers and drugs workers is not easy. Each group uses a different ideological approach to its 'customers', even though the customers are the same individuals. The work takes place in police space so that drugs workers are visitors and present on police terms. Management is a key issue: there are obvious drawbacks to police management, but the management of drugs workers based in custody suites by outside agencies can also result in problems.

Second, a more coercive approach has slowly been developing, but there are limits to such an approach. The legal and ethical implications of coercion with regard to drug testing and with enforcing attendance for assessment/treatment have been pushed to the margins. Such issues are exacerbated when testing takes place post-arrest but before charge. Increasing police involvement changes the nature of drug work in custody suites.

Third, having a coherent, well-organized system in place in custody suites is one thing, but this does not resolve issues about the number and quality of treatment agencies in the community. Waiting lists lead to serious difficulties; the quality of treatment offered by agencies needs to be monitored; contestability, i.e. putting services hitherto operated by the public sector out to tender, is likely to impact upon the availability of agencies; and effective data collection procedures are required to track clients through the treatment process.

Finally, a two-tier policy is now evident. The linking of arrest referral and drug testing to become the DIP does not apply equally to all custody suites in England and Wales, and this may lead to differences between intensive and non-intensive DIP areas. Arrestees' access to services may differ, sentences may differ, resources may differ – all of which would raise significant issues regarding equity and justice.

The 2008 Drug Strategy (Home Office, 2008c) makes it quite clear that the present approach will continue and develop as necessary. For the future, one can see testing and referral covering more locations and more arrestees, but whether national 24-hour coverage will ever be attainable is questionable, and there is a further question to be asked about its necessity. Whether alcohol use should be covered, and what to do about juveniles are two other matters that require consideration. As we have seen, there has been increasing police involvement via drug testing, but how far this process can continue is debatable. While bringing together arrest referral and drug testing is a major development, it is by no means the end of the journey – indeed it may be only a beginning.

Note

1. All Wirral cases were excluded as the arrangements in ARCH for collecting and holding information on arrest referral cases made it impossible for the researchers to access data; Merseyside Drugs Council routinely copied all completed forms to the researchers.

References

Advisory Council on the Misuse of Drugs (ACMD) (1991) *Drug Misusers and the Criminal Justice System. Part 1: Community Resources and the Probation Service*. London: HMSO.

Barton, A. (1999) 'Breaking the crime/drug cycle: the birth of a new approach?', *Howard Journal of Criminal Justice*, 33(2): 144–57.

Barton, A. and Quinn, C. (2002) 'Risk management of groups or respect for the individual? Issues for information sharing and confidentiality in Drug Treatment and Testing Orders', *Drugs: Education, Prevention and Policy*, 9(1): 35–43.

Bean, P. (2004) *Drugs and Crime*, 2nd edition. Cullompton: Willan Publishing.

Bean, P. and Nemitz, T. (2004) 'Introduction', in P. Bean and T. Nemitz (eds) *Drug Treatment: What Works?* London: Routledge.

Bennett, T. (1995) *A Feasibility Study of Drug Testing of Arrestees in England and Wales*. Cambridge: Institute of Criminology.

Bennett, T. (2000) *Drugs and Crime: The Results for the Second Development Stage of the NEW-ADAM Programme*, Home Office Research Study 205. London: Home Office.

Bennett, T. (2001) 'Recent developments in drug-testing arrestees for research purposes: an English perspective on an international phenomenon', *Addiction*, 96(6): 809–13.

Bennett, T. and Holloway, K. (2007) *Drug–Crime Connections*. Cambridge: Cambridge University Press.

Cabinet Office (1994) *Tackling Drugs Together: A Consultation Document on a Strategy for England 1995–1998*. London: HMSO.

Carver, J.A. (2004) 'Drug testing: a necessary prerequisite for treatment and for crime control', in P. Bean and T. Nemitz (eds) *Drug Treatment: What Works?* London: Routledge.

Cozart (2008) 'RapiScan on-site products', http://www.cozart.co.uk/rscan_test.php visited September 2008

Dorn, N. (1994) 'Three faces of police referral: welfare, justice and business perspectives on multi-agency work with drug arrestees', *Policing and Society*, 4: 13–34.

Edgar, K. and O'Donnell, I. (1998) *Mandatory Drug Testing in Prisons: An Evaluation*, Home Office Research Findings 75. London: Home Office.

Edmunds, M., Hough, M., Turnbull, P. and May, T. (1999) *Doing Justice to Treatment: Referring Offenders to Drug Services*, DPAS Paper 2. London: Home Office.

Edmunds, M., May, T., Hearnden, I. and Hough, M. (1998) *Arrest Referral: Emerging Lessons from Research*, DPI Paper 23. London: Home Office.

Garland, D. (1996) 'The limits of the sovereign state: strategies of crime control in contemporary society', *British Journal of Criminology*, 36(4): 445–71.

Hammersley, R., Forsyth, A., Morrison, V. and Davies, J.B. (1989) 'The relationship between crime and opioid use', *British Journal of Addiction*, 84(9): 1029–43.

Holloway, K., Bennett, T. and Williams, T. (2004) *The Results of the First Two Years of the NEW-ADAM Programme*, Home Office Online Report 19/04. London: Home Office.

Home Office (2002a) *Updated Drug Strategy*. London: Home Office.

Home Office (2002b) *Evaluation of Drug Testing in the Criminal Justice System in Three Pilot Areas*, Home Office Findings 176. London: Home Office.

Home Office (2003) *Evaluation of Drug Testing in the Criminal Justice System in Nine Pilot Areas*, Home Office Findings 180. London: Home Office.

Home Office (2004) *On-charge Drug Testing: Evaluation of Drug Testing in the Criminal Justice System*, Development and Practice Report 16. London: Home Office.

Home Office (2007a) *Operational Guidance for Implementation of Testing on Arrest: Required Assessment and Restriction on Bail*. London: Home Office.

Home Office (2007b) *Drug Interventions Programme: Operational Programme Guidance Frequently Asked Questions List*. London: Home Office.

Home Office (2007c) *Drug Testing Process Map, Drugs Intervention Programme*. London: Home Office. http://www.drugs.gov.uk/publication-search/dip/test_assess_map.

Home Office (2008a) *Drugs: Protecting Families and Communities. Action Plan 2008–2011*. London: Home Office.

Home Office (2008b) *Drug Interventions Programme: Conditional Cautioning and the DIP Condition. Operational Guidelines for Criminal Justice Integrated Teams and Partners*, Version 1.3. London: Home Office.

Home Office (2008c) *Drugs: Protecting Families and Communities. The 2008 Drug Strategy*. London: Home Office.

Hunter, G., McSweeney, T. and Turnbull, P. (2005) 'The introduction of drug arrest referral schemes in London: a partnership between drug services and the police', *International Journal of Drug Policy*, 16(5): 343–52.

Longshore, D., Prendergast, M.L. and Farabee, D. (2004) 'Coerced treatment for drug-using criminal offenders', in P. Bean and T. Nemitz (eds) *Drug Treatment: What Works?* London: Routledge.

Mair, G. (1999) *The U-Turn Project: A Preliminary Evaluation of an Arrest Referral Scheme for those with Drug and Alcohol Problems*. Liverpool: LJMU Centre for Criminal Justice.

Mair, G., Millings, M. and Palmer, C. (2002) *Arrest Referral on Merseyside: An Evaluation.* Liverpool: LJMU Centre for Criminal Justice.

Matrix and Nacro (2004) *Evaluation of Drug Testing in the Criminal Justice System,* Home Office Research Study 286. London: Home Office.

Oerton, J., Hunter, G., Hickman, M., Morgan, D., Turnbull, P., Kothari, G. and Marsden, J. (2003) 'Arrest referral in London police stations: characteristics of the first year. A key point of intervention for drug users?', *Drugs: Education, Prevention and Policy,* 10(1): 73–85.

O'Shea, J. and Powis, B. (2003) *Drug Arrest Referral: A Case Study of Good Practice.* London: Home Office.

Powell, C.L., Bamber, D. and Christie, M.M. (2007) 'Drug treatment in the criminal justice system: lessons learned from offenders on DTTOs', *Drugs: Education, Prevention and Policy,* 14(4): 333–45.

President of the Council (1998) *Tackling Drugs to Build a Better Britain: The Government's Ten-Year Strategy for Tackling Drug Misuse,* Cm 3945. London: The Stationery Office.

Sondhi, A., O'Shea, J. and Williams, T. (2002) *Arrest Referral: Emerging Findings from the National Monitoring and Evaluation Programme.* London: Home Office.

Turnbull, P., Webster, R. and Stillwell, G. (1996) *Get It While You Can: An Evaluation of an Early Intervention Project for Arrestees with Alcohol and Drug Problems,* DPI Paper 9. London: Home Office.

Turnbull, P., McSweeney, T., Webster, R., Edmunds, M. and Hough, M. (2000) *Drug Treatment and Testing Orders: Final Evaluation Report,* Home Office Research Study 212. London: Home Office.

6 Drug interventions in the remand process

Anthea Hucklesby

Introduction

The focus of this chapter is on the remand process and its use to engage defendants in drug treatment. It examines the introduction of Restriction on Bail (RoB) in England and Wales which enables magistrates' courts and the Crown Court to require defendants to attend drug assessment and treatment as a condition of court bail or face the possibility of being remanded in custody. The main aim of RoB is to channel defendants into drug treatment thereby reducing levels of offending on bail. A secondary aim is to divert defendants from custodial remands. This chapter draws on the findings of Home Office funded evaluation of the pilots to discuss issues raised by using the remand process to put defendants in contact with drug services (Hucklesby et al., 2005, 2007).

The RoB provisions were first legislated for in the Criminal Justice Act 2003 and subsequently amended by the Drugs Act 2005. These Acts amended the Bail Act 1976 to enable RoB to be imposed by the courts. Several conditions have to be met in order for RoB to be applied: defendants must be aged over 18 and have tested positive for a specified Class A drug. Consequently, for RoB to be imposed, drug testing arrangements must be in place at police stations. The basis on which drug tests are carried out is either that 'trigger offences' (which are mostly acquisitive offences) are alleged to have been committed or because the police suspect that the offences are drug-related (see Mair and Millings, Chapter 5 this volume). For RoB to be applied, courts must be 'satisfied that there are substantial grounds for believing that the offences were caused, wholly or partly, by defendants' misuse of specified Class A drugs or were motivated, wholly or partly, by drug use'. This test requires courts to link the alleged commission of offences directly to defendants' drug use. In practice, courts use positive drug tests to establish that offences are drug-related although there are a number of substantive arguments which raise questions about whether this is sufficient. These relate primarily to the complex nature of the drug–crime link and the fact that in many cases the link may not be direct or causal (see Bennett and Holloway, 2007; Reuter and Stevens, 2009). The issue is complicated further when testing occurs at the time suspects are charged because a considerable time may have elapsed between the commission of the alleged offence and the drug test. In theory, this provides defendants and solicitors with the opportunity to argue that alleged offences were not drug related. In practice, this avenue is rarely exploited by solicitors mainly because RoB is perceived to be in the best interests of their clients and because it is a mechanism by which defendants could avoid being remanded in custody. The introduction of testing on arrest has closed the potential to exploit this loophole in some cases but it is still a possible avenue to challenge courts' assumptions when time elapses between the commission of the alleged offence and the arrest of suspects.

If all three criteria for the imposition of RoB are met and courts grant bail, the application of RoB is mandatory. RoB is a condition of bail which requires defendants to undergo drug assessment and treatment as directed. If defendants refuse to undergo assessments or refuse to participate in any relevant follow-up (treatment or other support), they must be denied bail unless the court is satisfied that there is no significant risk of an offence being committed on bail. Therefore the presumption of bail is reversed, raising considerable issues about civil liberties given that defendants are not convicted of any offence and may never be. This part of RoB was strengthened by the Drugs Act 2005. Originally, the Criminal Justice Act 2003 provided more discretion to the courts when considering what to do if defendants refused to comply with RoB by using the legal wording 'shall' rather than 'must' in relation to remanding them in custody. This was the legal position during the period when the evaluation was taking place (May 2004 to October 2005). Subsequently, the Drugs Act 2005 took away nearly all of the courts' discretion but retained just enough to stymie any potential legal challenges on the basis of a breach of the Human Rights Act 1998.

Restriction on Bail is firmly embedded in current government attempts to tackle drug-related crime. It was one of the last pieces in the jigsaw of the Drug Interventions Programme (DIP) which aims to provide a comprehensive strategy to deal with drug-related offending throughout the criminal justice process. The aim of RoB was to plug the gap in the provision of drug services between arrest referral and sentencing. Its introduction was thought to be necessary because take-up of arrest referral schemes was relatively low and attrition rates were high (Sondhi et al., 2002; Mair and Mullings, Chapter 5 this volume). This resulted from a number of factors, including suspects being missed by arrest referral schemes and the fact that arrest referral schemes were voluntary resulting in a high proportion of the suspects who were referred into treatment failing to attend their appointments or dropping out subsequently. Consequently, arrest referral schemes were viewed as an imperfect way to channel suspects into drug treatment early on in the criminal justice process. Additionally, certain groups of suspects, including users from minority ethnic groups, older users and crack users, were identified as being particularly difficult to engage in voluntary arrest referral schemes (see, for example, Sangster et al., 2002; Witton and Ashton, 2002; Fountain et al., 2003; Inciardi, 2003; Gossop and Moos, 2008).

Restriction on Bail aimed to reduce attrition rates by engaging suspects who were missed by arrest referral schemes as well as those from hard-to-reach groups. Its main tool to achieve this was to introduce coercion into defendants' choices about whether to access drug assessment and treatment while waiting for their case to be dealt with by the courts. This took the form of incentives and disincentives in line with the Tough Choices programme whereby incentives to comply are juxtaposed with unpleasant consequences if defendants failed to comply. The incentive was rapid access to treatment. This was viewed as a vital component of the scheme because long waiting times and poor experiences of treatment had been identified as significant barriers to users' engagement with drug services (Sondhi et al., 2002). The disincentive was the threat of custodial remands if defendants failed to engage with either assessment or treatment. This aspect of RoB was the most controversial because it seemingly used the criminal justice process to coerce unconvicted and, therefore, legally innocent, defendants into drug assessment or treatment. The government strenuously denied RoB's coercive nature but strongly supported its place within its Tough Choices programme to reduce drug-related offending. The controversies and ethical issues surrounding coercing individuals into treatment are discussed elsewhere in this volume and will not be examined in detail here. Suffice it to say that at the time that RoB was introduced, research evidence was starting to suggest that coerced treatment was as effective as voluntary treatment, which was contrary to previous orthodoxies (Wild et al., 2002; Klag et al., 2005; Stevens et al., 2005; see also Stevens, Chapter 8 this volume).

Restriction on Bail was piloted in three areas (Manchester, Nottingham and Salford) between May 2004 and October 2005. During the pilot period, RoB was extended to a number of contiguous areas and was subsequently rolled out nationally to areas where drug testing was in place in March 2006. After the pilots, RoB became part of the Tough Choices project. This project was an extension of the Drug Interventions Programme and was launched by the government in 2006. It combined two elements introduced in the Drugs Act 2005, testing on arrest and required assessment, with the national roll-out of RoB (Skodbo et al., 2007). Together these measures moved drug interventions to earlier on in the criminal justice process, from post-charge to post-arrest. This raises pertinent issues about the appropriateness of using such measures for suspects who may never be charged or convicted thereby raising additional civil liberties concerns.

The evaluation

The evaluation of the RoB pilots was funded and managed by the Home Office. It aimed to provide evidence about the impact and effectiveness of RoB. The evaluation had three elements, namely process and impact evaluations and a monitoring exercise. The main aims of the evaluation were: to measure take-up of RoB; to identify who it was used for to measure its impact on the incidence of offending on bail, the prison population, entry into drug treatment and retention rates, and levels of drug use; and to explore defendants' and stakeholders' views of RoB (see Hucklesby et al., 2005, 2007).

The evaluation used a range of methods to collect both quantitative and qualitative data. Administrative data were collated by RoB staff in the three pilot sites between May 2004 and October 2005 and provided data on defendants appearing at magistrates' courts who had tested positive for opiates and/or cocaine when they were charged. Some cases were excluded because defendants were ineligible for RoB. A total of 2,831 cases were analysed, which equated to 1,876 defendants because 526 defendants appeared in the data more than once. Data on 984 cases involving defendants who tested positive for specified Class A drugs were collected from three magistrates' courts outside of the pilot areas where RoB was not operational and comprise the comparison sample. Police National Computer (PNC) data were obtained for 2,831 defendants from the pilot sites and 779 defendants in the comparison areas. These data relate to offending history and convictions for offending on bail.

Treatment data were collected from two sources, namely one of the pilot sites and the National Treatment Agency (NTA). The research team were denied access to treatment data in two of the three pilot sites and in all of the comparison sites because of issues of data protection and confidentiality. This was despite considerable efforts and assurances on the part of the research team whose original request was for a limited amount of data. This made it impossible to evaluate RoB effectively in terms of one of its key aims of channelling and retaining defendants into drug treatment. To partially compensate for this, the NTA provided aggregate data on treatment take-up and retention for defendants in both the pilot sites and the comparison sample. Data on 30 defined groups were obtained using criteria such as eligibility for RoB, imposition of RoB, and remand status for defendants who did not have RoB imposed. For example, one group comprised defendants who were eligible for RoB but who were remanded in custody. Another group were defendants who were ineligible for RoB and who were released on bail. While these data were useful, the fact that they were collated by the NTA from national records and could not be verified by the research team raises questions about their reliability and validity. The issues raised by accessing treatment data are discussed elsewhere in this volume (see Hucklesby and Wincup, Chapter 2). Suffice it to say that the effectiveness of drug interventions cannot be evaluated effectively without access to data pertaining to drug treatment and its outcomes.

Observations were also undertaken of remand hearings in each of the three pilot sites. The courtrooms in each court which dealt with the majority of remand cases were identified and court sessions were observed on random days. Information related to the remand process and defendants was collected, including information presented to the court and its source. A total of 1,105 cases were observed. Of these, 241 cases related to defendants who were identified as being eligible for RoB. Semi-structured interviews were carried out with a range of groups, including criminal justice practitioners ($n = 89$), for example magistrates, District Judges and legal advisers; stakeholders ($n = 35$), for example members of local and national steering groups; RoB staff ($n = 11$); and defendants ($n = 61$). The majority of interviewees, except the defendants, were interviewed twice, once in the initial stages and again in the final stages of the pilot.

Multi-agency working

The operation of RoB involves a large number of agencies from both the criminal justice sector and the health sector. It therefore provides a good case study of how the criminal justice and health sector work together. Traditionally, criminal justice agencies and drug agencies have been reluctant to work together mainly because they viewed themselves as having a different etho, culture and goals in relation to how to deal with drug users. At the time of the pilot, lines of communication were opening up between the two sectors mainly because of broader developments, including the DIP. However, the RoB pilot itself contributed to a growing sense of shared understanding and goals between all of the agencies involved and multi-agency working. This largely emanated from the need to solve considerable problems which arose during the pilots. All agencies demonstrated a commitment to the pilots and worked together to alleviate the problems which were encountered. This had a ripple effect, improving working relationships more broadly and resulting in an increase in collaborative working on RoB and other initiatives. Nevertheless, the process was not always smooth and some residual issues remained at the end of the evaluation which are discussed in the rest of this section.

Regional government offices were tasked with managing the pilots. They chaired the local steering groups for much of the pilot period and were responsible for bringing all of the agencies together. Initially, however, criminal justice agencies, and particularly the courts and the

Crown Prosecution Service (CPS), were poorly represented on local steering groups. A contributory factor in this was that the initiative was viewed as a drug initiative rather than criminal justice measure. This was probably inevitable given that RoB was firmly rooted within, and funded through, the DIP and that Drug Action Teams (DATs) were the lead agencies. However, it resulted in the importance of the role of criminal justice agencies being underestimated and criminal justice agencies feeling sidelined at the start of the pilot.

From a drugs perspective, the main challenge to implementing RoB was viewed as providing fast access to treatment. In reality, this was the part of the process which went relatively smoothly, possibly because the drug agencies, upon which responsibility for RoB had been firmly placed, needed to demonstrate that they could deliver their part of the project. Operational difficulties arose largely in the areas which were the responsibility of criminal justice agencies. This produced a lack of fit between the agencies with the most involvement in the management of the pilot and the parts of the process where the problems arose. For example, considerable difficulties arose in all of the pilot sites in ensuring that drug test results were available in courts.

The precursor for RoB to be imposed is that defendants must have tested positive for a specified Class A drug. Consequently, an important step in the process is for the test results to be available to courts so that they can identify eligible defendants. The identification process involves all of the major criminal justice agencies (the police, CPS and the courts) and was not directly under the control of DATs. Problems arose with the process so that not all eligible defendants were identified although the problem diminished with time (Hucklesby et al., 2007). Some sites were more successful than others at identifying eligible defendants. Manchester had the most problems with getting drug test results to courts. It appeared to be more than a coincidence that this was the area where the court administration was least involved in the pilots and where leadership from individuals running the courts was minimal. By contrast, the Deputy Legal Director in Nottingham was a champion of the pilots. Here, there was a high concordance rate between the number of defendants who tested positive at the police station and the number of these test results which were known to the courts from the start of the pilot (Hucklesby et al., 2007). Both the police and CPS also played a significant role in improving the flow of test results from the police to the courts during the pilot. This highlights clearly that, while RoB may be a drug-based initiative, it relies on criminal justice agencies to be able to identify potential defendants and impose the condition.

What seemed at face value to be a simple exercise of transferring test results from the police to the courts was complicated. The process involved a number of agencies, none of whom had responsibility for RoB nor were their performances measured in respect of RoB during the initial stages of the pilots. To take account of this, alterations were made to the management and accountability structures during the pilot. However, a recommendation made by the evaluation team that there should be a shift away from the drugs focus of the initiative towards a more criminal justice focus, demonstrated most visibly by the involvement of Local Criminal Justice Boards was not implemented fully. Local Criminal Justice Boards have the remit to coordinate activity and share responsibility for delivering criminal justice in their areas. To this end, membership includes all the local chief officers of criminal justice agencies. There may be many reasons why the recommendation was not taken forward but a significant contributory factor was that the RoB was funded through the DIP rather than criminal justice budgets. Such demarcation between criminal justice and health agencies which can result in no agencies taking responsibility for issues which arise is likely to persist and potentially be exacerbated by the split between the Ministry of Justice and the Home Office. Consequently, the DIP comes under the auspices of the Home Office while much of the implementation of it, and especially RoB, relies on agencies which come under remit of the Ministry of Justice. This is not conducive to multi-agency working in relation to initiatives which cut across both government departments. The result was that the CPS and the courts in particular were never fully integrated into the management structures for RoB although levels of assimilation of these agencies varied between pilot sites.

Restriction on Bail, like DIP more generally, operates largely as an add-on to the criminal justice process rather than being fully integrated within it. It has a tendency to run parallel to the criminal justice process, often reinventing procedures and policies rather than using existing structures, and duplicating work. Some examples of this can be seen by examining the position of the Probation Service in the RoB pilots. It was never envisaged that the Probation Service would have a role in RoB and it was not represented on local steering groups. Given the focus of RoB on drugs and its funding stream, this might have been expected. However, the Probation Service has considerable experience of operating in the courts generally, and particularly in the provision of reports to magistrates and judges. From this perspective, it could have provided (and did provide in one pilot site) valuable guidance on the operation of RoB, particularly the court process. Probation services had operated bail information schemes in the 1990s which had faced many of the same issues as the RoB process, for example identifying eligible defendants, and Probation's experience of operating other procedures such as breaches could have been invaluable. Probation Service staff also played a valuable role in ensuring that defendants who had tested positive were identified in court (Hucklesby et al., 2007). This role evolved because it became apparent that RoB workers could not always be in court when RoB cases were dealt with. Another consequence of the parallel existence of RoB was a lack of coordination between RoB and sentencing. Despite this being seen as an essential component of the RoB process, at the time of the pilots very few links had been made between the pre-trial RoB process, sentencing and subsequent case management, mainly because of the different responsibilities of the agencies.

The main advantage to having DIP outside the rest of the criminal justice process is that specialist assistance is given to drug users and that the resources for doing this are ring-fenced and do not get siphoned off into other areas of the criminal justice process. It also enables ethical issues in relation to the provision of drug services to defendants and offenders to be sidestepped. However, the disadvantages are significant. The focus on defendants' drug use can militate against other needs being dealt with simultaneously. It can also mean that resources are duplicated, with drug and probation staff dealing with the same issues or needs such as housing. Conversely, defendants' needs may not be dealt with because they fall through the gap between drug and criminal justice agencies. Running two parallel systems is also costly in terms of resources such as staffing and accommodation. It also ties up experienced drugs workers in routine court work which could be undertaken by less specialist individuals (Hucklesby et al., 2007).

Take-up of Restriction on Bail

A total of 1,315 defendants were granted bail with RoB during the pilots (Hucklesby et al., 2007). This represents almost three-fifths (59 per cent) of the defendants who were eligible (i.e. had tested positive for a specified Class A drug). Table 6.1 demonstrates that take-up varied between pilot sites. It shows that around two-thirds of eligible defendants were bailed with RoB in Nottingham (69 per cent) and Salford (63 per cent),

Table 6.1 Whether or not RoB was imposed

	Manchester		Nottingham		Salford		Total	
	n	%	n	%	n	%	n	%
Yes	310	41	856	69	149	63	1,315	59
No	438	58	388	31	86	37	912	41
Not known	2	1	0	0	0	0	2	>1
Total	750	100	1,244	100	235	100	2,229	100

compared with just over two-fifths (41 per cent) in Manchester (Hucklesby et al., 2007). Nearly two-thirds (63 per cent) of eligible defendants were remanded in custody. Over one-quarter (29 per cent) of eligible defendants were granted bail without RoB despite its being a condition which should have been considered. Three-quarters (75 per cent) of this group were bailed unconditionally. The results clearly suggest that RoB was not routinely applied in cases where unconditional bail was deemed suitable. Indeed, it was not common practice for RoB to be imposed when defendants had been released on bail by the police. In such cases, RoB was often not considered by the courts partly because cases were not identified to them. Consequently, RoB was not the blanket decision that was intended. Instead it concentrated on defendants who were higher bail risks. This largely resulted from its being viewed as a measure to divert defendants away from custodial remands. This may be viewed positively because it concentrated resources where they were most needed and also militated against net-widening which results in more individuals being drawn into the criminal justice system and to a greater degree. Yet net-widening was a real possibility with the use of RoB because there is a risk that it could have resulted in defendants being remanded in custody as a consequence of non-compliance, offending or up-tariffing if they were charged with other offences when they were never originally at risk of going to prison.

Restriction on Bail was used for both men and women, and gender did not appear to be a significant factor in decisions about whether to impose RoB. However, questions were raised by the evaluation about the way in which RoB was used for different ethnic groups (Hucklesby et al., 2007). Defendants from minority ethnic groups were less likely to be bailed with RoB than white defendants. Table 6.2 shows that this pattern was apparent in all sites but was most marked in Manchester. The differences were not explained by any measureable factors, although other factors such as differences in offending and bail histories could not be explored because data were unavailable. This mirrors previous research which suggests that defendants from minority ethnic groups are less likely to be bailed (Brown and Hullin, 1993). But criminal-justice-related factors may not tell the

Table 6.2 Proportion of cases where RoB imposed, by ethnic origin

	Manchester		Nottingham		Salford		Total	
	n	%	n	%	n	%	n	%
White	267	33	750	63	137	56	1,154	51
BME	43	22	106	57	12	40	161	40

BME = black and minority ethnic.

whole story because research has also highlighted how the provision of drug services for members of minority ethnic groups are inadequate and largely fail to cater for their needs (Sangster et al., 2002). It also suggests that members of minority ethnic groups view drug services as catering for the white population and that negative direct or indirect experiences of drug treatment can prevent them from attending again (see Fountain et al., 2003).

Drug treatment

The three pilot sites were all phase one sites for DIP. On national measures, the sites had the infrastructure in place to operate RoB, including a range of treatment services. Generally, pilot sites had waiting times below the national average and retention rates around the national average at the time of the evaluation (Hucklesby et al., 2007). Most of the treatment delivered through RoB was Tier 3 which is defined by the NTA as community-based drug treatment with involves regular sessions undertaken as part of a care plan. It may include prescribing, structured day programmes and psychosocial interventions (NTA, 2009a). The interventions available in the three sites varied.

Two models of the provision of services through RoB operated during the pilot. Manchester and Salford operated a health-based approach integrating RoB fully into existing drug services. In these areas, few problems were reported in terms of treatment provision. In theory, defendants were provided with a holistic service, including access to the whole range of treatment and other services which were available from the beginning of their time on RoB. In these areas, the aim of RoB was the same as for drug services generally, namely to retain defendants in treatment and deal with drug use in the longer term. It was incidental that they came into treatment through the criminal justice process. This impacted upon compliance and enforcement issues where a degree of discretion was used and other mechanisms were utilized to ensure attendance at appointments such as providing lifts for defendants. If defendants were already in treatment when RoB was imposed, this was treated as an opportunity to review progress and the treatment that defendants were receiving.

The approach in Nottingham was different and emphasized a criminal justice approach to RoB. RoB was operated largely outside existing structures to deal with drug use such as the Criminal Justice Intervention Team (CJIT) and treatment services. Instead, RoB workers case-managed defendants who were typically referred to the Rapid Prescribing Service (RPS) specifically set up to work with defendants on RoB because of concerns about the lack of treatment provision in the area. In theory, defendants stayed for an initial period of two to four weeks until their drug use was stabilized, after which they were referred on to core treatment services. The main advantage of this approach was the speed at which substitute prescribing was available. But it was less successful at getting defendants into appropriate treatment; providing holistic services including the provision of accommodation; and ensuring a broad understanding and support for RoB from the range of individuals and agencies involved in drug services. Nottingham's approach meant that services were narrowly focused on drug use and the short-term goals of getting defendants through their bail periods without offending. To this end, RPS dealt with any immediate issues such as access to cash and substitute drugs but did not provide other support or deal with long-term problems which underlay drug use or offending. Nottingham also operated a strict enforcement policy in terms of non-compliance in line with its criminal justice ethos. No review process existed for defendants already receiving treatment when RoB was imposed.

Lack of timely access to appropriate treatment services has been one of the barriers to the provision of drug treatment (Strang et al., 2004; Donmall et al., 2005). This issue posed significant challenges for RoB because the time awaiting trial may be short and its length is often unpredictable because of uncertainty about how the case is going to proceed. Furthermore, the focus on reducing delays in the criminal justice process has meant that remand periods have shortened for some defendants, particularly those charged with relatively straightforward offences such as shoplifting which made up a major constituency of defendants who were bailed with RoB (Home Office, 1997; 2006; DCA, 2007; Ministry of Justice, 2008). The average period of time spent subject to RoB was eight weeks (Hucklesby et al., 2007). Yet, in half of the cases, defendants spent a month or less on RoB which includes just under one-fifth of defendants who spent a week or less subject to RoB (Hucklesby et al., 2007). An additional challenge for the provision of drug treatment was that the success of RoB was to be measured in relation to short-term goals, i.e. reducing rates of offending on bail. Consequently, a crucial element in the operation of RoB was speedy access to drug treatment. The pilots were quite successful in this regard. Nearly 90 per cent of defendants were assessed within a week of being bailed with RoB and nearly all (96 per cent) received treatment appointments within two weeks of being assessed. Some sites were quicker than others but data are muddied by the different functions of assessments and initial treatment appointments between sites (see Hucklesby et al., 2007). Manchester and Salford were less successful than Nottingham at getting defendants quick access to treatment. In Manchester, access to treatment was generally slow and periodic blockages occurred whereas in Nottingham the RPS usually provided prescriptions within a few days. The downside of Nottingham's approach was that the provision of mainstream services and other types of support was the same as for individuals who came into treatment through other routes, resulting in lengthy periods on waiting lists after initial stabilization of their drug use. Despite these differences, defendants viewed the quick access to treatment as one of the main advantages of RoB. As one interviewee explained:

> [I] had tried to get treatment before but had to wait four weeks if not more for the first appointment. With RoB I was seen in two weeks. This is much better. Anyone who wants to get treatment, really wants it, RoB is good. I had a script within two weeks.

Another interviewee concurred:

> I'm desperate for treatment. Before this came out it used to take months to get treatment. Now if you want it, it's there straight away.

Restriction on Bail was relatively successful at channelling defendants into assessment and subsequent treatment. Over 90 per cent of defendants who had RoB imposed attended their assessment and over 90 per cent of this group were referred into drug treatment. Even if defendants dropped out of treatment subsequently, RoB facilitated contact between defendants and drug services which may increase the likelihood that subsequent interactions with treatment episodes are sustained and effective (NDEC, 2004). However, a significant number of defendants referred into treatment after drug assessments were already in treatment although it was not recorded where this was. On average, around one-third of defendants were identified as being already in treatment although NTA data suggested that numbers were significantly higher. The proportion of defendants already in treatment increased throughout the pilot period, from one-fifth in the first six months to two-fifths in the final six months. This suggests that there was an element of recycling happening whereby RoB was increasingly picking up defendants who had already accessed treatment, either through RoB, other criminal justice interventions or self-referral, and that the pool of drug users eligible for interventions is limited.

The number of defendants subject to RoB who were already in treatment raises the issue of whether it was necessary for RoB to be imposed in such circumstances. On the one hand, the main aim of RoB was already being fulfilled and resources were arguably wasted on the assessment process. On the other hand, if the alternative is a custodial remand then it is more cost effective to duplicate assessments. Furthermore, RoB may produce added value, for instance by focusing defendants' minds and emphasizing the importance of engaging with treatment services, resulting in longer periods of engagement and/or more effective outcomes. It also provides an opportunity to review progress.

Individuals who stay in treatment for at least 12 weeks are more likely to have successful outcomes (Gossop et al., 2001; NTA, 2005, 2009b). On this measure, RoB had high rates of retention, with four-fifths of defendants staying in treatment for 12 weeks or more. Retention rates were significantly higher for defendants who were already in treatment (87 per cent) than for those who were not in treatment at the time RoB was imposed (56 per cent). At first sight these data appear to suggest that treatment which is not voluntarily entered into is less effective than voluntary treatment. However, the original route into treatment was unknown so it is possible that defendants who were already in treatment were mandated to be there through another criminal justice intervention such as Drug Treatment and Testing Orders or Drug Rehabilitation Requirements. Consequently, the only conclusion that can be drawn is that defendants who entered treatment as a result of RoB being imposed were less likely to be retained in treatment than defendants who entered treatment by other means. One possible explanation for this is that RoB reinforces defendants' commitment to treatment by introducing an element of coercion.

Four issues arose in relation to drug treatment during the pilot. Firstly, there was a great deal of confusion about what should be done with defendants who were deemed not to require treatment. Courts are under an obligation to impose RoB if legal conditions are met. Consequently, the provision catches defendants who either define themselves as recreational users of drugs or are assessed as not in need of treatment. This caused particular problems in Nottingham because services providing support and advice were not readily available. In the other sites, defendants would be provided with some advice, but even here there was a lot of uncertainty about how to deal with this group. It also raises questions about the way in which blanket provisions such as RoB ensnare individuals who are not in immediate need of assistance with their drug use and whose drug use is unrelated to their offending. Similarly, problems arose when defendants stated that they did not want treatment. Legally, these defendants should have been breached, but in Manchester and Salford, a more health-focused approach was taken. In Manchester, defendants were provided with general advice on harm reduction and allowed to continue on RoB. In Salford, it was reported that defendants were encouraged rather than forced into treatment.

The second issue related to fair and equal access to treatment services. Defendants on RoB received priority access to drug services which may have resulted in other non-offending individuals waiting longer. It was pointed out, therefore, that the quickest way to receive drug treatment is to commit an offence. This raises ethical issues which link into wider debates about rights of suspects, defendants and offenders, and how and where finite resources should be made available.

A third issue was that, in practice, treatment options were often narrow, focusing around heroin users and substitute prescribing, while counselling and other support were less likely to be available, although the type of treatment available varied between sites. Concentrating on substitute prescribing potentially deals with the short-term targets of reducing drug use and perhaps offending while defendants are subject to RoB. Yet, it does not deal with longer-term issues or the often deep-seated problems which resulted in defendants using drugs in the first place. For this reason, some defendants questioned its long-term impact on their drug use and offending. One interviewee explained: '. . . would like help with all aspects of my life. Methadone is not enough'. The lack of available options and diversity of treatment also meant that a few defendants failed to engage with treatment services because they felt that it did not cater for their needs.

A fourth issue was what happens to defendants when their bail period ends in relation to their drug treatment. There was an implicit assumption that defendants would be convicted and continue to receive treatment whether they were sentenced to a community or to a custodial sentence. However, there will be a number of defendants who are acquitted or whose cases are dropped or who receive a fine. No data are available from the pilot, but around one-fifth of defendants remanded by magistrates' courts and the Crown Court are acquitted or not proceeded against and a further one-fifth are fined in magistrates' courts (Ministry of Justice, 2008). It may be that the acquittal rate is lower for defendants subject to RoB because of the nature of much of their offending. Nevertheless, there appeared to be no clear strategy for dealing with these circumstances, which may mean that defendants do not continue to receive treatment or that they have a less positive experience of it. Even for defendants who were sentenced to community or custodial sentences it was not clear how the transition from defendant to offender was managed and what processes were put in place to ensure the continuity of treatment.

Compliance

Defendants were asked about their compliance with RoB. Most defendants reported attending drug assessments and at least one treatment session. The reasons provided by interviewees for complying fell into two broad categories. The first set of reasons related to deterrence and the possible consequences of non-compliance, for example the possibility of being remanded in custody. The second set of reasons related to their own motivation to comply. This included defendants who wanted to stop or reduce their drug use or change their lifestyle. Defendants' reasons for complying changed over the lifetime of their time on RoB. Fear of custodial remands was a more prevalent reason for complying at the assessment stage whereas defendants' own motivation assumed greater importance once they were receiving treatment.

One of the dangers of the Tough Choices approach is that it may encourage individuals to play the system, presenting a veneer of complying while having no intention of engaging with the process. In other words, they formally rather than substantively comply (Robinson and McNeill, 2008). A few defendants disclosed complying with the minimum requirements of orders, i.e. turning up for appointments, therefore technically complying but continuing to use drugs and having no intention of desisting. The way in which RoB operates encourages this approach because the only way to prevent being remanded in custody, something that most defendants would want to avoid, is to consent to the RoB condition. Indeed, solicitors who were interviewed were well aware of this danger and gave examples of defendants who 'played the scheme'. One danger of this approach is that defendants who do not intend to address their drug use prevent defendants and others from accessing timely drug treatment. Additionally, there was some confusion about what complying actually meant and whether formal compliance, i.e. turning up for appointments, was enough or whether substantive compliance through active engagement was necessary. Formal compliance is relatively easy to assess but substantive compliance is much more difficult although there is a range of assessment tools available to measure motivation to change (Robinson and McNeill, 2008; Hucklesby, 2009a). For these reasons, breaches on the basis of missed appointments were the norm. Practitioners, however, struggled with issues about how to deal with defendants who failed to engage with their treatment but continued to turn up for appointments.

Research on the enforcement of Drug Treatment and Testing Orders has highlighted issues with the uneven use of breach policies and variability in workers' readiness to enforce orders (Turnbull et al., 2000). These findings were mirrored in relation to RoB. During the pilots some drug workers were uncomfortable with breaching defendants. This was a particular issue in one of the sites where drug workers refused to be directly involved in the breach process. Instead, procedures had to be put in place so probation-based RoB staff rather than drug service staff dealt with breaches. Confidentiality was also an issue because drug workers were reluctant to pass on information about the treatment being received or defendants' engagement. Consequently, there was something of a black hole once defendants had entered treatment because no further information was forthcoming unless non-compliance was reported to RoB workers. This gives drug workers a great deal of discretion about when it may be appropriate to breach

Table 6.3 Compliance rates for defendants bailed with RoB

	Manchester		Nottingham		Salford		Total	
	n	%	n	%	n	%	n	%
Full	214	79	364	49	110	75	688	59
Partial	3	1	26	3	20	14	49	4
Breach	53	20	356	48	17	12	426	37
Total	270	100	746	100	147	100	1,163	100

defendants. RoB workers raised concerns about this because it could potentially result in unfair and inconsistent decisions being reached.

Compliance rates for RoB compared favourably with other initiatives (Turnbull et al., 2000; Best et al., 2003). Table 6.3 shows that defendants were recorded as fully compliant, attending all their appointments, in three-fifths of cases. A further four per cent were partially compliant, missing their assessment or a small number of treatment appointments. Table 6.3 shows also that compliance rates varied between pilot sites. Around three-quarters of defendants were recorded as fully complying in Manchester and Salford compared with half of the defendants in Nottingham. Partial compliance rates were negligible in Manchester and Nottingham but over one-tenth in Salford ($n = 20$, 14 per cent). The different levels of compliance are likely to partially reflect the variations in breach policies between the three pilot sites but it is notable that Nottingham, whose approach was more criminal justice focused, had a significantly higher breach rate than the other two sites. Variations in breach policies mean that conclusions cannot be drawn about whether a criminal justice or a health based approach to drug treatment while defendants await trial is more effective.

Defendants subject to RoB can breach bail in two ways: by not complying with the RoB condition or by failing to comply with other bail conditions such as residence or curfews. No national or local statistics are available on the prevalence of non-compliance with bail conditions. During the pilot, most breaches which were recorded were RoB related rather than breaches of other bail conditions, but this may simply result from RoB teams being unaware of breach proceedings for conditions other than RoB. Table 6.4 shows that over two-thirds (69 per cent) of RoB-related breaches were for non-attendance at treatment. Only one-tenth (11 per cent) of breaches were for not complying with treatment. Nottingham was the only pilot site to breach defendants for not engaging in treatment and this reason accounted for just over one-tenth (13 per cent) of its breaches. Non-attendance at initial assessments was linked to the location of the

Table 6.4 RoB-related breaches

	Manchester		Nottingham		Salford		Total	
	n	%	n	%	n	%	n	%
Non-attendance at assessment	2	4	81	20	10	63	93	20
Non-attendance at treatment	48	96	268	67	6	37	322	69
Not complying with treatment	0	0	54	13	0	0	54	11
Total	50	100	403	100	16	100	469	100

assessment centres. In the pilot sites where treatment centres were not easily accessible, i.e. some distance from the court or outside of the city centre, lower attendance rates were recorded.

There are a number of other reasons why breach rates varied between pilot sites. Firstly, the sites had different breach policies for the majority of the pilot, ranging between a 'one strike' and a 'three strike' policy. Only in the latter part of the pilots did the Home Office issue guidance on breach, implementing a universal 'one strike' policy in line with procedures for breaches of other bail conditions whereby defendants should automatically be returned to court. According to interviewees, the reasons for this zero tolerance approach were twofold: (a) it communicated the seriousness in which RoB was viewed, particularly in relation to its place as an alternative to custodial remands, and (b) it gave out an explicit and simple message to defendants thus helping to ensure that individuals had a very clear understanding of what was required of them. By contrast, some practitioners believed that defendants should be given a second chance, arguing that it was more important to retain defendants in treatment than to breach them, demonstrating the tension between criminal justice and health goals.

The second explanation for the variations between sites was the different approaches taken by RoB workers, and in particular how they operationalized breach policies. The approach taken in Nottingham allowed less discretion and was stricter than the other two areas. For example, in Nottingham defendants were breached if they did not attend their appointments on time, whereas in the other two sites defendants were given more leeway. Practitioners in these sites recognized that defendants often had chaotic lifestyles and the goals of reducing offending and drug use in the longer term were ultimately more important than short-term compliance.

A third explanation for different breach rates was the priority given to executing warrants and the speed at which this took place. In Nottingham, warrants were executed within 48 hours, but blockages and delays oc-curred in the other two sites. This resulted in some bail periods finishing before breaches were completed. A final explanation for the high breach rate in Nottingham was the treatment regime. In this area the treatment regime had two stages: initial assessment and stabilizing with the RPS fol-lowed by a referral to a local drug service. This may have contributed to non-compliance because it required a change in the place, regime and workers involved in treatment. The incentive to attend the drugs service was also not as compelling as it was to attend RPS. This was because defen-dants who attended the drug services had to pick up their scripts from a different location whereas picking up scripts and attending appointments were co-located in the RPS. In conjunction with differences in rates of non-attendance at assessment, this suggests that a key influence on com-pliance is the location and continuity of treatment provision.

Disagreements surfaced during the pilots in relation to what happened to defendants who were breached, particularly in relation to whether they should be re-bailed or remanded in custody. These arose largely because of tensions between competing goals. On the one hand, criminal justice goals required that the credibility of RoB in the eyes of defendants and practitioners was upheld by using custodial remands in response to non-compliance. On the other hand, health goals required that defendants were kept in treatment for as long as possible, and using custodial remands militated against this. Longer-term criminal justice goals of reductions in offending may also be met by a longer-term, more health-focused strategy. Most interviewees thought that the policy of reimposing RoB following a breach, especially on multiple occasions, was too lenient. However, this was tempered by an acknowledgement that change was unlikely to hap-pen overnight and that tackling drug use took time and often involved relapses. For this reason, most interviewees were satisfied that defendants who breached should be given one further chance as long as the RoB work-ers agreed to have them back on the scheme. However, practice differed from this policy, with multiple breaches by the same defendants being re-bailed to the same extent as first breaches. This is likely to be linked to the need for decision makers to temper the use of custodial remands for defendants charged with less serious offences which would not nor-mally result in remands in custody. A good example of such an offence is shoplifting, which accounted for a significant proportion of the offences committed by defendants subject to RoB (Hucklesby et al., 2007). This demonstrates that there is often a large gap between the rhetoric of Tough Choices and the practicalities of operating it, particularly in a climate in which prisons generally, and local prisons specifically, are overcrowded.

Around one-quarter of defendants who were breached were remanded in custody, leaving nearly three-quarters of defendants who were re-bailed, mostly with RoB. The lack of local or national data on outcomes of breaches of bail conditions makes it impossible to compare these outcomes with those relating to breaches of other bail conditions. Breaches were dealt with differently in the three pilot sites (Hucklesby et al., 2007). In Manchester, three-fifths of breaches resulted in custodial remands compared with half in Salford and one-fifth in Nottingham. Almost all of the cases in which defendants were re-bailed with RoB were in Nottingham. This highlights interesting differences in how the sites dealt with breaches which make it impossible to uncover comparable breach rates. In Nottingham, nearly all defendants were formally breached whatever the seriousness of their non-compliance and were taken back to court where courts often re-bailed them back onto the scheme. In Manchester, less serious breaches, such as being late for appointments, were dealt with informally without recourse to the criminal justice system. Consequently, only defendants who had committed more serious breaches were taken back to court and, by their very nature, these were much more likely to result in custodial remands. In Salford, the small number of breaches and comments from staff suggested that their approach was similar to Manchester's.

Offending

The findings of the evaluation in relation to offending on bail were inconclusive. Offending on bail rates varied from one-third to one-quarter depending on which measures were used (Hucklesby et al., 2007). Both of these figures were likely to underestimate the prevalence of offending on bail because they captured only offending known to criminal justice agencies (see Hucklesby and Marshall, 2000). There are also no recorded rates of offending on bail kept locally or nationally with which to compare these rates. They were, however, compared with data from comparison groups. The findings varied between sites, with one area recording higher levels of offending on bail for defendants on RoB compared with defendants who were bailed without RoB, whereas another area showed the opposite. The inconclusive findings are what might have been expected given a number of factors. One, defendants generally had long criminal careers and it is unrealistic to expect that one short-term intervention will lead to immediate desistance. Two, persistent shoplifters were the main group captured by RoB. They are likely to pose significant risks in terms of offending on bail but the relatively low seriousness of their offences meant that this group of defendants were unlikely to be remanded in custody. For these reasons changes in the severity, frequency and timing of offending on bail may be more useful measures of RoB's effectiveness. However, no significant changes were recorded in any of these measures.

Self-report data from defendants provides a slightly different picture suggesting that defendants had generally reduced their levels of offending while on RoB (Hucklesby et al., 2007). However, it is important to bear in mind that defendants may have reasons for under-reporting their criminal activities while subject to RoB. Two-thirds of the interviewees claimed not to have offended while on RoB. Around one-quarter linked this directly to reductions in or cessation of drug use. One-third of the interviewees admitted offending on bail but none of them claimed to have increased levels of offending in terms of frequency or severity during their period of RoB. Indeed, over four-fifths of the group reported reducing offending. Most of the offending was theft-related and did not appear to be any more serious than the offending which was reported before RoB was imposed.

Drug use

Restriction on Bail aims to channel defendants into drug treatment in order to reduce or stop their drug use. Routine drug testing is not part of the regime of RoB so data are available only on defendants' self-reported drug use captured during interviews. These demonstrate that interviewees had long drug-using careers and that the majority of them perceived that they had a drug problem spanning a substantial period of time (Hucklesby et al., 2007). Two-thirds of interviewees had previously been in treatment although half of them had not been in treatment for at least five years. The treatment received previously was normally substitute prescriptions (Hucklesby et al., 2007).

All but two of the 61 interviewees reported using drugs in the month before they were bailed with RoB (Hucklesby et al., 2007). Most users were polydrug users, with the majority of interviewees using two or three drugs. Interviewees were placed in one of four categories according to their pattern of drug use in order to measure changes in drug use:

1. *Heroin and crack/cocaine users*. All 36 interviewees in this group used heroin and either crack or cocaine. All of them used either heroin, crack or cocaine daily and at least another one of these drugs more frequently than weekly. They described themselves as dependent drug users.
2. *Heroin users*. These 10 interviewees used heroin daily. All but one interviewee described their use as dependent. The interviewee who did not, spent £300 per day on heroin.
3. *Crack/cocaine users*. Four interviewees used cocaine or crack daily and described themselves as dependent drug users.
4. *Recreational*. This group of nine interviewees includes one recreational user of cannabis and ecstasy, three recreational cannabis

Table 6.5   Changes in drug use between the month prior to RoB being imposed and while on RoB

	Drug user group one month before bailed with RoB					
	Heroin and crack/ cocaine	Heroin	Crack/ cocaine	Recreational/ controlled	Non-users	Total
No change	**13**	**5**	**3**	**2**	**1**	**24**
Total reductions	**21**	**2**	**1**	**5**	**0**	**29**
Desister	3	0	1	3	0	7
Frequency	11	2	0	0	0	13
Frequency and stopped at least one drug type	3	0	0	1	0	4
Stopped at least one drug type	4	0	0	1	0	5
Total increases	**1**	**3**	**0**	**1**	**1**	**6**
Frequency	1	1	0	1	0	3
Frequency and new drug type	0	0	0	0	1	1
New drug type	0	2	0	0	0	2
Total	**35**	**10**	**4**	**8**	**2**	**59**

users who six months before being bailed with RoB were using heroin and crack/cocaine but who were in treatment the month before RoB was imposed, and three recreational crack/cocaine users who reported using no more frequently than monthly.

Findings in relation to drug use were mixed. Half of the interviewees reported reducing their drug use, just under half reported no change and a small number reported increasing their drug use. Further details about changes in patterns of drug use are shown in Table 6.5. The table demonstrates that seven out of the 59 interviewees who were using in the month prior to RoB being imposed claimed to have stopped using while on RoB. A further 22 interviewees reported reducing their drug use during this time. Over half of these interviewees reported reducing the frequency of use of at least one drug. A further nine interviewees stopped using at least one drug type while on bail with RoB. For example, six of the seven pre-RoB heroin and crack/cocaine users reported that they had not used crack or cocaine while on RoB but continued to use heroin. Four interviewees reported reducing the frequency of drug use and ceasing the use of at least one drug. Conversely, six interviewees claimed to have increased their drug use while on RoB. Five of this group reported increased use of crack. Few interviewees changed drug-using groups. Four heroin and crack/cocaine users became heroin-only users during their time on RoB and three reported becoming recreational users. By contrast, two heroin-only users became heroin and crack/cocaine users and one non-user became a recreational user.

A significant number of defendants reported continuing to inject while on RoB. Twenty-seven of the 59 interviewees using drugs in the month prior to RoB being imposed reported injecting. Seven claimed to have stopped while on RoB. Eighteen interviewees reported injecting while subject to RoB, two of whom reported not injecting in the month before RoB was imposed. One of these claimed to have started injecting while on RoB whereas the other defendant reported restarting injecting having not reported injecting in the month prior to RoB being imposed.

The amount that defendants/offenders spend on drugs is important in the context of DIP because it is assumed that the proceeds of offending are used to fund drug use. Consequently, if the amount spent on drugs is reduced, the need to offend diminishes or disappears altogether. RoB appeared to be quite successful in this regard. Interviewees suggested that the average daily spend on drugs dropped from £96 in the month before RoB was imposed to £43 while on RoB (Hucklesby et al., 2007). Expenditure dropped in all groups except the recreational/controlled users which rose from £10 to £24 per week.

Substitute prescribing is one of the ways in which expenditure on drugs can be reduced. It is an important element of RoB because it assists it to meet the short-term criminal justice goal of reducing offending on bail. However, an important issue uncovered during interviews was the widespread 'topping-up' being practised by defendants while being prescribed methadone. Two-fifths of defendants using the month prior to RoB being imposed reported using methadone as well as other drugs during this period (Hucklesby et al., 2007). Similarly, three-quarters of defendants using methadone or subutex while on RoB also reported heroin use. Such widespread 'topping up' largely leaves health goals unfulfilled and raises issues about policies which rely on substitute prescribing as their main or only method of drug treatment.

Conclusion

The evaluation of the pilots of RoB suggests that it is one way of getting drug users into contact with drug services thereby opening up the possibility of their entering and being retained in drug treatment. This is a positive outcome in terms of health goals. However, RoB's ability to meet its criminal justice goal of reducing levels of offending on bail is less certain. The unpredictability and short time span of many remand periods makes the long-term goals of desistence from offending and drug use difficult to achieve through RoB alone. However, viewing RoB as the start of a case management process for drug-using offenders means that it arguably has value because drug users are channelled into treatment early on in the criminal justice process, increasing the likelihood of successful outcomes. Nevertheless, RoB raises substantial civil liberties issues because it coerces legally innocent defendants into treatment and is one of many examples of defendants' right to bail being eroded without due consideration (Hucklesby, 2002, 2009b). Stakeholders were generally of the view that this was acceptable because of the positive outcomes that could be achieved. Yet, some defendants were concerned, not because it threatened their civil liberties, but because unmotivated defendants would be clogging up services which others needed.

Two very different models of operating RoB emerged during the pilots. Crudely, one focused on short-term criminal justice goals of getting defendants through their bail period without offending, using predominantly substitute prescribing to achieve this. The second focused of long-term health goals of tackling drug use and it was largely incidental whether it also achieved more short-term criminal justice goals. At this stage it is impossible to say if one approach is more effective than the other, but what is certain is that defendants in the different pilot areas experienced RoB, and especially the breach procedures, differently. This only exacerbates concerns about whether it is appropriate to use the remand process to coerce defendants into drug treatment.

Acknowledgements

This chapter is based on a Home Office funded evaluation undertaken by Anthea Hucklesby, Catherine Eastwood, Angela Spriggs and Toby Seddon who at the time were based in the Centre for Criminal Justice Studies, University of Leeds (see Hucklesby et al., 2005, 2007).

References

Bennett, T. and Holloway, K. (2007) *Drug–Crime Connections*. Cambridge: Cambridge University Press.

Best, D., Ho Man, L., Rees, S., Witton, J. and Strang, J. (2003) *Evaluating the Effectiveness of Drug Treatment and Testing Orders*. London: National Addiction Centre.

Brown, I. and Hullin, R. (1993) 'Contested bail applications: the treatment of ethnic minority and white offenders', *Criminal Law Review*, 107–13.

Department of Constitutional Affairs (DCA) (2007) *Delivering Simple, Speedy, Summary Justice: An Evaluation of the Magistrates' Courts Tests*, http://www.dca.gov.uk/publications/reports_reviews/mag_courts_evaluation.pdf (accessed on 13 February 2009).

Donmall, M., Watson, A., Millar, T. and Dunn, G. (2005) *Outcome of Waiting Lists (OWL) Study*. London: National Treatment Agency and Department of Health.

Fountain, J., Bashford, J. and Winters, M. (2003) *Black and Minority Ethnic Communities in England: A Review of the Literature on Drug Use and Related Service Provision*. London: National Treatment Agency.

Gossop, M., Marsden, J. and Stewart, D. (2001) *NTORS after Five Years: Changes in Substance Use, Health and Criminal Behaviour during the Five Years after Intake*. London: National Addiction Centre.

Gossop, M. and Moos, R. (2008) 'Substance misuse among older adults: a neglected but treatable problem', *Addiction*, 103(3): 347–8.

Home Office (1997) *Review of Delay in the Criminal Justice System* (Narey Report). London: Home Office.

Home Office (2006) *Delivering Simple, Speedy, Summary Justice*. London: Home Office. http://www.dca.gov.uk/publications/reports_reviews/delivery-simple-speedy.pdf.

Hucklesby, A. (2002) 'Bail in criminal cases', in M. McConville and G. Wilson (eds) *The Handbook of the Criminal Justice Process*. Oxford: Oxford University Press.

Hucklesby, A. (2009a) 'Understanding offenders' compliance: a case study of electronically monitored curfew orders', *Journal of Law and Society*, 36(2): 248–71.

Hucklesby, A. (2009b) 'Keeping the lid on the prison remand population: the experience in England and Wales', *Current Issues in Criminal Justice*, 21(1): 3–23.

Hucklesby, A., Eastwood, C., Seddon, T. and Spriggs, A. (2005) *Restriction on Bail Pilots: Implementation Lessons from the First Six Months*, Home Office Online Report 36/05. London: Home Office.

Hucklesby, A., Eastwood, C., Seddon, T. and Spriggs, A. (2007) *The Evaluation of Restriction on Bail Pilots: Final Report*, RDS On-line Report 06/07. London: Home Office.

Hucklesby, A. and Marshall, E. (2000) 'Tackling offending on bail', *Howard Journal of Criminal Justice*, 39(2): 150–70.

Inciardi, J.A. (ed.) (2003) 'Health services research among hard to reach populations: special issue', *Journal of Psychoactive Drugs*, 35(4): 415–18.

Klag, S., O'Callaghan, F. and Creed, P. (2005) 'The use of legal coercion in the treatment of substance abusers: an overview and critical analysis of thirty years of research', *Substance Use and Misuse*, 40(12): 1777–95.

Ministry of Justice (2008) *Criminal Statistics: England and Wales 2007. Statistical Bulletin.* London: Ministry of Justice.

National Drug Evidence Centre (NDEC) (2004) *Treatment Effectiveness: Demonstration Analysis of Treatment Surveillance Data about Treatment Completion and Retention.* London: National Treatment Agency.

National Treatment Agency (NTA) (2005) *Retaining Clients in Drug Treatment.* London: NHS.

National Treatment Agency (NTA) (2009a) *Explaining the Tier system.* http://www.nta.nhs.uk/about_treatment/the_tier_system.aspx (accessed 13 February 2009).

National Treatment Agency (NTA) (2009b) *Retaining Clients in Treatment.* http://www.nta.nhs.uk/areas/facts_and_figures/retention.aspx (accessed 13 February 2009).

Reuter, P. and Stevens, A. (2009) 'Assessing UK drug policy from a crime control perspective', *Criminology and Criminal Justice*, 8(4): 461–82.

Robinson, G. and McNeill, F. (2008) 'Exploring the dynamics of compliance with community penalties', *Theoretical Criminology*, 12(4): 431–50.

Sangster, D., Shiner, M., Sheikh, N. and Patel, K. (2002) *Delivering Drug Services to Black and Minority Ethnic Communities*, DPAS Paper 16. London: Home Office.

Sondhi, A., O'Shea, J. and Williams, T. (2002) *Arrest Referral: Emerging Findings from the National Monitoring and Evaluation Programme*, DPAS Paper 18. London: Home Office.

Strang, J., Best, D., Ridge, G. and Gossop, M. (2004) *Randomised Clinical Trial of the Effects of Time on a Waiting List on Clinical Outcomes in Opiate Users Awaiting Out-patient Treatment.* London: National Treatment Agency and Department of Health.

Stevens A., Berto D., Heckmann W., Kerschl V., Oeuvray K., Van Ooyen M., Steffan E. and Uchtenhagen A. (2005) 'Quasi-compulsory treatment of drug dependent offenders: an international literature review', *Substance Use and Misuse.* 40(3): 269–83.

Turnbull, P., McSweeney, T., Webster, R., Edmuds, M. and Hough, M. (2000) *Drug Treatment and Testing Orders: Final Evaluation Report*, Home Office Research Study 212. London: Home Office.

Wild, T.C., Roberts, A.B. and Cooper, E.L. (2002) 'Compulsory substance abuse treatment: an overview of recent findings and issues', *European Addiction Research.* 8: 84–93.

Witton, J. and Ashton, M. (2002) *Treating Cocaine and Crack Dependence*, Research into Practice Briefing 1a. London: National Treatment Agency.

7 Drug courts: lessons from the UK and beyond

Gill McIvor

The international development of drug courts

Drug courts were established initially in the USA in the late 1980s, initiated by sentencers who were frustrated at the limited range and effectiveness of existing criminal justice measures for dealing with drug-related crime. The first drug court was introduced in Dade County, Florida, in 1989. The impetus for the establishment of drug courts in North America came from a growing acknowledgement of the link between drug misuse and crime along with increasing evidence of the efficacy of drug treatment, including treatment that is compelled rather than undertaken on a voluntary basis (for example, Hough, 1996; Farabee et al., 1998; Gebelein, 2000; and, more recently, McSweeney et al., 2007). Operationally, drug courts vary across jurisdictions, but all are designed to reduce drug use and drug-related offending by combining drug treatment with ongoing supervision and court-based review. Drug courts – and other 'problem-solving' courts – represent an approach to criminal justice processing that has been termed 'therapeutic jurisprudence' (Wexler and Winick, 1992) which refers to capacity of legal processes and procedures (including the actions and approaches of criminal justice professionals) to have therapeutic or anti-therapeutic outcomes. Under traditional court models, rehabilitation may be an *aim* of criminal justice processing, but within a model of therapeutic jurisprudence it is *intrinsic* to the process.

This chapter examines the introduction and expansion of drug courts and the key features of their structure and operation, locating the more recent development of drug courts in the UK in an international context. Drawing upon process and outcome evaluations, the operation of drug courts in England and Wales and in Scotland is compared and contrasted and emerging findings related to the wider international literature, with a particular emphasis upon operational barriers and concerns (including the development of multi-professional teamwork and the capacity of drug courts to accommodate diversity). The chapter also examines the evidence regarding the capacity of drug courts to impact upon drug use and drug-related crime and identifies the features of drug courts that appear to be important in this respect.

Although there are wide differences in the manner in which they operate, drug courts are characterized by a number of key features, including: the use of a non-adversarial approach; the 'fast-tracking' of participants into treatment; the provision of a continuum of treatment, rehabilitation and related services; frequent testing for illicit drugs (and usually, in the USA, alcohol); effective teamwork between judge, prosecution, defence and treatment providers to secure compliance; the application of rewards and sanctions ('smart punishment') to provide external motivation; ongoing judicial review of progress in individual cases; and partnerships with public agencies and community-based organizations (Gebelein, 2000; Freiberg, 2002a). Longshore et al. (2001) have developed a conceptual framework for the classification of drug courts, which they suggest may vary in terms of: *leverage* (where they are located in the criminal justice process and the available system of sanctions and rewards); *population severity* (the nature of the targeted population in terms of drug use and offending history); *programme intensity* (the frequency of testing, supervision meetings and review, and types of treatment available, for example, residential versus non-residential); *predictability* (the consistency and certainty of judicially imposed rewards and sanctions and their compliance with the drug court protocol); and *rehabilitative emphasis* (the degree of collaborative decision making, attention to offenders' needs and flexibility with respect to procedures).

From modest beginnings, the drug court 'movement' (Nolan, 2001) in the USA grew exponentially. By 1999 there were 472 drug court programmes in operation, and by 2007 this had increased to 2,147 (Huddleston et al., 2008). The impetus to the expansion of drug courts in the mid-1990s came from the provision of federal funding through the Violent Crime Control and Law Enforcement Act 1994. Federal funding was intended to have a pump-priming function after which drug courts were required to compete for local and state funding for their continued survival. Between 1989 and 1997, drug courts were provided with around $80 million of federal funding and $45 million funding from state and local governmental and non-governmental sources (Wilson et al., 2006). Increasingly, drug courts are becoming integrated as part of the mainstream judicial function (Goldkamp, 2003).

The numerical increase in drug treatment courts is also matched by their growing specialization and diversity. A national survey conducted in 2007 revealed that 'traditional' adult drug treatment courts remained most common, comprising 1,174 of the 2,147 drug courts in operation. However, the USA also had 435 juvenile drug courts[1] (dealing with delinquency and status offending linked to drug or alcohol use); 301 family drug courts (focusing upon parental substance misuse); 110 designated Driving While Impaired (DWI) courts; 72 tribal drug courts; 24 re-entry courts (facilitating release from local or state correctional facilities); 6 campus courts (targeting students involved in excessive substance misuse); and 5 federal district courts (based on early discharge from prison under intensive drug treatment and supervision) (Huddleston et al., 2008). There has also been a trend towards drug courts dealing with more serious offences and offenders. The early drug courts tended to focus on pre-plea diversion from prosecution of offenders charged with minor drug offences (such as possession of cannabis), but there is now a greater emphasis upon post-plea procedures, with 78 per cent of drug courts estimated to operate in this way (Huddleston et al., 2008).

Internationally, drug courts have been introduced in a number of jurisdictions, including Canada, Australia, Ireland, Brazil, Jamaica and Bermuda. The first Canadian drug court was introduced in Toronto in 1998 followed by a second court in Vancouver in 2001 (Fischer, 2003). More recently, drug treatment courts have been established in Edmonton, Regina, Winnipeg and Ottawa (Werb et al., 2007). The first Australian drug court was set up in New South Wales in 1998, and by 2003 drug courts were also operational in Western Australia, South Australia, Victoria and Queensland (Indermaur and Roberts, 2003). A further drug court pilot was introduced in Tasmania in 2007.

The introduction of drug courts in the UK

The UK, in common with other Western jurisdictions, has sought to develop more effective ways of responding to drug-related crime. Although the link between drug use and crime is complex; it is recognized that much acquisitive crime occurs through the need of individuals with drug problems to obtain the financial resources necessary to maintain a regular supply of drugs. In the 1990s, policy attention shifted towards demand reduction through the provision of drug treatment to individuals whose offending was related to the misuse of drugs. The criminal justice system was perceived as a suitable route into treatment for individuals with drug problems in view of emerging research findings that indicated that mandated treatment could be as effective as treatment accessed voluntarily (Hough, 1996). Consequently, as Stevens (2007: 90) has argued, 'the emphasis in drug policy has been strongly in favour of an increased role for the criminal justice system', as indicated in the White Paper *Tackling Drugs Together* (HM Government, 1995), the subsequent ten-year drug strategy (HM Government, 1998) and the latest drug strategy (HM Government, 2008a).

The introduction of drug courts in the UK has followed a slightly different trajectory from that in other jurisdictions, where drug courts filled an important gap in the range of community-based sanctions available to the courts to deal with drug-related crime. In the UK some of the key features of drug courts (such as regular testing and judicial review) were incorporated into Drug Treatment and Testing Orders (DTTOs), introduced through the Crime and Disorder Act 1998 (see Stevens, Chapter 8 this volume).

Pilot DTTO schemes were introduced in England in 1998 in three pilot sites, with varying degrees of success (Turnbull et al., 2000) and in two pilot sites in Scotland in 1999/2000 (Eley et al., 2002a) prior to wider national roll-out.[2] Although DTTOs represented an innovative criminal justice response to drug-related offending, they attracted some criticism. Bean (2002), in particular, described them as 'watered down' versions of drug courts because they contained some of their elements but not the coordinated multi-professional team approach that characterized drug courts in other jurisdictions.

Shortly after the introduction of DTTOs in Scotland, and following a review of international developments in drug courts (Walker, 2001), the Scottish government agreed to fund pilot drug courts in the same location as the earlier DTTO pilots (Glasgow and Fife). The Glasgow drug court became operational in November 2001 and the Fife drug court made its first orders in September 2002. Initial funding of the pilot drug courts was extended following a broadly positive evaluation (McIvor et al., 2006), though there appear to be no immediate plans by the government to introduce further drug court pilots in Scotland, with the most recent strategy document from the Scottish government indicating that the success and effectiveness of the pilot drug courts would be reviewed in 2009 (Scottish Government, 2008).

Pilot drug courts (referred to as dedicated drug courts, DDCs) were introduced in England and Wales in 2005. West London and Leeds magistrates' courts were selected by the Home Office as the pilot sites, though a drug court model had already been operational in Leeds for a number of years. A process evaluation of the pilots in London and Leeds provides some early data on the implementation and operation of the pilot drug courts (Matrix Knowledge Group, 2008) but very limited information about treatment, testing and outcomes. Nonetheless, the Secretary of State for Justice announced on 1 April 2008 that further drug court pilots would be introduced in four more sites, the location of which would be decided following consultation with the judiciary, court staff and other key parties. The expansion of drug courts (subject to evaluation of the pilots) was identified as a key action in the most recent government strategy on drugs (HM Government, 2008a) aimed, along with a number of other proposals at 'proactively targeting and managing drug misusing offenders' (HM Government, 2008b).

The characteristics and operation of the UK drug courts

The Scottish drug court pilots

The Scottish drug court pilots shared many features with similar courts in other jurisdictions. It was agreed from the outset, however, that they would target repeat offenders whose offending was assessed as being directly related to their misuse of drugs and who were at immediate risk of receiving a custodial sentence. They were, therefore, located within the Sheriff Summary Courts – the middle level of court in Scotland with sentencing powers of up to six months' imprisonment for individual offences.

The sentencing options available to the drug courts were the same as those available to any Sheriff Court operating under summary proceedings. In practice, however, the majority of orders made in the first two years were DTTOs (78 per cent of cases in both Glasgow and Fife) (McIvor et al., 2006). Probation orders were likely to be imposed where offenders were identified as having additional problems that required intervention and support or where the sheriff wanted to review offenders' progress more than once a month. Deferred sentences were often used in respect of additional or further offences to provide sheriffs with a means of rewarding good progress or sanctioning offenders who were not responding well.

Assessments of offenders' suitability for the drug courts were undertaken by a supervision and treatment team, and offenders were bailed for one month for this purpose. If a drug court order was recommended by the team and the court agreed with the recommendation, a DTTO and/or probation order would be imposed for between six months and three years, during which time the offender would be linked into a treatment service (usually methadone), seen regularly by their supervising social worker and addiction worker, subjected to regular drug testing (typically three times per week in the early stages of the order) and brought back to court regularly (at least once a month) to have their progress reviewed by the drug court sheriff. Subject to progress, the offender could have specific requirements of their order(s) amended such as the frequency of testing and reviews increased or decreased.

A central tenet of the drug courts was the recognition that drug misuse is a relapsing condition and for this reason concerted efforts were made to retain offenders on their orders. In the event of non-compliance the court could impose sanctions such as varying the frequency of reporting and/or testing. If good progress was made on an order (as indicated by negative drug tests and cooperation with other requirements), the order would run to the termination date or could be discharged early if a stage was reached where no further progress was deemed to be required. When the drug courts were initially introduced there were no legislated sanctions available to deal with serious or persistent non-compliance, other than to terminate the order and impose an alternative (usually custodial) sentence. Since July 2003, however, the drug courts have had the power to impose short prison sentences (of up to 31 days cumulatively) or short periods of community service while allowing a drug court order to continue. Although the Scottish drug court sheriffs were not operating *explicitly* within a model of therapeutic jurisprudence (Wexler and Winick, 1992), it is clear that a central concern was in creating the conditions through which the drug court process could encourage and support participants in their efforts to become drug free. The vehicle for ongoing contact between sentencers and participants was the regular court-based review. Although reviews are also a feature of non-drug court DTTOs, in the drug court they were preceded by multi-professional pre-review meetings aimed at furnishing the sheriff with an improved quality and range of information to facilitate decision making.

While both drug courts operated in broadly similar ways, there were important organizational and operational differences across the two pilot sites (McIvor et al., 2006). In Glasgow, the drug court team comprised two sheriffs who sat in the court on alternative weeks, a dedicated procurator fiscal (prosecutor), a dedicated clerk and court officer and the drug court supervision and treatment team. The latter consisted of a team leader, supervising social workers, addiction workers, treatment providers and medical staff who were located together in shared premises. A drug court coordinator, who was seconded from the Procurator Fiscal Service, facilitated the work of the drug court team.

Glasgow Sheriff Court is the largest court of its level in Europe and it was not considered feasible for the drug court to deal with the anticipated volume of cases that might be referred to it. Instead, when initially established the drug court targeted accused persons who had been detained in police custody and who were prepared to tender a guilty plea to the offences with which they had been charged. This process was meant to ensure that offenders could be 'fast-tracked' into treatment. The other sheriffs in Glasgow retained the capacity to make DTTOs in respect of offenders who came into the court system through other routes. Two hundred and seventy-one cases were referred for a drug court assessment during the first two years of the Glasgow pilot, 150 of which resulted in a drug court order (McIvor et al., 2006).

In Fife the drug court was presided over by one sheriff (with back-up) who sat in one court for two days per week and in a second court for one day per week. A designated sheriff clerk provided the appropriate administrative support. The drug court Supervision and Treatment team consisted of a team leader, social workers and assistants, addiction workers, medical officers, ten nurses and two project workers from a local drug and alcohol project. They were organized into three multi-professional sub-teams which covered different geographical areas served by the drug court. There was no dedicated prosecutor and no drug court coordinator in Fife.

All potential drug court cases in Fife were identified by sheriffs presiding over other summary courts (sometimes brought to their attention by defence agents or, less usually, social workers). Offenders were referred across to the drug court at the sentencing stage if the adjudicating sheriff thought that a drug court disposal might be appropriate. Sheriffs in Fife had agreed that from its inception only the drug court would impose DTTOs and all *existing* DTTOs were transferred into the drug court when it became operational in September 2002. In the first two years of operation, 872 referrals were made to the drug court, involving 382 offenders, 205 of which resulted in a drug court order being made (McIvor et al., 2006).

The English dedicated drug court pilots

Dedicated drug courts (DDCs) were introduced in two pilot sites in England in 2005. As in Scotland, the DDC model was intended to provide a framework to facilitate partnership working between criminal justice and drug treatment agencies. The objectives of the pilots were: to reduce reoffending and drug use; to introduce improved processes to support inter-agency working and a holistic approach to drug misuse; to be cost neutral; and to be capable of replication (Martix Knowledge Group, 2008).

The two sites chosen for the pilot were high crime areas characterized by high levels of acquisitive and potentially drug-related crime. The Leeds magistrates' court DDC built upon an existing model that had been operating for a number of years, using a model that was almost identical to the proposed pilot. West London magistrates' court was the second pilot site. Here the judiciary and court staff were enthusiastic about the drug court concept and had already begun working towards the creation of a drug court.

As the evaluation of the pilot DDCs indicates (Matrix Knowledge Group, 2008), the underpinning framework consisted of a number of central elements: specialist court sessions (with the DDCs handling cases to completion or breach); continuity of sentencers across hearings; the provision of additional training for sentencers and other court staff; improved processes to facilitate the flow of information between key parties; and an emphasis upon partnership characterized by multi-disciplinary work with other criminal justice agencies and professionals.

The DDCs in each area were supported by professionals responsible for treatment and the supervision of court orders. The composition of the bench differed across the two sites, though in both the intention was to maximize sentencer continuity throughout an offender's order. In Leeds, where 40 magistrates had volunteered to sit in the DDC, panels of four or five magistrates were formed from which panels of three magistrates were drawn for any one hearing. The intention was that at least one of the panel of three magistrates (and ideally more) would have sat on the panel when the offender previously appeared in court. The sentencers in West London comprised three District Judges (magistrates' courts) and three benches of three magistrates each of whom presided over the drug court every six weeks (Matrix Knowledge Group, 2008).

Offenders who were considered eligible for the drug courts were those deemed eligible for a Drug Rehabilitation Requirement (DRR) as part of a community order or suspended sentence order. In Leeds, potentially eligible cases were referred to the DDC for a DRR assessment by a probation officer. In West London, a slightly more complex assessment process was initiated by the magistrates' court, with cases remitted to the DDC only if, following an initial and full assessment, the offender was considered suitable for a DRR (Matrix Knowledge Group, 2008). It is worth noting that in the English pilots offenders were remanded in custody while assessments of suitability for the drug courts were carried out. In Scotland, by contrast, potential drug court participants were assessed in the community since this was believed to provide a more accurate assessment of their motivation to change. Any early concerns by sentencers about the attendant risk of reoffending were soon offset by the perceived increase in the quality of the resulting assessments (Eley et al., 2002b; McIvor et al., 2006).

Although the DDCs could, technically, make use of any available court disposal, those sentenced in the DDCs were made subject to community orders with Drug Rehabilitation Requirements. Under these orders offenders were required to attend treatment, undergo regular testing for drug use and attend court-based reviews. Little detail is provided by the process evaluation on the types of orders made (such as the use and nature of other requirements attached and the relative use of community orders and suspended sentence orders), though it was noted that the average sentence length was ten months and the average length of participation in the DDC was six months. The level and intensity of orders made was intended to be informed by the offence seriousness and by the offender's history of drug use. Community orders most commonly consisted of supervision for a period of between nine and twelve months and a six-month DRR (Matrix Knowledge Group, 2008).

The number of orders made in the pilot courts, especially in West London, was reported to be lower than expected: 276 new cases per year in Leeds and 60 in London. For this reason, few quantitative data are presented in the process evaluation, and those which are relate to Leeds. In this pilot site the average age of participants was 30 years, 74 per cent were male and 87 per cent were white. They had an average of more than 14 previous convictions and 85 per cent reported heroin as their main drug of choice (Matrix Knowledge Group, 2008). In terms of age, sex, criminal history and type of drug use, the profile of the Leeds DDC participants was very similar to those given drug court orders in Glasgow and Fife (McIvor et al., 2006).

Key operational differences

While drug courts across jurisdictions share a common aim of reducing drug use and drug-related crime, a distinctive feature of the drug court 'movement' has been the development of diverse procedures and practices. Even within a single jurisdiction, these are likely to vary across courts. For example, the nature and range of locally available drug treatment services will have a bearing on whether a single treatment provider or multiple treatment providers are engaged in providing services to drug court clients. In Scotland, the geographical location of the drug courts (one in the largest city and the other in a predominantly rural area) had important implications for potential capacity and throughput of cases which, in turn, were reflected in different routes of referral. However, even greater procedural differences can be found between the drug courts north and south of the border.

A central feature of drug courts in the UK and in other jurisdictions is the role of the sentencer in overseeing progress of offenders. In the English pilots, offenders in Leeds were reviewed in court every four weeks whereas in West London reviews took place every six weeks (Matrix Knowledge Group, 2008). By contrast, court-based reviews of drug court orders in Scotland were usually conducted at least every month, and often fortnightly, especially in the early stages when frequent court reviews were considered necessary by sentencers and by supervision and treatment staff as a means of encouraging and sustaining offenders' motivation to change. Although such a high frequency of reviews was not permissible under DTTO legislation, sheriffs made creative use of probation orders and deferred sentences to bring offenders back to court as often as was deemed to be required (McIvor et al., 2006).

The review process in the English and Scottish pilot drug courts differed in other important ways. In particular, an important feature of the review process in the Scottish pilots (and in drug courts on other jurisdictions) was the pre-review meetings that were held in court each morning to discuss the progress of offenders who were appearing before the sheriff for a review hearing in the afternoon. These meetings brought the sheriff together with the key professionals involved in offenders' supervision and treatment: criminal justice social workers, medical officers, nurses and addiction workers. Although convened in the courtroom, they were fairly informal in nature, being characterized by open sharing of information and discussion. In this regard, the Scottish drug court pilots – despite some resolved and some ongoing inter-professional tensions – operated very much as a multi-disciplinary team convened by the sheriff. Sheriffs valued highly the direct input from different professionals involved with a case and regarded these meetings as invaluable for providing 'an overall picture' of each participant and in so doing helping the sheriff to decide 'which buttons to push' in their subsequent dialogue with offenders in court (McIvor et al., 2006; McIvor, 2009).

In the English pilots, however, court reviews were dependent upon written reports prepared by the supervising probation officer and presented to the magistrates or judge in court. These reports were compiled by the probation officer using information provided by the different professionals contributing to the supervision and treatment of offenders, but it appears that sentencers had little time to digest the content of reports and to respond to offenders accordingly, and that only the probation officer was present in court to speak to issues or concerns (Matrix Knowledge Group, 2008). It seems that there was little – other than enhanced continuity of bench and, perhaps, the frequency of reviews – to differentiate the approach of the DDCs from the earlier DTTOs. Although multi-professional teamwork may have been good (despite some communication difficulties between different professional groups in the two sites), it is unlikely that the regular meetings of the multi-professional steering group would have been sufficient to engender the shared understanding, commitment and purpose that characterized the drug court pilots in Scotland (McIvor et al., 2006).

The English and Scottish pilots also differed in terms of the options open to sentencers in the event of offenders' non-compliance with the requirements of their orders. In the DDCs, sentencers had a rather limited range of options available to sanction participants who were failing to comply: they could vary the requirements of orders upon an application for breach or revoke the order and re-sentence offenders for the original offence (Matrix Knowledge Group, 2008). In Scotland, sheriffs were reluctant to resort to revocation of a drug court order and endeavoured to retain offenders on orders if possible. They therefore welcomed the introduction, through the Criminal Justice (Scotland) Act 2003, of legislated intermediate sanctions to deal with non-compliance.

Operational and procedural concerns

Process evaluations of drug courts in the UK and elsewhere have high-lighted the importance of effective structures and processes to facilitate inter-agency working and the promotion of a shared agenda with common goals (McIvor et al., 2006; Matrix Knowledge Group, 2008). For example, one of the perceived strengths of the drug court in New South Wales was the multi-professional approach (Taplin, 2002). The scale of the challenge presented by the multi-disciplinary approach was highlighted by Wager (2002: 2), who observed that drug courts are 'created from one of the most mismatched partnerships...a marriage between health and justice'. While some studies have identified philosophical and professional differences between treatment providers and the court, these generally appear to lessen over time (Taplin, 2002; McIvor et al., 2006). Research has also, however, highlighted a number of procedural issues that have the potential to undermine drug court effectiveness.

Attrition

High levels of attrition are common in drug courts as a result of non-compliance with testing and failure to appear for treatment and other appointments, linked to the vulnerability of drug court clients and the complexity of their problems. Studies of US drug courts generally report relatively high rates of retention and low rates of recidivism (Sanford and Arrigo, 2005), no doubt reflecting the drug and offending histories of participants (Freiberg, 2002b). By comparison, completion rates in the Canadian drug courts – which target more 'serious' offenders – were found to be low: 14 per cent in Vancouver and 16 per cent in Toronto (Public Safety Canada, 2007, 2008). Attrition rates in Australian drug courts have also been high: for example, in New South Wales 42 per cent of drug court programmes had been terminated for non-compliance (Briscoe and Coumarelos, 2000). Taplin (2002) identified a concern among some professionals that criteria for graduation were overly onerous, making it likely that few participants would graduate from the programme. Furthermore, Indermaur and Roberts (2003) have suggested that the range of demands placed upon participants in the South Queensland drug court may have resulted in participants being 'set up to fail'. High levels of programme failure could have an overall net-widening effect by drawing more offenders into the prison system for longer periods than would have been warranted by their original offence.

Werb et al. (2007) have argued that the emphasis placed on abstinence and the limited tolerance of relapse in North American drug courts make it more likely that those with severe drug dependence will fail. In Scotland, where 'high-risk' offenders were targeted, but where relapse was recognized by sheriffs as likely and some allowance made accordingly, relatively high completion rates (47 per cent and 30 per cent in Glasgow and Fife respectively) were obtained (McIvor et al., 2006).

Drug testing

Random testing is a feature of drug courts. Testing usually occurs more frequently at the beginning of orders and decreases in frequency as participants make progress. Amendments to the frequency of testing can be made to reward progress or to sanction non-compliance. A reduction in the number of tests may also be offset by an increased proportion of random tests.

UK research into criminal justice drug interventions in which drug testing is a component have suggested that for some offenders regular drug testing can serve as a 'carrot' or a 'stick', encouraging either continued compliance or deterring further drug use (see, for example, Turnbull et al., 2000; Eley et al., 2002a). However, drug testing of itself is unlikely to serve as an incentive to reduce drug use, particularly if testing is used primarily to monitor compliance rather than for therapeutic ends (McSweeney et al., 2008). Concerns have been expressed, for example, that drug testing fails to detect and reflect *reductions* in drug use thereby limiting its potential to accurately reflect progress made by offenders on their court orders (Eley et al., 2002a; McSweeney et al., 2008).

Makkai (2002) identified a number of issues that arose in relation to drug testing in the Australian drug courts. These included concerns that drug testing was often not random, and reluctance on the part of health workers to pass on negative test results to the court because of uncertainty about how sentencers might interpret and respond to this information. Access to supervised testing facilities has proved problematic in some jurisdictions owing to the wide geographical areas covered by some drug courts.

Dealing with diversity

The ability of drug courts to deal effectively with diverse populations has also arisen as a concern. In the USA this provided the impetus for the creation of drug courts aimed at specific populations, with the first female drug court being established in 1992 in Kalamazoo, Michigan, and tribal drug courts subsequently being introduced to deal with indigenous offenders (Huddleston et al., 2008). In other jurisdictions the ability of drug courts to engage effectively with female and indigenous or offenders from minority ethnic groups has been questioned. For example, professionals in Scotland expressed concern at the absence of treatment and other services that were suited to female offenders and sentencers identified compliance as a particular problem for women (McIvor et al., 2006). In New South Wales, the perceived lack of suitable treatment options for female drug court participants was considered to be a barrier to participation and the percentage of women entering the drug court would have been higher if it reflected the real level of need. For example, few residential rehabilitation facilities were said to be willing to accept women with their children at short notice and the high level of commitment required by the drug court regime may have disadvantaged those with parenting commitments who found it more difficult to comply (Taplin, 2002).

Internationally, evidence regarding completion rates and outcomes for women is somewhat mixed, with some studies suggesting lower retention rates for women (for example, McIvor et al., 2006) and others indicating higher rates of drug court programme completion (for example, Dannerbeck et al., 2002). A qualitative study of female drug court participants in northern California suggested that women welcomed the support, concern and understanding offered by sentencers and drug court staff and valued individualized treatment, services that accepted children, female counsellors (given their previous experiences of trauma and abuse) and the opportunity to participate in work or education (Fischer et al., 2007).

With respect to ethnicity, Taplin (2002) suggests that the number of aboriginal clients accepted onto the drug court programme in New South Wales was low because most had previous convictions for alcohol-related violence, and violent offenders were explicitly excluded from the drug court. In addition, some South-east Asian offenders who might otherwise have been eligible were excluded because they or their parents could not speak English. The Perth drug court was also found not to have engaged with many indigenous offenders because the drug court model – with its onerous requirements – was not well suited to them and because of the absence of appropriate community-based treatment facilities for this group of offenders (Crime Research Centre, 2003).

Other practical and procedural issues

In some jurisdictions, resource constraints have made it difficult for treatment agencies to incorporate 'high-demand' clients. The resource-intensive nature of drug courts is often underestimated, resulting in under-staffing (Eley et al., 2002b). As Makkai (2002) has observed, caseloads that might be considered 'normal' for other court disposals (such as probation) may need to be adjusted down to accommodate the needs of drug court participants. Equally, it is becoming clear that there needs to be sufficient follow-up support for participants once they have 'graduated' from a drug court programme, highlighting the importance of services and supports aimed at enhancing participants' social inclusion and integration (Taplin, 2002; McIvor et al., 2006).

The identification of culturally appropriate sanctions and rewards has also proved challenging for drug courts outside the USA. The applauding in court of participants' achievements is a feature of most of the drug courts in Australia but would not be regarded as fitting easily with the court culture in the UK. Observation of courts in which magistrates and others reward participants with a round of applause corroborates that this can constitute a powerful source of positive reinforcement for participants, confirming their sense of achievement and boosting their self-esteem. Beyond this, however, rewards most commonly take the form of progress from one stage of a programme to another or (as in Scotland) the varying of specific drug court requirements. As Lawrence and Freeman (2002: 74) observed, 'the NSW Drug Court Team were not comfortable with replicating the razzmatazz of buttons, t-shirts, hugs, cheering and tears, which is evident in some US drug courts'.

In the Scottish pilots there was a broad consensus among relevant professionals regarding the eligibility criteria for the drug courts, though some believed that younger offenders should have the opportunity to be given orders. It was agreed that a pattern of relatively minor but persistent offending linked to drug use would signal potential suitability for orders, but reservations were expressed regarding the appropriateness of the drug court for offenders with coexisting mental health problems or convictions for violence (Eley et al., 2002b; McIvor et al., 2006). Elsewhere, professionals have also expressed concern about the incidence of mental health problems among drug courts participants and their implications for offender management and about the lack of clarity regarding the definition of 'violent conduct' with respect to eligibility for a drug court order and the potential consequences for staff and public safety (Taplin, 2002).

A further challenge for the Scottish drug court pilots was the increasing incidence of cocaine use (especially in Glasgow) and lack of existing treatment resources. It was envisaged by professionals that a wider range of resources, including residential rehabilitation, would be required and recognized that this would have important resource implications (McIvor et al., 2006). Similar issues have arisen with respect to methamphetamine and cocaine use in Australia (Weatherburn et al., 2001) and the USA (Huddleston et al., 2008).

Finally, as Freiberg (2002a) and Nolan (2001) have commented, concerns have been expressed that drug court models place too much power in the hands of individual judges with the result that the courts may become less legal and more personalized. This may result in inconsistencies between sentencers and, where there is little or no limit on court intervention, sanctions may be overly onerous and the length of order imposed disproportionate to the offence. Freiberg (2002a) has further cautioned that that drug courts may compromise the adversarial system and undermine the role of the prosecution and defence by rendering them too ambiguous. However, the relative informality and absence of an adversarial approach appear to be important elements of the drug court process. The challenge, it seems, lies in ensuring that sufficient checks and balances are in place to foster a problem-solving orientation while at the same time safeguarding the interests and rights of the offenders concerned.

Are drug courts effective?

It is still too early to say whether and to what extent drug courts in the UK will have a measurable impact upon drug use and drug-related offending, though initial findings are encouraging. In the Scottish pilots there was a steady decline in the proportions of participants testing positive drug for opiates and benzodiazepines over the course of drug court orders and most offenders reported marked reductions in drug use and drug-related crime. Fifty per cent of offenders were reconvicted within 12 months and 71 per cent within two years, though the reconviction rate was lower among completers (67 per cent) after 24 months than among those whose orders had been breached (76 per cent). There was a significant reduction in the frequency of convictions among those who successfully completed a drug court order (McIvor et al., 2006).

A robust quantitative analysis of the impact of the English pilot DDCs has not yet been possible. However, interviews with offenders in the Leeds and West London DDCs revealed confidence among them that participation in the DDC could reduce their drug use and impact positively upon their lives over time, with the encouragement shown by those involved in the operation of the drug court being a significant factor in this respect. If levels of motivation were not particularly high when offenders entered the drug court, they appeared to increase over time: offenders in Leeds reported that their compliance with treatment and review increased as their order progressed (Matrix Knowledge Group, 2008).

Despite frequent methodological limitations, local and national evaluations of drug courts in the USA have been generally encouraging. There is accumulating evidence that participation in drug courts can contribute to reductions in drug use and drug-related offending and improvements in health and well-being (for example, Gebelein, 2000; Goldkamp et al., 2001; Freeman, 2002; Lind et al., 2002; Makkai and Veraar, 2003; Wilson et al., 2006). Belenko (1998, 2001) concluded that drug courts achieved better completion rates than traditional courts and brought about reductions in drug use and recidivism while offenders were participating in the programme. Latimer et al.'s (2006) meta-analysis suggests that, if anything, the benefits of drug court may actually *increase* over time.

Recent meta-analyses[3] have suggested that drug courts are associated with clear and significant reductions in recidivism (for example, Lowenkamp et al., 2005; Latimer et al., 2006; Shaffer, 2006; Wilson et al., 2006). Latimer et al. (2006) estimated that drug treatment courts reduced the recidivism rate of participants by 14 per cent compared with offenders in control or comparison groups. Similarly, Wilson et al. (2006) concluded that the reduction in offending attributable to drug court participation (in comparison to 'traditional' processing) was 26 per cent across all studies and 14 per cent for the two studies that employed randomized controls.

According to Sanford and Arrigo (2005), recidivism rates for drug court graduates are usually lower than for non-graduates and those for dropouts are usually higher than for comparison cases. Roman et al.'s (2003) survey of 2,020 graduates from 95 drug courts identified rearrest rates of 16.4 per cent and 27.5 per cent after 12 and 24 months respectively. They also found, however, that rearrest rates varied across courts and appeared to be related to the targeted population: for example, courts with higher rearrest rates tended to accept offenders who were cocaine and heroin users and who were classified by drug court staff as having moderate or severe drug problems.

Generally encouraging results have also been reported from evaluations of drug courts in Australia (Makkai and Veraar, 2003; Wundersitz, 2007; Payne, 2008; but see Crime Research Centre, 2003, for a less positive conclusion). For example, in New South Wales there were lower levels of recidivism among 'successful' drug court participants than among those whose programmes were terminated and among randomized controls. Non-terminated participants remained offence free for longer and had fewer new offences involving shoplifting, other theft, house breaking and possession of drugs (Lind et al., 2002). Spending on illicit drugs reduced significantly when offenders participated in the programme, with this lower rate of spending maintained at eight and twelve months. Significant improvements were also found in participants' health and social functioning as assessed by standardized questionnaires (Freeman, 2002). However these benefits were somewhat offset by the high rate of attrition, leading Freeman (2002) to recommend that the court should target offenders who were facing lengthy prison sentences and who would therefore be more likely to comply with the programme.

Identifying effective features of drug courts

Given the multifaceted nature of drug court programmes, there is growing interest in which features of drug courts are associated with success.

For instance, Wilson et al. (2006) have argued that there is a need for more rigorous evaluations and a clearer focus upon the 'black box' of drug treatment courts (Goldkamp, 2004). While a review of drug court evaluations by the US Government Accountability Office (2005) was unable to find evidence that any specific drug court components (such as the behaviour of the judge or the amount of treatment received) were associated with reduced recidivism, other analyses have identified particular aspects of the drug court approach that appear to be instrumental in bringing about change. These include effective participant screening (Sanford and Arrigo, 2005), the use of graduated sanctions (Goldkamp et al., 2001; Goldkamp, 2004; Sanford and Arrigo, 2005); programme duration (Latimer et al., 2006); the creation of a multi-professional team that interacts with the judge to inform decision making (Olson et al., 2001); and the use of a single treatment provider (Wilson et al., 2006). Sanford and Arrigo (2005) highlight the need for further research on the role of *treatment* in drug courts. While researchers agree that this is likely to be a key component (Goldkamp, 2004), there has been little research into its significance in relation to other elements of the drug court programme (Banks and Gottfredson, 2003; Wilson et al., 2006).

Makkai (2002) has suggested that the most significant change brought about by drug courts has been the linking of treatment directly with the judge whereby 'the notion of an impartial arbitrator is replaced with a caring, but authoritarian, guardian' (Payne, 2005: 74). Evidence that sentencers may have a key role to play in determining drug court outcomes is provided by a long-term study of a drug court in Oregon. Recidivism rates differed widely among judges, with reductions of recidivism varying from 4 per cent to 42 per cent (Finigan et al., 2007). Although Sanford and Arrigo (2005) found no consistent evidence that the *frequency* of judicial reviews was associated with improved drug court outcomes, Marlowe et al. (2004, 2005) found that more frequent reviews resulted in improved outcomes for higher-risk offenders.

Consistency of sentencers appears, however, to be linked to drug court success. For example, Goldkamp (2004) found that higher levels of contact with the same judge resulted in lower levels of recidivism while the process evaluation of the DDCs in England found that continuity of sentencer across court appearances was associated with enhanced compliance with court hearings, lower levels of positive drug tests for heroin, an increased rate of completion of orders and a reduced frequency of reconviction (Matrix Knowledge Group, 2008). A review of specialist courts in different jurisdictions commissioned by the then Department of Constitutional Affairs concluded that judicial monitoring of offenders was related to their success (Plotnikoff and Woolfson, 2005).

Wexler (2001) has suggested that judicial involvement in specialist courts can promote rehabilitation by contributing to the 'desistance narratives' (Maruna, 2001) that help to facilitate and sustain desistance from crime. McIvor (2009) has argued that the exchanges that take place between sentencers and offenders in drug courts can enhance procedural justice,[4] which confers greater legitimacy upon judges and increases the responsiveness of participants to exhortations that they should change. Support for such an argument can be found in Gottfredson et al.'s (2007) finding that judicial review directly reduced drug use and indirectly reduced criminal behaviour by increasing participants' perceptions of procedural fairness.

Differences in effectiveness across different groups

There is also some evidence that drug courts may be differentially effective with different groups of offenders. The low number of women on drug court orders in the UK pilots has thus far precluded a gendered analysis of outcomes. However, Roman et al. (2003) found that female drug court graduates did better in terms of subsequent rearrest than male graduates. In a study of the Brooklyn Treatment Court in New York (Harrell et al., 2001), women who participated in the drug court programme were found to have lower levels of self-reported drug use and recidivism than women in a comparison group who were eligible for the drug court but who lived outside its catchment area. No other benefits in terms of financial status and health were, however, observed.

Roman et al. (2003) found that rearrest rates among drug court graduates were lowest among white, highest among black, and intermediate among Hispanic offenders. These differences in recidivism by ethnicity appear to be closely linked to the types of drugs favoured by different groups and associated differences in drug-related offending. Overall, there is some tentative evidence that drug courts do better with more drug-dependent offenders with longer criminal histories (for example, Marlowe et al., 2006). This would be consistent with the finding that younger offenders appear not to benefit from drug court involvement (Eardley et al., 2004; Latimer et al., 2006), and would echo the views of practitioners in Scotland that younger offenders (i.e. those under 21 years of age) were unlikely to be sufficiently motivated to meet the rigorous demands of a drug court regime (McIvor et al., 2006).

Cost effectiveness

Given that a central feature of drug courts is their high levels of supervision, treatment and support (including regular court-based reviews), it is not surprising that they are resource intensive compared with other community sanctions. The process evaluation in Leeds estimated that DDC DRRs were associated with additional costs of £4,633 for a 12-month order and £6,792 for a 24-month order compared with non-DDC DRRs (Matrix Knowledge Group, 2008). In Scotland, the cost of a drug court order across the two pilot sites was, on average, £4,401 more than a non-drug-court DTTO, though this unit cost difference could have been reduced through an increase in the number of referrals in Glasgow and the introduction of a more efficient assessment process in Fife (McIvor et al., 2006). The costs of drug court orders (£18,486 in Scotland based on data for 2001–04) also need to be set alongside the cost of alternative sentences and the cost savings from possible reductions in drug use and crime. The Scottish Prison Service estimated that in 2003–04 the cost of six months in prison was £15,336 while 12 months in prison cost £30,672 (Scottish Executive, 2005). It was also found that self-reported expenditure on drugs among drug court participants in Scotland reduced, on average, by £402 per week, resulting, it was estimated, in reductions in property crime to the value of approximately £1,200 per participant per week (McIvor et al., 2006).

A break-even analysis of the Leeds DDC suggested that between 8 per cent and 14 per cent of participating offenders would need to stop taking drugs for five years from completion of the sentence for DDCs to provide a net economic benefit to society (Matrix Knowledge Group, 2008). Recidivism data are not yet available for the English DDC pilots; however, as we have seen, the Scottish evaluation found that 29 per cent of drug court participants remained free of further convictions in the two-year period after drug court orders were imposed. Although it is likely that the rate of reconviction will increase in subsequent years, it is also well established that most offenders who are going to be reconvicted following a community sentence or imprisonment will be reconvicted within two years. That being so (and assuming that the reconviction rates achieved in Scotland are also achieved by the English pilots), it can be assumed that drug courts in the UK are likely to prove at least cost neutral and probably cost beneficial in the longer term.

There is also international evidence to suggest that drug courts may be cost effective: although they are more expensive than traditional court processing, when the costs of alternative sentences are taken into account the benefits of US drug courts have often been assessed to outweigh the costs (see, for example, Finigan, 1999; Belenko, 2001). In Australia, the economic evaluation of the New South Wales drug court suggested that the court was cost effective in comparison with the sentences that it replaced. Although the cost per day for an individual placed on a drug court programme was slightly higher than the per diem cost for the control group, it was estimated to cost more to avert further shoplifting and drug possession offences using alternative sanctions (Lind et al., 2002).

Conclusions

Although drug courts are a new phenomenon in the UK they are now well established in other jurisdictions and the international evidence in support of drug courts' effectiveness, in terms of their ability to bring about reductions in offending, is increasingly persuasive. The findings from meta-analyses and narrative reviews of drug court evaluations generally support the conclusion that drug courts can be effective in reducing drug use and drug-related crime. Attention is now turning to the identification of aspects of the drug court model that appear critical to its success.

However, the wide range of contexts in which drug courts have been introduced and the wide variations in whom they target and how they operate mean that detailed and rigorous local evaluations are necessary to determine whether and how, in a particular jurisdiction, drug courts are a viable and effective means of supporting offenders in drug treatment and breaking the link between drug use and crime. Changes from outside the drug court can have a strong effect upon drug court operation and effectiveness (Sanford and Arrigo, 2005). Often, however, decisions about drug court expansion appear to have been made in the absence of a sufficiently solid empirical base (Werb et al., 2007).

In the UK, while the initial results of process and outcome evaluations are broadly encouraging, rigorous analyses of recidivism, drug use and costs with large enough samples of offenders over a sufficient follow-up period are still required to determine the added economic and social value that drug courts can provide. It is envisaged, however, that the resource intensiveness and high unit costs associated with drug courts will mean that they are viable only in high crime areas where a throughput of cases can be guaranteed, where there is commitment and enthusiasm among sentencers and where there is existing capacity to provide the treatment and other services that are necessary to support those whose offending is related to their misuse of drugs.

Even if they are unlikely for pragmatic reasons to constitute a universal response to drug-related offending, the wider impact of drug courts on criminal justice processes needs to be acknowledged. An important impact of the drug court 'movement' in the USA, UK and elsewhere has been the impetus that drug courts have provided to the development of other forms of specialist, problem-solving courts. These include domestic abuse courts, mental health courts, disability courts (for offenders with learning difficulties or 'cognitive disabilities') and community courts (which adopt a community-focused problem-solving approach to local crime). As Goldkamp (2003: 203) has argued, through 'method and substance, its philosophy and values' and through its transformation to a more generalised problem-solving approach, the drug court model has served in various jurisdictions as a major catalyst for judicial change.

Notes

1. Juvenile drug courts were introduced in the USA in 1990. Compared with adult drug courts, they involve the cooperation of a wider range of community agencies (for example, child protection, education etc.) and require the development of a more collaborative relationship between the court and the offender's family. Sanford and Arrigo (2005) suggest that juvenile drug courts face additional challenges posed by young people's indifferent attitudes towards drug treatment programmes, the influence of gang membership or delinquent peers, and young people's lack of maturity.
2. In England and Wales (but not Scotland) DTTOs have been replaced by community orders with Drug Rehabilitation Requirements.
3. A meta-analysis is a statistical technique for combining the results from a number of separate studies to assess the size of effect produced by an intervention.
4. Procedural justice refers to the fairness and transparency with which legal proceedings are conducted (see Tyler, 1990).

References

Banks, D. and Gottfredson, D. (2003) 'The effects of drug treatment and supervision on time to arrest among drug treatment court participants', *Journal of Drug Issues*, 33(2): 385–412.

Bean, P. (2002) *Drugs and Crime*. Cullompton: Willan Publishing.

Belenko, S. (1998) *Research on Drug Courts: A Critical Review*. New York: National Center on Addiction and Substance Abuse at Columbia University.

Belenko, S. (2001) *Research on Drug Courts: A Critical Review 2000 Update*. New York: National Center on Addiction and Substance Abuse at Columbia University.

Briscoe, S. and Coumarelos, C. (2000) *New South Wales Drug Court Monitoring Report: Crime and Justice Bulletin*, Contemporary Issues in Crime and Justice No. 52. Sydney: New South Wales Bureau of Crime Statistics and Research.

Crime Research Centre (2003) *Evaluation of the Perth Drug Court Pilot Project: Final Report*. Perth, WA: West Australian Department of Justice.

Dannerbeck, A., Sundet, P. and Lloyd, K. (2002) 'Drug courts: gender differences and their implications for treatment strategies', *Corrections Compendium*, 27(12): 1–5, 24–6.

Eardley, T., McNab, J., Fisher, K. and Kozlina, S. (2004) *Evaluation of the New South Wales Youth Drug Court Pilot Program: Final Report*. Sydney: Social Policy Research Centre, University of New South Wales.

Eley, S., Gallop, K., McIvor, G., Morgan, K. and Yates, R. (2002a) *Drug Treatment and Testing Orders: Evaluation of the Scottish Pilots*. Edinburgh: Scottish Executive Social Research.

Eley, S., Malloch, M., McIvor, G., Yates, R. and Brown, A. (2002b) *Glasgow's Pilot Drug Court in Action: The First Six Months*. Edinburgh: Scottish Executive Social Research.

Farabee, D., Prendergarst, M. and Anglin, M.D. (1998) 'The effectiveness of coerced treatment for drug-abusing offenders', *Federal Probation*, 62: 3–10.

Finigan, M.W. (1999) 'Assessing cost off-sets in a drug court setting', *National Drug Court Institute Review*, 2(1): 59–92.

Finigan, M.W., Carey, S.M. and Cox, A. (2007) *The Impact of a Mature Drug Court over 10 Years of Operation: Recidivism and Costs*. Portland, OR: NPC Research.

Fischer, B. (2003) 'Doing good with a vengeance: a critical assessment of the practices, effects and implications of drug treatment courts in North America', *Criminal Justice*, 3(3): 227–48.

Fischer, M., Geiger, B. and Hughes, M.E. (2007) 'Female recidivists speak about their experience in drug court while engaging in appreciative inquiry', *International Journal of Offender Therapy and Comparative Criminology*, 51(6): 703–22.

Freeman, K. (2002) *New South Wales Drug Court Evaluation: Health, Well-Being and Participant Satisfaction*. Sydney: New South Wales Bureau of Crime Statistics and Research.

Freiberg, A. (2002a) 'Specialised courts and sentencing'. Paper presented at Probation and Community Corrections: Making the Community Safer, conference organized by the Australian Institute of Criminology and the Probation and Community Corrections Officers' Association, Perth, WA. http://www.aic.gov.au/conferences/probation/freiberg. html.

Freiberg, A. (2002b) 'Australian drug courts: a progress report'. Paper presented at Policing–Prevention–Innovation–Beyond Enforcement, 2nd Australian Conference on Drug Strategy, Perth, WA.

Gebelein, R.S. (2000) 'The rebirth of rehabilitation: promise and perils of drug courts', *Sentencing and Corrections: Issues for the 21st Century*. Washington, DC: National Institute of Justice.

Gottfedson, D.C., Kearley, B.W., Najaka, S.S. and Rocha, C.M. (2007) 'How drug treatment courts work: an analysis of mediators', *Journal of Research in Crime and Delinquency*, 44(1): 3–35.

Goldkamp, J.S. (2003) 'The impact of drug courts', *Criminology and Public Policy*, 2(2): 197–206.

Goldkamp, J.S. (2004) 'Judicial "hands on" in drug courts: moving from whether to how drug courts work'. Paper presented at the 1st Key Issues Conference of the International Societies of Criminology, Paris.

Goldkamp. J.S., White, M.D. and Robinson, J.B. (2001) *From Whether to How Drug Courts Work: Retrospective Evaluation of Drug Courts in Clark County (Las Vegas) and Multnomah County (Portland)*. Philadelphia, PA: Crime and Justice Research Institute.

Harrell, A., Roman, J. and Sack, E. (2001) *Drug Court Services for Female Offenders, 1996–99: Evaluation of the Brooklyn Treatment Court*. Washington, DC: Urban Institute.

HM Government (1995) *Tackling Drugs Together: A Strategy for England 1995–1998*, Cmd 2846. London: HMSO.

HM Government (1998) *Tackling Drugs to Build a Better Britain: The Government's Ten-Year Strategy for Tackling Drugs Misuse*, Cmd 3945. London: HMSO.

HM Government (2008a) *Drugs: Protecting Families and Communities. The 2008 Drug Strategy*. London: HM Government. http://drugs.homeoffice.gov.uk/publication-search/drug-strategy/drug-strategy-2008?view=Binary.

HM Government (2008b) *Drugs: Protecting Families and Communities. Action Plan 2008–2011*. London: HM Government. http://drugs.homeoffice.gov.uk/publication-search/drug-strategy/drug-action-plan-2008-2011?view=Binary.

Hough, M. (1996) *Drug Misuse and the Criminal Justice System: A Review of the Literature*. London: Home Office.

Huddleston, C.W., Marlowe, D.B. and Casebolt, R. (2008) *Painting the Current Picture: A National Report Card on Drug Courts and other Problem-Solving Court Programs in the United States*. Alexandria, VA: National Drug Court Institute.

Indermaur, D. and Roberts, L. (2003) 'Drug courts in Australia: the first generation', *Current Issues in Criminal Justice*, 15(2): 136–54.

Latimer, J., Morton-Bourgan, K. and Chretien, J. (2006) *A Meta-Analytic Examination of Drug Treatment Courts: Do They Reduce Recidivism?* Ottawa: Department of Justice Canada.

Lawrence, R. and Freeman, K. (2002) 'Design and implementation of Australia's first drug court', *Australian and New Zealand Journal of Criminology*, 35(1): 63–78.

Lind, B., Wratherburn, D., Chen. S., Shanahan, M., Lancsar, E., Haas, M. and De Abreu Lourenco, R. (2002) *New South Wales Drug Court Evaluation: Cost-Effectiveness*. Sydney, NSW: New South Wales Bureau of Crime Statistics and Research.

Longshore, D., Turner, S., Wenzel, S., Morral, A., Harrell, A., McBride, D., Deschenes, E. and Iguchi, N. (2001) 'Drug courts: a conceptual framework', *Journal of Drug Issues*, 31(1): 7–26.

Lowenkamp, C.T., Holsinger, A.M. and Latessa, E.J. (2005) 'Are drug courts effective? A meta-analytic review', *Journal of Community Corrections*, 15(4): 5–10, 28.

Makkai, T. (2002) 'The emergence of drug treatment courts in Australia', *Substance Use and Misuse*, 37(12–13): 1567–94.

Makkai, T. and Veraar, K. (2003) *Final Report on the South East Queensland Drug Court*, Australian Institute of Criminology Technical and Background Paper Series No. 6. Canberra, ACT: Australian Institute of Criminology.

Marlowe, D.B., Festinger, D.S., Dugosh, K.L. and Lee, P.A. (2005) 'Are judicial status hearings a "key component" of drug court? Six and twelve month outcomes', *Drug and Alcohol Dependence*, 79(2): 145–55.

Marlowe, D.B., Festinger, D.S. and Lee, P.A. (2004) 'The judge is a key component of drug court', *Drug Court Review*, 4(2): 1–34.

Marlowe, D.B., Festinger, D.S., Lee, P.A., Dugosh, K.L. and Benasutti, K.M. (2006) 'Matching judicial supervision to clients' risk status in drug court', *Crime and Delinquency*, 52(1): 52–76.

Maruna, S. (2001) *Making Good: How Ex-inmates Reform and Rebuild their Lives*. Washington, DC: American Psychological Association.

Matrix Knowledge Group (2008) *Dedicated Drug Court Pilots: A Process Report*. London: Ministry of Justice.

McIvor, G. (2009) 'Therapeutic jurisprudence and procedural justice in Scottish drug courts', *Criminology and Criminal Justice*, 9(1): 29–49.

McIvor, G., Barnsdale, L. Malloch, M., Eley, S. and Yates, R. (2006) *The Operation and Effectiveness of the Scottish Drug Court Pilots*. Edinburgh: Scottish Executive Social Research.

McSweeney, T., Stevens, A., Hunt, N. and Turnbull, P. (2007) 'Twisting arms or a helping hand? Assessing the impact of "coerced" and comparable "voluntary" drug treatment options', *British Journal of Criminology*, 47(3): 470–90.

McSweeney, T., Stevens, A., Hunt, N. and Turnbull, P. (2008) 'Drug testing and court review hearings: uses and limitations', *Probation Journal*, 55(1): 39–53.

Nolan, J. (2001) *Reinventing Justice: The American Drug Court Movement*. Princeton, NJ: Princeton University Press.

Olson, D.E., Lurigio, A.J. and Alberston, S. (2001) 'Implementing the key components of specialized drug treatment courts: practice and policy considerations', *Law and Policy*, 23(2): 171–96.

Payne, J. (2005) *Final Report on the North Queensland Drug Court*. Canberra ACT: Australian Institute of Criminology.

Payne, J. (2008) *The Queensland Drug Court: A Recidivism Study of the First 100 Graduates*. Canberra, ACT: Australian Institute of Criminology.

Plotnikoff, J. and Woolfson, R. (2005) *Review of the Effectiveness of Specialist Courts in other Jurisdictions*. London: Department of Constitutional Affairs.

Public Safety Canada (2007) *Toronto Drug Treatment Court Project: Evaluation Summary*. Ottawa: National Crime Prevention Centre.

Public Safety Canada (2008) *Drug Treatment Court of Vancouver (DTCV): Evaluation Summary*. Ottawa: National Crime Prevention Centre.

Roman, J., Townsend, W. and Bhati, A.S. (2003) *Recidivism Rates for Drug Court Graduates: Nationally Based Estimates*. Washington, DC: Urban Institute.

Sanford, J.S. and Arrigo, B.A. (2005) 'Lifting the cover on drug courts: evaluation findings and policy concerns', *International Journals of Offender Therapy and Comparative Criminology*, 49(3): 239–59.

Scottish Executive (2005) *Costs, Sentencing Profiles and the Criminal Justice System 2003: Section 306*. Edinburgh: Scottish Executive.

Scottish Government (2008) *The Road to Recovery: A New Approach to Tackling Scotland's Drug Problem*. Edinburgh: Scottish Government.

Shaffer, D.K. (2006) *Reconsidering Drug Court Effectiveness: A Meta-analytic Review*. Las Vegas, NV: Department of Criminal Justice, University of Nevada.

Stevens, A. (2007) 'When two dark figures collide: evidence and discourse on drug-related crime', *Critical Social Policy*, 27(1): 77–99.

Taplin, S. (2002) *The New South Wales Drug Court Evaluation: A Process Evaluation*. Sydney, NSW: New South Wales Bureau of Crime Statistics and Research.

Turnbull, P.J., McSweeney, T., Webster, R., Edmunds, M. and Hough, M. (2000) *Drug Treatment and Testing Orders: Final Evaluation Report*, Home Office Research Study 212. London: Home Office.

Tyler, T.R. (1990) *Why People Obey the Law*. New Haven, CT: Yale University Press.

US Government Accountability Office (2005) *Adult Drug Courts: Evidence Indicates Recidivism Reductions and Mixed Results for other Outcomes*. Washington, DC: US Government Accountability Office. http://www.gao.gov/new.items/do5219.pdf.

Wager, J. (2002) 'The drug court: can a relationship between health and justice really work?'. Paper presented at Alcohol and other Drugs: Collaborating for Better Care, Inaugural Alcohol and other Drug Symposium, Fremantle, WA.

Walker, J. (2001) *International Experience of Drug Courts*. Edinburgh: Scottish Executive Central Research Unit.

Weatherburn, D., Jones, C., Freeman, K. and Makkai, T. (2001) *The Australian Heroin Drought and its Implications for Drug Policy*, Crime and Justice Bulletin 59. Sydney, NSW: New South Wales Bureau of Crime Research and Statistics.

Werb, D., Elliott, R., Fischer, B., Wood, E., Montaner, J. and Kerr, T. (2007) 'Drug treatment courts in Canada: an evidence-based review', *HIV/AIDS Policy and Law Review*, 12(2/3): 12–17.

Wexler, D.B. (2001) 'Robes and rehabilitation: how judges can help offenders "make good"', *Court Review*, Spring: 18–23.

Wexler, D.B. and Winick, B.J. (1992) 'The potential of therapeutic jurisprudence: a new approach to psychology and the law', in J.R.P. Ogloff (ed.)

The Law and Psychology: The Broadening of the Discipline. Durham, NC: Carolina Academic Press.

Wilson, D.B., Mitchell, O. and Mackenzie, D. (2006) 'A systematic review of drug court effects on recidivism', *Journal of Experimental Criminology*, 2(4): 459–87.

Wundersitz, J. (2007) *Criminal Justice Responses to Drug and Drug-Related Offending: Are They Working?* Canberra, ACT: Australian Institute of Criminology.

8 Treatment sentences for drug users: contexts, mechanisms and outcomes

Alex Stevens

Introduction

Readers who have made it through to this eighth chapter will not need reminding of the strong correlation between dependent drug use and offending. Large numbers of drug users end up in court, with a judge deciding what will happen to them. For many, and especially those unfortunate enough to be facing a judge in the USA, their fate will involve a locked cell. It is well known that the rise in imprisonment of drug users has contributed substantially to the massive increase in the US prison population since the early 1970s. For example, the total number of people incarcerated in federal and state prisons and local jails for drug offences increased from 38,680 in 1972 to 480,519 in 2002 – an increase of 1,242% (Caulkins and Chandler, 2006). It is less well known that there has also been a rapid increase in the use of imprisonment for drug law offenders in England and Wales. Between 1994 and 2006, the number of months given in prison sentences for drug offences increased by 150 per cent, while the increase in the use of imprisonment for other offences was limited to 27 per cent (Reuter and Stevens, 2008). As the previous chapter on drug courts noted, widespread disillusionment in the results obtained by this extended use of prison has led to a search for more effective alternatives.

Various international bodies, including the United Nations (1990) and the Council of Europe (1999), have endorsed credible alternative sentences as means for reducing the use of imprisonment and improving protection of human rights. The drug court is just one example of the attempt to realize these aspirations. There are several other models available to courts in various countries which involve providing treatment to dependent drug users through the encouragement, supervision and control of the criminal justice system. This chapter examines the development of such sentences in England and Wales. It describes the political purposes that have motivated the development of the Drug Treatment and Testing

Order and the Drug Rehabilitation Requirement. It then places these English orders alongside international perspectives on contexts, targeting, treatment content and approaches to non-compliance. It moves on to discuss the processes and effects of such quasi-compulsory treatment (QCT), with a specific emphasis on the link between coercion, motivation and outcome. It uses the available literature on QCT, combined with a specific study which was led by the author, called QCT Europe.

The QCT Europe study

QCT Europe was a prospective, quasi-experimental evaluation of quasi-compulsory treatment for drug-dependent offenders in five countries (England, Austria, Italy, Germany and Switzerland). It included structured interviews (based on the European Addiction Severity Index; see Kokkevi and Hartgers, 1995) with a random sample of offenders who were entering QCT at purposively selected treatment sites in each country, as well as a comparison group of dependent drug users who were entering treatment at the same sites without the constraint of the criminal justice system. The total sample was 845 people, including 157 people in England. These people were interviewed at intake. Follow-up response rates were 68 per cent at six months, 53.2 per cent at 12 months and 46.5 per cent at 18 months. A sub-sample of 138 people in the QCT group were also engaged in semi-structured qualitative interviews, as were 82 professionals, including drug treatment workers and managers, probation officers, lawyers and judges. The study was funded by the European Union's Fifth Framework Research and Development Programme and was separately ethically approved in each participating country. More details on methodology and results from the QCT Europe study can be found in Stevens et al. (2006a, 2007), McSweeney et al. (2007) and Schaub et al. (2009).

The development of drug treatment sentences for offenders in England

In England and Wales, there has been significant evolution in sentences that involve an order to attend treatment. As far back as 1970, the Magistrates' Association was arguing that magistrates should be able to order drug users into treatment, on the grounds that drug dependence is an illness that needs be treated no differently from others under the Mental Health Act 1959 (Young, 1971). The Powers of the Courts Act 1973 permitted courts to attach a condition of treatment to a probation order, as long as a qualified medical practitioner confirmed that the offender had a treatable condition (Bean, 2008). This Act was not specifically aimed at drug users and was infrequently used for them.

The Criminal Justice Act 1991 introduced a power that was specifically aimed at drug-using offenders: the Schedule 1A(6) order. One London study found that this sentence tended to target (as was intended) those offenders with the heaviest patterns of drug use. These offenders were able to reduce their offending and drug use more than others whose orders did not include a condition to attend treatment (Hearnden, 2000). However, a different study found two-year reconviction rates of 91 per cent for a small group of offenders who were given Schedule 1A(6) orders in two other areas (Hough et al., 2003). Whatever its benefits, this order was rarely used, with sentencers apparently preferring to use more mainstream community sentences (South, 1998). There was no significant expansion of court-ordered drug treatment in England and Wales until 2000.

The Labour Party in opposition had famously promised to be tough both on crime and on its causes. It successfully won the initiative from the Conservative Party on the politically sensitive issue of law and order. Labour had identified drug use as the cause of crime it could afford to be tough on (Straw, 1996), and was under pressure to prove that it could deliver on its promise to be doubly tough. It planned to expand drug treatment, but it also needed to show that treatment could be tough. The party had already received a ready-made policy proposal which met these needs. A Labour Party researcher, Justin Russell, worked closely with Shadow Home Secretary Jack Straw while Labour was in opposition, and went on to be Tony Blair's special adviser on home affairs when Blair became Prime Minister. He had taken a Harkness Fellowship study visit to drug courts in the USA in 1993 and had returned home with the suggestion that an adapted version should be implemented in the UK (Russell, 1994). He based this recommendation on three key findings from his American sojourn. One was that 'treatment works'. The second was that it works better the longer the drug user stays in treatment. And the third was that drug users who are legally coerced into treatment can do at least as well as volunteers. He concluded that, '[f]or politicians, treatment programmes for offenders offer a potential middle ground between "lock 'em up" type strategies, which are popular, but expensive and generally ineffective, and early interventions, for example pre-school and after school provision, which are cheap and effective, but take years to make an impact' (Russell, 1994: 6).

This archetypically 'third way' proposal fell on fertile political ground and was included, in the form of the Drug Treatment and Testing Order (DTTO), in the Crime and Disorder Act 1998. The DTTO enabled courts to order offenders whose offending was considered to be linked to their drug use to attend drug treatment (initially at least 20 hours per week)

for between six months and three years. Mechanisms to ensure compliance included regular drug testing, court review and disciplinary procedures for breaching the order. Probation officers were expected to institute
breach proceedings if the offender had two 'unacceptable' failures to comply (for example, missing a day in treatment without an acceptable reason)
(National Audit Office, 2004). The DTTO was initially piloted in three areas. The researchers found that only one of these areas had been able to establish a viable programme. Dropout rates were high, although there were
reductions in drug use and offending among those who stayed in treatment (Turnbull et al., 2000). A later analysis suggested that only 30 per
cent of the offenders in the pilot DTTO completed the sentence without
the order being revoked for non-compliance. The two-year reconviction
rate was 80 per cent (Hough et al., 2003). Other small-scale studies have
been done on the DTTO, and have tended to show reductions in drug
use and offending (especially for those who stay on the order), despite
difficulties in establishing effective inter-agency working (Ricketts et al.,
2002; Turner, 2002, 2004; Robinson, 2003; Falk, 2004; McSweeney et al.,
2007; Naeem et al., 2007).

The DTTO was rolled out nationally in 2000, before the results of the
pilot had been published. This roll-out rapidly expanded the number of
sentences that included a condition of drug treatment (see Figure 8.1 on
page 167). It reflected a cross-party policy consensus that drugs were a major cause of crime and that the criminal justice system was the appropriate
mechanism to force drug users to address their drug-using and offending
behaviour. I have criticized the faulty methodology and political rhetoric
behind these assumptions elsewhere (Stevens, 2007). The practical consequences were a proliferation in the legal measures available for use in
encouraging drug-using offenders to seek treatment, and a large expansion in the number of people who went through them. The DTTO was
followed by measures such as the Drug Abstinence Order and the Drug
Abstinence Requirement. These enabled courts to order that offenders
submit to drug testing. Evaluation found that these orders did not make
a significant difference to rates of Class A drug use, but did significantly
increase the number of offenders whose orders were breached, leading
to more of them being imprisoned (Matrix Research & Consultancy and
Nacro, 2004).

In 2003, Labour passed a Criminal Justice Act and hoped to reassure the
public that it was still serious about tackling crime. The Act was widely criticized for introducing several measures that increased the punitive scale
of the criminal justice system without any sound evidence that crime
would be reduced. One eminent criminologist went so far as to call it 'full
of misconceived, bound-to-fail and repressive measures' (Tonry, 2004: 4).
The Act's authors claimed that it would ensure that prison was reserved

for serious and violent criminals, while simultaneously ensuring that the public was protected from the most dangerous offenders. The intention to increase sentence lengths for violent offenders has been fulfilled, largely by the creation and enthusiastic use of indeterminate sentences for public protection. But there has been no commensurate reduction in the use of imprisonment for lower-level offenders (House of Commons Justice Committee, 2008). The government's diagnosis of the problem was that courts and the public lacked confidence in the confusing array of community sentences that were available to them. So the Act replaced the previous range of orders (including the DTTO) with one generic 'community order' that could have any one of twelve types of requirement attached to it. One of these potential requirements was the Drug Rehabilitation Requirement (DRR). The DRR replaced the DTTO when the Act came into force in April 2005.

In some ways, the DRR is more flexible than the DTTO. It is available to offenders with less serious offences than those who were considered eligible for the DTTO. This may make wider groups of people – including more women and homeless people – whose offending is petty but persistent, eligible for court-ordered drug treatment (Hollingworth, 2008). But it also increases the possibility of more intensive orders being given to people who would otherwise have received community sentences (with no treatment conditions) that were easier to complete without breaching. Courts can make DRRs at three different levels of intensity, which involve different amounts of weekly time in treatment for the offender. However, the level of intensity is based on the seriousness of the offence rather than on the offender's level of need for drug treatment. Probation areas struggled to reconcile the tension between offence seriousness and treatment need in allocating offenders to treatment programmes, leading to inconsistent practice (HM Inspectorate of Probation, 2006). The DRR was less flexible than the DTTO in terms of courts' response to non-compliance. They could no longer take no action or impose a fine in response to breach. Rather, courts were expected either to impose 'more onerous' requirements or to revoke the order and re-sentence (for example, to prison) (National Probation Directorate, 2005).

Also in 2005, a new Drugs Act was rushed through Parliament in the run-up to the May general election. This introduced a range of dubious measures. For example, it put unprocessed psilocybe mushrooms into Class A, on the basis of selective evidence of an increase in the use of magic mushrooms (and no evidence of increase in harm from their use). It introduced an assumption, which has since proved to be unworkable, that people carrying more than an unspecified – and evidently impossible to decide – weight of drugs should be sentenced as drug suppliers. It also empowered the police to require people who were arrested for a range of acquisitive offences to be tested for drugs. Previously, this power had applied only to those who were charged. People who test positive can now be ordered, on pain of committing a criminal offence if they refuse, to attend a meeting where their need for drug treatment is assessed. Concerns expressed over the implications of this law for the human right to privacy (Joint Committee on Human Rights, 2004) were brushed aside and have yet to be tested in court.

More recently, as discussed in the previous chapter, the government has piloted dedicated drug courts (DDCs) in Leeds and West London. These introduced more of the US drug court model than had been imported into the DTTO/DRR. In the USA, the relationship between judge and offender has been a crucial component in the development of drug courts as a new form of 'therapeutic justice'. Interaction with the offender is highly valued, at least by American drug court judges themselves (Nolan, 2001). This was not a role that many English sentencers were keen to take on in the early stages of the DTTO. Judge Justin Phillips of the West London drug court does not share this reticence, and has followed the charismatic style of US judges in developing his court and evangelizing for its model. As he told a 2007 conference of the Association of Chief Police Officers: 'drug court review work can never be a success in a big, busy remand court with the defendant in the dock and the bench on a raised platform miles away' (Phillips, 2007). In our QCT Europe, we received similar reports from probation officers, lawyers and offenders (McSweeney et al., 2008a). We observed attempts at communication between a robed judge on a raised dais and the dishevelled drug users beneath him that were so comically ineffectual that they led to giggling from the wigged barristers waiting for their own cases to appear.

Alongside these innovations, government set a central target of directing at least 1,000 drug-using offenders per week into treatment through the criminal justice system by March 2008. This was exceeded by January 2008 through the expansion of drug treatment sentences and the government's Drug Interventions Programme (Home Office, 2008). Figure 8.1 shows, however, that the increase in the numbers of offenders being sentenced to drug treatment did not lead to a commensurate reduction in the number of people being sent to prison. In 2007, over 12,000 people were sentenced to non-custodial drug treatment, compared with under 2,000 in 1995. The figures for new prison sentences were 91,740 and 89,173 respectively. It seems – in line with Cohen's (1985) gloomy prediction of 'net-widening' – that DTTOs and DRRs have been used in addition to, rather than as a replacement for, imprisonment.

In addition to the failure to reduce the use of imprisonment, other concerns have been expressed about the use of drug treatment as a criminal

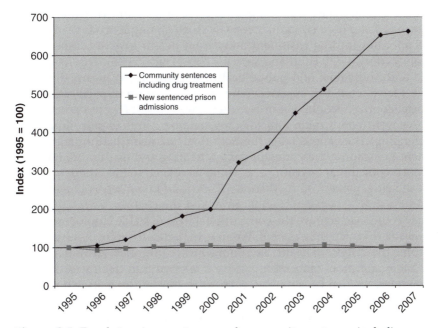

Figure 8.1 Trends in prison sentences and community sentences including condition of drug treatment, 1995–2007
Source: Calculated from figures given by RDS NOMS, 2007, and Ministry of Justice, 2009

sentence. One is that it creates an incentive for drug users who may be unable to get treatment any other way, to commit an offence in order to get treatment. This criticism was frequently heard from drug users' families in the early days of the DTTO. It was also included in a report by a treatment agency (Turning Point, 2004) and in a recent statement to the Home Affairs Select Committee by the father of singer Amy Winehouse (Winehouse, 2009). There may have been such cases, but the offenders we interviewed for the QCT Europe study were not among them. They were offending quite frequently as it was, with no need for extra incentives from drug treatment entry processes. We found that, rather than act as an initiator of offending, the possibility of a drug treatment sentence made them rather less worried about getting arrested for offences they were already committing. One of our interviewees commented that if he got away with his theft, he got to buy heroin, but if he did not, at least he could get into treatment. Now that waiting lists have plummeted, following the huge expansion in treatment availability since 1998, it is even less likely that drug users are responding directly to this incentive to commit crimes.

This does not mean that the expansion of drug treatment sentences has not had some poor consequences. One such consequence is the shifting of priorities in drug treatment away from health towards crime reduction (Barton, 1999; Hunt and Stevens, 2004; Duke, 2006). This has effects on both individual and public health. Individually, it means that drug users have tended to experience treatment as a form of pacification and social control. People whom we interviewed on DTTOs recognized that the government's main aim for drug treatment was to stop drug users offending. They appreciated the help that treatment had initially given them in escaping the vortex of daily offending and heroin use, but they were sceptical that anything else would be offered to help them move on from being 'parked' on methadone. They found themselves caught in an endless shuttle between the jobcentre and the chemist, wondering how they could ever achieve the conventional lives of stable employment and housing to which they aspired. Women, in particular, were disadvantaged during the shift from health to criminal justice priorities. We noticed how, as more and more male offenders were referred into treatment day programmes, women became scarce; crowded out by the men, whom they often knew already as dealers, violent abusers, or both.

There were also serious implications for treatment providers of the change in their accountabilities. Treatment services, whether NHS or voluntary, have traditionally seen their role as supporting their users and improving their health. They have defended the right of these service users to confidentiality and emphasized this over competing priorities, such as public protection. With the introduction of DTTOs, and the increasing entanglement of the treatment and criminal justice systems, this tradition has been challenged. We were told of several cases in England where treatment had been allocated according to the court's order rather than on the basis of clinical need.[1] As noted above, the different tariffs of the DRR formalize this prioritization. As predicted (for example by Wild et al., 2001), there have been clashes between the differing aims and philosophies of treatment and criminal justice professionals. A case at one of the English treatment centres included in the QCT Europe study exemplifies this. The manager of the centre excluded a man who was on a DTTO and had been found smoking heroin in the centre's toilets. The man consequently could not attend treatment and was therefore breached by probation. At the breach hearing, the magistrate insisted that the treatment service had no right to exclude this man as he was in treatment by order of the court. The manager of the service was summoned to appear before the court and spent some uncomfortable time defending her decision before reason prevailed and a solution was found.

Problems like this may be ironed out as the system develops (although they were still being reported several years after the national roll-out of the DTTO). They highlight the shift in emphasis from the relationship between the treatment provider and the client, to include the demands of a criminal justice system which is less likely to have a nuanced understanding of the drug user's (and the drug worker's) needs. Indeed, treatment clients often complained in interviews with us that probation officers were writing ill-informed reports for the court, when it was the treatment staff who had much better knowledge of both the issues they were facing and the progress they were making.

At the level of public health, there has been an alarming ignoring of the risks posed by drug-related deaths and infections, which are on the rise among injecting drug users in the UK (especially among recent initiates to injecting) (Health Protection Agency, 2008). The action plan which accompanied the government's 2008 drug strategy did not include any details on these public health issues. Neither HIV, hepatitis C nor death are mentioned even once in a government update on the drug strategy, which plays heavily on the role of drug treatment in combating crime (HM Government, 2009).

International perspectives on quasi-compulsory treatment sentences

So far, we have examined the political contexts in which treatment sentences have been created and used in England and Wales, and some consequences of these developments for the treatment system and its users. We have seen that the introduction of the DTTO and subsequent developments have been heavily influenced by the US drug court model. But we should also recognize that there is a larger international context that we can use in analysing these sentences. Many European countries have been using treatment sentences as alternatives to prison for longer than either the USA or the UK. Their experiences provide valuable perspectives in understanding the development and effects of such sentences in the UK.

Sentences which enable offenders to enter treatment instead of prison have been described as quasi-compulsory treatment (QCT). There are some countries where treatment ordered by the criminal justice system is fully compulsory. Sweden and Norway provide perhaps the best-known examples of systems in which people who are considered to be addicts can be sent to treatment without having any kind of choice in the matter (Heckmann, 1997). The Netherlands is a more surprising example (for those who like to see it as an island of tolerance) of a country where offenders who are also drug users can be placed in a drug treatment institution against their will (van 't Land et al., 2005). Such compulsory systems are not discussed in detail in this chapter, which focuses on QCT sentences in which the offender retains an element of choice over whether to enter treatment. The option of taking a different punishment (usually imprisonment) is still on the table, and is sometimes chosen. A variety of QCT systems are practised in Europe. Some of them include the possibility to divert offenders from prosecution into treatment, whereas others leave this diversion until the stage of sentencing and punishment (Werdenich et al., 2004). A comparison of various features of the sentences that were included in the QCT Europe study is given in Table 8.1.

It is important to note that QCT sentences can only be compatible with human rights if they are based on due process and are not longer or more restrictive of liberty than the usual sentence for the offence (Gostin, 1991; Gostin and Mann, 2004; Stevens et al., 2005b). These standards are not always applied in practice. For example, the DTTO and the DRR in England and Wales frequently last longer than the usual community or prison sentence for the offence. And there have been many cases in the USA where offenders who are sentenced to treatment have not been able to test reports of non-compliance in court, and so have been reimprisoned without due process (Burns and Peyrot, 2003).

Not all QCT sentences are the same. These differences mean that there is a choice not just between prison and an alternative sentence to treatment, but also of what type of QCT to apply. Diversity is explored here in order to show the range of potential alternatives.

Context

There are at least three elements of the context for QCT which deserve attention. These include the cultural context, the legal context and the socio-economic context. If we follow Douglas's (1992) conception of culture, we can see it as a system within which people hold each other accountable for their adherence to expected standards of behaviour. There are great differences between cultures and countries in these standards, especially when it comes to the consumption of psychoactive substances. One of the most important distinctions between the USA and many European countries is the greater cultural emphasis on abstinence that has influenced American policy and practice. Perhaps the clearest symbol of this is the difference between the UK and USA in the decisions that were taken in the early twentieth century on the acceptability of providing psychoactive substances as medical treatment. The US Supreme Court, in the 1919 *Doremus* and *Webb* cases, affirmed that physicians could be prosecuted for giving heroin to addicts, whereas the 1926 Rolleston Committee instituted the 'British system' of prescribing heroin to dependent users (Nolan, 2002). This reflects a wider tension between US and European cultures on the moral acceptability of taking mind-altering substances.

Table 8.1 Types of QCT order available in the countries of the QCT Europe study

Country	Type of order	Stage of CJS	Targeted offenders	Type of diversion
Austria	§35 SMG Vorläufige Zurücklegung der Anzeige durch den Staatsanwalt (preliminary suspension of the complaint by the prosecution)	From police custody or during the prosecution process	Drug crimes Acquisitive crimes	Suspension of prosecution
	§37 SMG Vorläufige Einstellung durch das Gericht (preliminary suspension of court-hearings)	From police custody or or pre-trial detention	Drug crimes Acquisitive crimes	Suspension of court hearings
	§39 SMG Aufschub des Strafvollzuges (delay of sentence) Therapie statt Strafe (therapy instead of punishment)	From pre-trial detention or at court hearings	Any crime committed by an offender who is substance dependent	Suspension of prison sentence
England & Wales[a]	Drug Treatment and Testing Order	At trial sentencing	Any crime considered serious enough to attract a prison sentence, but not so serious as to demand one	Specific order of the court
	Drug Rehabilitation Requirement	At trial sentencing	For a wider group of offenders facing low to high seriousness community sentences	Condition attached to a community order
Germany	§35, 36 BtMG Strafaussetzung Therapie statt Strafe (suspension pending therapy instead of punishment)	Pre-trial detention, pre-trial hearings, or during sentence	Offenders facing prison sentences of less than two years	Suspension of sentence under probation supervision
	§37 BtMG Zurückstellung der Strafe im Rahmen der Ermittlung (deferment of punishment during investigation)	Deferment of prosecution because of low seriousness of offence	Offenders who are already participating in a treatment programme and who commit minor crimes	Suspension of prosecution
	§38, 39 BtMG Aussetzung der Strafe um Rahmen der Strafverfolgung (suspension of punishment during prosecution)	Pre-trial detention, or youth/juvenile detention	Offenders facing prison sentences of less than two years	Suspension of sentence under probation supervision
	§56 StGB Bewährungsauflage (probation order)	Court hearings	Crimes committed in connection with drugs	Specific order of the court
Italy	Ex art. 91 c. 3 T. U. 309/90	Court hearings, or during sentence	Drug-dependent offenders facing less than six years remaining of a prison sentence (except Mafiosi)	Suspension of imprisonment under supervision of probation

[a] The DTTO was available for offences committed prior to 4 April 2005. The DRR applies for offences committed on or after that date.

171

With its specifically Protestant origins, American culture has been more influenced by the call to curtail sensory pleasures in favour of embodying the purity of scripture. This contrasts with European cultures which retain the influence of medieval Catholicism in celebrating the sensuous carnality of consumption (Mellor and Shilling, 1997). For example, the temperance movement was much larger (and more influential) in America than in the less Protestant cultures of Europe. These attitudes to unearned pleasure and intoxication have been transferred onto more recently imported psychoactive substances, with significant consequences for the aims and methods adopted by drug treatment in general, and by QCT sentences in particular.

This cultural context also affects both the legal and socio-economic contexts for QCT. If we compare, for example, the sentences used for the possession and distribution of illicit drugs, we find that US legislatures have transferred their taste for abstinence into much longer penalties and a much wider use of imprisonment than their European counterparts. In many European countries, it is comparatively rare for people to be sent to prison for drug possession alone. For example, in 2003 in Scotland, the rate of imprisonment for convicted drug offenders other than drug traffickers was 0.6 per 100,000 population (despite a relatively high prevalence of heroin and cannabis use by European standards). This rate was 5.4 in Germany and 13.6 in Switzerland (Council of Europe, 2006). In the USA in 2004, the most serious offence committed by 28 per cent of state convicts and 5 per cent of federal convicts was drug possession (Mumola and Karberg, 2006), implying a convict imprisonment rate for possession of at least 24 per 100,000 population. This higher rate may be partly explained by higher rates of drug use in the USA (see Reuter and Stevens, 2007) and the imprisonment of people under conviction for possession who actually had roles in drug distribution (Sevigny and Caulkins, 2004). However, there is other evidence for a more punitive approach to drug offenders in the USA. Looking at maximum sentences, we find that Sweden, which is considered to be America's strongest European ally in upholding drug prohibition, has a maximum prison sentence of only 10 years, even for serious trafficking offences (ELDD, 2008). By contrast, 10 years is the *minimum* sentence an Alabama court can give to *any* drug seller, provided that the sale occurs within three miles of both a school and a housing project (Greene et al., 2006). The disparity in sentencing between the USA and Europe creates a radically different legal context for the use of alternatives to imprisonment. In the USA, a much larger group of drug offenders is prone to much longer sentences than their European counterparts. In practice, it means that treatment alternatives are used for much less serious offenders in the USA.

As Weber (1954) noted, the less contested influence of Protestantism in the USA has led to a purer form of capitalism. The broader social base of the capitalist 'spirit' in the USA, and the individualism it inspired, has led to less intervention by the state in providing health care and welfare support. US social policy has been described as the archetype of the individualist 'liberal' system and contrasted with the interventionist 'corporatist' and 'social democratic' welfare systems of continental Europe (Esping-Anderson, 1990). Weber argued that the American Protestant sect was a more exclusive institution than the European guild. It relied on people proving their worth and respectability in order to join and remain within the trusted membership. This exclusivity has deepened the increasing social exclusion which characterizes societies that have taken the USA as their model in late modern society (Young, 1999). These different socio-economic cultures imply that people who go through alternatives to prison will also be expected to live up to different standards of respectability as evidence of their success. In the USA, the intended outcome of treatment is much more likely to include both abstinence and paid employment, while the European alternatives are more likely to tolerate continued reliance on prescribed or illicit drugs and enrolment in social welfare systems.

Targeting

As noted above, the pool of people who are liable to imprisonment for drug offences is much bigger in the USA. This might imply that there is a larger group who might be considered eligible for alternatives, but this would depend on how far up the scales of seriousness of offence and offender US authorities are prepared to countenance diversion from prison. And this varies widely between jurisdictions.

Many drug courts follow the model of the original Dade County prototype in limiting eligibility to offenders charged with possession or purchase of controlled substances and excluding people with a history of violent offences. Even if there has been a historical pattern of drug courts expanding their eligibility criteria as they have matured, with more serious and violent offenders being included as eligible (Saum et al., 2001), the main target group of drug courts is still one that would face a much lower risk of imprisonment in most European countries. The California drug courts, for example, explicitly exclude people who have committed offences of sale or production of illicit drugs (Burns and Peyrot, 2003). The Urban Institute surveyed 600 US drug courts in 2005 and found that 88 per cent excluded offenders with any history of violent offending and 49 per cent excluded people with prior treatment history (Singh Bhati et al., 2007).

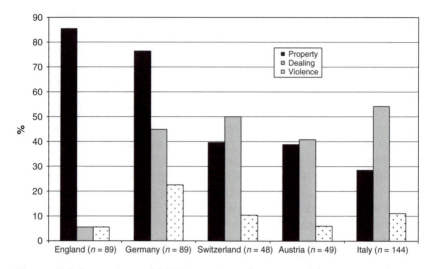

Figure 8.2 Proportions of QCT Europe sample sentenced for property, drug dealing or violent offences, by country

Note: Some respondents reported being sentenced for more than one category of crime. Each reported category is included in this figure.

In European systems, the imprisonment of people for possession alone is comparatively rare (see, for example, Mwenda, 2005). But there are wide disparities within Europe in the type of offender that receives QCT. In the QCT Europe study, we selected research sites purposively, so did not recruit a truly random sample of QCT entrants. However, our findings on the type of offences they had committed in order to receive their QCT sentence did indicate that some countries provide such measures for more serious offenders than others. Figure 8.2 shows that a large majority of people entering DTTOs in England had been convicted of property offences. They were typically people who were financing lengthy heroin (and other drug) habits through daily shoplifting, with the occasional foray into fraud and burglary when the occasion allowed. The English sentencers whom we interviewed expressed their exasperation with this group. Many of them had appeared frequently before the courts, and had received community sentences, which they typically breached. Sentencers described short terms of imprisonment as an appropriate response to repeated failures to heed the warnings of the court. This attitude was also prevalent among people whom we interviewed on entry to their DTTO. Some of them considered themselves fortunate to have escaped prison despite their lengthy criminal records.

The proportion of property offenders among QCT entrants was lower in the other countries of the study, where drug dealers and violent offenders made up larger proportions of the group who were given sentences to

Table 8.2 Indicators of social exclusion among people entering QCT in the QCT Europe study

	England	Italy	Austria	Switzerland	Germany
Sample size	*89*	*144*	*53*	*49*	*92*
Average years in education	10	8	11	9	10
Unemployed	79%	20%	49%	38%	44%
Homeless	32%	7%	13%	27%	33%
Has chronic medical problem	37%	56%	55%	43%	64%
Been treated for mental illness	26%	31%	17%	29%	10%
Has no close friends	41%	50%	32%	21%	25%

treatment instead of prison. These data suggest that England and the USA are locking up many offenders who would not be considered to warrant imprisonment in other countries. Most offenders in each country of the QCT Europe study also had significant prior experience of treatment,[2] which would have excluded them from many US drug courts.

If we look in more detail at the people who were getting QCT sentences (see Table 8.2), we find that they tended to follow the pattern that has been found for problematic drug users in a variety of European cities (March et al., 2006). They were vulnerable to different forms of social exclusion. Most of them had not stayed in secondary education until the usual age of graduation. Large proportions, especially in England, were unemployed. Homelessness was relatively common. There were high rates of chronic physical and mental health problems. Large proportions of them did not have anyone they could call a close friend. A common response when we asked them about friendship was, 'I don't have any real friends, just people I do drugs with.'

All of these indicators of social exclusion were more prevalent among the QCT group than among the 'volunteers' who were being treated at the same locations. This, combined with the higher levels of drug use among the QCT group, suggests that people entering treatment under QCT tended to have more serious combinations of drug and other problems than 'voluntary' treatment entrants.

Treatment content

There were also differences between countries in the QCT Europe study in the type of treatment provided to these offenders, with English offenders more likely to be ordered to participate in community-based day programmes, often while receiving an opiate substitution prescription, whereas the other countries made more use of drug-free, intensive, residential treatment. Drug-free treatment, whether residential or ambulatory, is also the dominant mode of treatment in US treatment alternatives. Methadone substitution is often denied to participants in these treatments, despite its proven effectiveness in reducing offending and illicit drug use (Jaeger, 2002). The Urban Institute survey found that only 18 per cent of the estimated number of people in drug court treatment were receiving methadone. The remainder were in drug-free treatment (Singh Bhati et al., 2007). Abstinence, as Bean (2002: 72) has written, 'has the obvious virtue of making treatment compatible with the goals of criminal justice'. From this he concludes that 'the sole aim of drug treatment agencies working within a criminal justice setting... must be compliance with the law' Bean (2002: 72), but he does not explain whether this should rule out legal treatment that is non-abstinent, or whether compliance with the law (for example, not using cannabis) is more important than the long-term prevention of offending through successful retention in drug treatment.

Approach to non-compliance

The dilemma posed by treatment content is also visible in the different approaches taken by various treatment alternatives to the definition and sanctioning of non-compliance. In the US drug courts, any renewed drug use can lead to action by the court. In the English DTTO and other systems in the QCT Europe study, continued drug use was often tolerated, with offenders providing repeated positive drug tests with little risk of being punished. A more important indicator of compliance for the DTTO was the person's attendance in treatment. As noted above, they were supposed to attend a minimum of 20 hours' treatment per week, with the treatment providers contracted to report on attendance to the Probation Service. In turn, the Probation Service was expected to institute breach proceedings (leading to a court review of the DTTO sentence) if the offender had more than two days of unexplained absence from the treatment programme. Many offenders fell foul of this standard. Other countries in the QCT Europe project used a more flexible approach to compliance, based more on professional discretion than on rigid rules and standards.

US drug courts, while having a stricter attitude to compliance, tend to have more flexibility when responding to it, as they use a wider range of sanctions. In the European systems, the reviewing courts could either continue or terminate treatment orders, perhaps with the inclusion of various conditions, such as different hours or frequencies of mandated treatment or drug tests. US drug courts have these options, but also employ others, such as ordering offenders to attend extra days in court, or to go to prison for short spells during their drug court participation. Indeed, the use of such prison time as a punishment for non-compliance can be so extensive as to eliminate any differences in the use of prison for drug court participants and comparable offenders who do not go through drug courts (Harrell, 2003). In this Baltimore example at least, the drug court operated as an adjunct to imprisonment rather than as an alternative. In the UK, high rates of non-compliance with the DTTO led to large numbers of participants being re-sentenced to prison and to one interviewee describing the DTTO as 'an expensive precursor to imprisonment'. The approach to non-compliance is therefore crucial in analysing whether QCT is, in practice, used as an *alternative* to imprisonment.

Bean (2004) has argued that flexibility in responding to non-compliance is vital for success. In the USA there are some advocates of the 'graduated sanctions' approach, with non-compliant offenders facing an escalating range of punishments (Harrell and Roman, 2001). But more research is needed on how offenders experience such sanctions and their effect on patterns of drug use and offending (Maxwell, 2000; Wild, 2006). One English study found that stricter enforcement of rules on breaching errant probation offenders did not appear to make any difference to their reconviction rates. The authors suggest that ways should be found to reward compliance and deal with non-compliance in ways that do not lead to revocation of the community sentence (Hearnden and Millie, 2003).

Mechanisms and outcomes in QCT

Having examined differences in the contexts and contents of QCT, let us turn to outcomes for the drug users who go through them. Some sweeping claims have been made about the effectiveness or failure of QCT. For example, Allen has stated that a 'volume of evidence' shows that coerced treatment does not work. But he does not cite any particular studies (Allen, 2007: 126). Perhaps this is because successive reviews of the literature have shown that there are several studies suggesting that coerced treatment, as Russell (1994) found, can work. Of course, we need to be clear about what we mean by effectiveness and coercion before we can judge whether coerced treatment really 'works'. The usual standards that are applied for effectiveness – reductions in drug use and crime – may not be the most relevant to drug users themselves. They may be seeking a better quality of life, including more satisfying experiences of work and family life. In the general context of socio-economic deprivation, stigmatization and marginalization that are experienced by dependent drug users, these outcomes are harder to achieve. They have also generally been neglected in drug treatment evaluation.

There is, however, a wealth of studies showing that drug treatment generally 'works' in reducing drug use and offending of the individuals who go through treatment (including Prendergast et al., 2002; Stevens et al., 2006b; NICE, 2007a,b,c,d; UNODC and WHO, 2008). There have also been reviews of the evidence published in English on drug treatment that is ordered through the criminal justice system (Leukefeld and Tims, 1990; Anglin and Hser, 1991; Gostin, 1991; Farabee et al., 1998; Belenko, 2001; Wilson et al., 2006; McSweeney et al., 2008b). Taken together, these studies suggest that, despite fairly disastrous results at compulsory treatment facilities in the USA before 1960, modern forms of QCT tend to have similar outcomes to treatment that is entered into 'voluntarily'. Some evidence published in other languages (for example, German and French) suggests that, as Allen also argues, some drug users are just not ready for treatment, and that their presence may harm treatment for people who are more deeply committed to changing their lives (Stevens et al., 2005a). These difficulties suggest that we need to look at what works for whom and under what circumstances.

The other crucial aspect of research on QCT sentences is the issue of coercion. Does it, as Allen seems to claim, doom treatment to failure?

Coercion and motivation

The argument that treatment works, but not for QCT clients, makes two separate and questionable assumptions. The first is that successful clients who are not coerced by the courts are entering treatment of their own free will. The second is that QCT clients have no intrinsic motivation to change. The idea that people enter treatment 'voluntarily' assumes that their dependence on drugs does not do away with their ability to exercise free will. This is an assumption that would be disputed by those who see dependence as a brain disease that fundamentally compromises free will (Erickson, 2003). But even without accepting this controversial definition of addiction, we can see that people may experience pressure to enter treatment from other sources than the courts. They may have friends, families and employers who tell them to get help for their drug use. They may be under threat of having their children taken away from them if they do not enter treatment. And they may experience the constant danger and hassle of their drug-using lifestyle as a source of considerable pressure. As a treatment client once told me, when I asked her why she entered treatment, 'It was either this or die on the street. What sort of choice is that?' While pressure from the state to enter treatment is qualitatively different from pressure from family, friends and the person's own fear of death (Stevens et al., 2005b), it is still the case that many drug users enter non-QCT treatment under some form of pressure.

The common presence of these other sources of pressure was why Gregoire and Burke used inverted commas around the word 'volunteer' in their 2004 article on the relationship between legal coercion and readiness to change. In a sample of 295 consecutive admissions to US drug treatment, they found that 'legal coercion was associated with greater readiness to change after controlling for addiction severity, prior treatment history and gender' (Gregoire and Burke, 2004: 337). They conclude from this that increasing legal coercion on drug users may be a way to increase motivation, and thereby improve treatment outcome. This conclusion is unsubstantiated in their data, challenged by results from the QCT Europe study, and potentially dangerous in the light of policy proposals to increase coercion on drug users (and not just those who have committed other offences) in ways that further harm their human rights (see, for example, PMSU, 2003; Gyngell, 2007).

The reason that this conclusion cannot safely be drawn from their data is that they ignore the complexity of the relationships between legal status, perceived coercion and motivation. They assume that all clients who are subject to legal pressure experience this as a form of coercion. In contrast, clients interviewed for the QCT Europe often stated that they did not feel pressured to be in treatment, despite being subject to a court order. A common response was, 'I wanted to get treatment anyway'. The QCT Europe study used a questionnaire (adapted from Simpson and Knight, 1998) to ask the treatment clients to rate how much pressure they felt from a range of sources, including families or friends, medical professionals, employers, the legal system and other sources. Unsurprisingly, those people who entered treatment through QCT reported perceived pressure scores that were significantly higher than the 'volunteers'. But 65 per cent of the 'volunteers' reported feeling some external pressure, and 22 per cent of the QCT group reported feeling no external pressure. A large proportion of people who enter treatment without a court order do feel pressured to be there by some other source. Families and social services were commonly mentioned. And many people who enter treatment through QCT, which is commonly seen as coerced treatment, did not feel under any external pressure to be there. Rather, they reported experiencing it as their own choice.

The assumption that increasing pressure can improve outcome is made even more problematic by QCT Europe's findings on the link (or lack of it) between perceived pressure and readiness to change. Allen (2007) argues that many drug users see treatment as an 'irrelevance that is forced on them by others'. According to common sense on taking horses to water, and its more sophisticated formulation in Deci and Ryan's (1985) theory of self-determination, this external coercion should destroy motivation to change in drug treatment. In the QCT Europe study, we used the Readiness to Change Questionnaire (Rollnick et al., 1992) to allocate treatment entrants to a stage in the 'cycle of change' (DiClemente and Prochaska, 1982). The stages could be, in increasing order of readiness to change, precontemplation, contemplation and action. In bivariate analysis, people who were in the QCT group were no more or less likely than the 'volunteers' to be at a higher stage of readiness to change. And the average perceived external pressure scores were not significantly different between people who were in different stages of motivation. This suggested that neither the objective presence of legal pressure nor the subjective experience of pressure were important in influencing motivation.

Drug use and offending outcomes

The idea that legal coercion damages motivation to such an extent that QCT cannot work is also challenged by the results on outcome from QCT Europe. We gathered information in a number of areas of outcome, including drug use, offending, physical and mental health. In none of these areas were outcomes significantly different between people who were in QCT or 'voluntary' treatment, in any of the countries included in the study. Results from the English sample, comparing people who went through DTTOs to comparable volunteers, are shown in the graphs below. They are representative of the results found in each of the countries of the QCT Europe study.

The EuropASI drug use score was used as a primary measure of drug use severity in the past 30 days, as it combines measures of the frequency of all the categories of drug use, of days experiencing drug problems and spending on drugs. As shown in Figure 8.3, there were significant reductions in the scores for both groups from intake to follow-up phases. The mean score for the DTTO group, which had been significantly higher than for the 'voluntary' group at intake, was slightly (but not significantly) lower at 18 month follow-up.

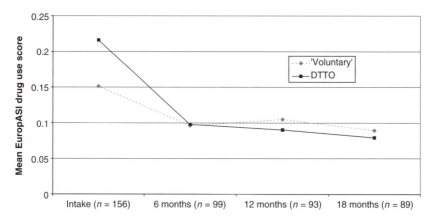

Figure 8.3 Mean EuropASI drug use scores over the phases of the study

In order to check the effects of study attrition on this analysis, it was repeated using last observation carried forward to impute missing scores at follow-up phases. This did not alter the pattern of significant reductions in the first six months, which were maintained over the following two phases. Translating the EuropASI scores into more easily comprehensible indicators of outcome, we found that there was a reduction, in both 'voluntary' and QCT groups, of about a half in the average number of days in the past month that treated clients used illicit drugs between intake and follow-up phases. There were also significant reductions, for both the DTTO group and the 'volunteers', in the proportion reporting injecting drugs. For those on DTTOs, this fell from over 50 per cent before entry to the DTTO to under 20 per cent 18 months later.

The number of days that these people reported committing offences also reduced significantly for both groups, as shown in Figure 8.4. The reduction was larger for the QCT clients, who reported higher levels of offending at intake. The proportion of people who reported committing any offending crimes in the previous 30 days also fell substantially for both groups from intake to 18 month follow-up. It fell from 96 per cent to 64 per cent for the DTTO group, and from 57 per cent to 34 per cent for 'volunteers'. Again, the largest reductions were observed in the first six months after treatment entry. Repeating these analyses using last observation carried forward again suggested that they were robust to the possibility of selection bias due to study attrition. These findings suggest that drug treatment does not eliminate offending for all those who enter it (many people continue to offend), but it does tend to substantially reduce the level of

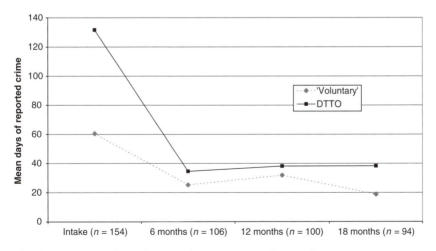

Figure 8.4 Mean days of reported crime in past six months

their offending, whether they enter treatment 'voluntarily' or on a QCT order.

Of course, these are average reductions. Outcomes varied between individuals, places and treatment agencies. For example, two treatment agencies in the English sample had particularly poor rates of retention and outcome. One of these agencies, which adhered to the 12 Step Minnesota model, demanded abstinence from all illicit drugs at a very early stage of treatment. Many QCT clients found it difficult to comply and so dropped out of treatment. In the qualitative interviews, it became clear that issues of matching treatment to clients' expectations and needs and, crucially, the establishment of relationships of trust between drug users and the professionals who were working with them, were vital in developing motivation and retaining clients in treatment (Stevens et al., 2006a). When such therapeutic alliances were created, clients in both QCT and 'voluntary' treatment were able to make substantial reductions to their drug use and offending.

It would be difficult to draw broader and stronger generalizations than this from the QCT Europe study. It was not a true experiment, as the members of the sample were not randomly assigned to either the QCT or 'voluntary' group. There were many people who dropped out of the study. These may have been the people who had, in Allen's (2007) terms, the most 'natural' attitude to drugs and so felt that treatment was not relevant to their needs. This attrition limited the application of an intention-to-treat design. We did include people who dropped out of treatment (many of whom ended up in prison) in the follow-up phases of the study. We also carried out analysis using 'last observation carried forward' to check that the results still held if we assumed that people who dropped out of the study maintained their previous levels of drug use and offending. Findings of this analysis were consistent with findings from the raw data. We can conclude that legal pressure does not always damage (or increase) motivation to change and that QCT sentences are not inherently doomed to failure.

Conclusions

Whatever we think about the rights and wrongs of criminalizing people for their drug use, it is still the case that some people who develop problematic patterns of consumption will also commit harmful acts that warrant some form of intervention. Too often, in the USA and the UK especially, these interventions have come in the form of expensive and futile prison sentences. This chapter has shown that there is a range of alternatives available, but that we should think very carefully about how best to implement and expand them. One particular danger, as highlighted in Figure 8.1 above, is that we will further widen and tighten the net of penal control. The rapid increases in treatment sentences in England and Wales have not produced a reduction in the use of imprisonment, despite the evident fall in crime since the 1995 peak (Walker et al., 2006). The use of imprisonment to encourage compliance with QCT sentences seems to have eliminated any reduction in the use of imprisonment in at least one QCT example (Harrell, 2003).

We should also be careful in making claims on the general effectiveness of QCT sentences in combating crime. The original advocate of the DTTO warned about what he called 'the funnel of crime' (Russell, 1994). At the top of this funnel is the wide and ever-changing population of offences and offenders. Due to attrition at each stage of the criminal justice system, from reporting crimes through to finding and sentencing individual offenders, only a much smaller number of offenders emerges at the bottom of the funnel. This means that sentences that are applied to this relatively tiny group are unlikely to have much effect on the general rates of crime that affect the population. Treatment sentences for offenders may be individually effective and less expensive than prison. But we still need to invest in tackling the wider, social causes of crime if we really intend to create large and sustained improvements in community safety.

Finally, if we continue to discuss QCT sentences and coerced treatment as if such sentences are all identical and applied to a homogeneous group of unmotivated offenders, we will not grasp the potential opportunities and dangers that exist in actual practice. QCT appeals to some drug users who have grown sick and tired of the struggle to obtain drugs every day. They find in it a chance to escape the repetitive grind of drug consumption, crime and imprisonment in which they have become stuck. Many of them are able to use QCT to create relationships which help them to recover from their dependence. But this does not mean we should unthinkingly corral ever-increasing numbers of drug users into treatment. To do so would not only threaten the human rights to which all of us are entitled, but also damage the principles of successful treatment which appear to apply equally to the increasingly large number of people who enter it through the criminal justice system.

Notes

1. This seemed to be less of a problem in other countries of the QCT Europe study, where treatment decisions were more likely to be left to clinical and professional discretion. In Germany, this was assisted by the payment method. In England, the treatment was typically commissioned in blocks for groups of DTTO offenders. In Germany, the treatment was paid for by the individual drug users' social insurance. This meant that the funding followed the drug users as they chose between treatment options.

2. Eighty-five per cent of the QCT sample across the countries had at least one prior treatment episode. The average number of prior treatment episodes was six.

References

Allen, C. (2007) *Crime, Drugs and Social Theory: A Phenomenological Approach*. Aldershot: Ashgate Press.

Anglin, M.D. and Hser, Y.I. (1991) 'Criminal justice and the drug-abusing offender: policy issues of coerced treatment', *Behavioral Sciences and the Law*, 9: 243–67.

Barton, A. (1999) 'Sentenced to treatment? Criminal justice orders and the health service', *Critical Social Policy*, 19(4): 463–83.

Bean, P. (2002) *Drugs and Crime*. Cullompton: Willan Publishing.

Bean, P. (2004) *Drugs and Crime*, 2nd edition. Cullompton: Willan Publishing.

Bean, P. (2008) *Drugs and Crime*, 3rd edition. Cullompton: Willan Publishing.

Belenko, S. (2001) *Research on Drug Courts: A Critical Review 2001 Update*. New York: National Centre on Addiction and Substance Abuse.

Burns, S.L. and Peyrot, M. (2003) 'Tough love: nurturing and coercing responsibility and recovery in California drug courts', *Social Problems*, 50(3): 416–38.

Caulkins, J.P. and Chandler, S. (2006) 'Long-run trends in incarceration of drug offenders in the United States', *Crime Delinquency*, 52(4): 619–41.

Cohen, S. (1985) *Visions of Social Control*. Cambridge: Polity Press.

Council of Europe (1999) *Recommendation R(99)2 of the Committee of Ministers to Member States concerning prison overcrowding and population inflation*. Strasbourg: Council of Europe Committee of Ministers.

Council of Europe (2006) *European Sourcebook of Crime and Criminal Justice Statistics*. The Hague: WODC, Ministry of Justice.

Deci, E.L. and Ryan, R.M. (1985) *Intrinsic Motivation and Self-Determination in Human Behavior*. New York: Plenum Press.

DiClemente, C.C. and Prochaska, J.O. (1982) 'Self-change and therapy change of smoking behavior: a comparison of processes of change in cessation and maintenance', *Addictive Behaviors*, 7(2): 133–42.

Douglas, M. (1992) *Risk and Blame*. London: Routledge.

Duke, K. (2006) 'Out of crime and into treatment? The criminalization of contemporary drug policy since "Tackling Drugs Together"', *Drugs: Education, Prevention and Policy*, 13(5): 409–15.

ELDD (2008) *Illegal Posession of Drugs*. Lisbon: EMCDDA European Legal Database on Drugs.

Erickson, C. (2003) 'Addiction is a disease', *Addiction Today*, Jan./Feb., pp. 17–19.

Esping-Anderson, G. (1990) *The Three Worlds of Welfare Capitalism*. Princeton: Princeton University Press.

Falk, C. (2004) 'Are DTTOs working? Issues of policy, implementation and practice', *Probation Journal*, 51(4): 398–406.

Farabee, D., Prendergast, M. and Anglin, M.D. (1998) 'The effectiveness of coerced treatment for drug-abusing offenders', *Federal Probation*, 62(1): 3–10.

Gostin, L.O. (1991) 'Compulsory treatment for drug-dependent persons: justifications for a public health approach to drug dependency', *The Milbank Quarterly*, 69(4): 561–93.

Gostin, L. and Mann, J. (2004) 'Toward the development of a human rights impact assessment for the formulation and evaluation of public health policies', in K. Malinowska-Sempruch and S. Gallagher (eds) *War on Drugs, HIV/AIDS and Human Rights*. New York: International Debate Education Association.

Greene, J., Pranis, K. and Ziedenberg, J. (2006) *Disparity by Design: How Drug-Free Zone Laws Impact Racial Disparity – and Fail to Protect Youth*. Washington, DC: Justice Policy Institute.

Gregoire, T.K. and Burke, A.C. (2004) 'The relationship of legal coercion to readiness to change among adults with alcohol and other drug problems', *Journal of Substance Abuse Treatment*, 26: 337–43.

Gyngell, K. (2007) *Breakthrough Britain: Ending the Costs of Social Breakdown. Vol. 4: Addictions*. London: Conservative Party.

Harrell, A. (2003) 'Judging drug courts: balancing the evidence', *Criminology and Public Policy*, 2(2): 207–12.

Harrell, A. and Roman, J. (2001) 'Reducing drug use and crime among offenders: the impact of graduated sanctions', *Journal of Drug Issues*, 31(1): 207–31.

Health Protection Agency (2008) *Shooting Up: Infections among Injecting Drug Users in the United Kingdom 2007. An Update*. London: Health Protection Agency.

Hearnden, I. (2000) 'Problem drug use and probation in London: an evaluation', *Drugs: Education Prevention and Policy*, 7(4): 367–80.

Hearnden, I. and Millie, A. (2003) *Investigating Links between Probation Enforcement and Reconviction*, Online Report 41/03. London: Home Office Research, Development and Statistics Directorate.

Heckmann, W. (1997) 'Schwedische Gardinen: Zur Tradition der Zwangsbehandlung Suchtkranker und -gefährdeter in Schweden', *Sucht. Zeitschrift für Wissenschaft und Praxis*, 43(3).

HM Government (2009) *The 2008 Drug Strategy: One Year On*. London: Home Office.

HM Inspectorate of Probation (2006) *Half Full and Half Empty: An Inspection of the National Probation Service' Substance Misuse Work with Offenders*. London: Home Office.

Hollingworth, M. (2008) 'An examination of the potential impact of the Drug Rehabilitation Requirement on homeless illicit drug-using offenders', *Probation Journal*, 55(2): 127–38.

Home Office (2008) *Departmental Report 2008*. London: Home Office.

Hough, M., Clancy, A., McSweeney, T. and Turnbull, P.J. (2003) *The Impact of Drug Treatment and Testing Orders on Offending: Two-Year Reconviction Results*, Findings 184. London: Home Office Research, Development and Statistics Directorate.

House of Commons Justice Committee (2008) *Towards Effective Sentencing. Fifth Report of Session 2007–08*, HC 184-1. London: The Stationery Office.

Hunt, N. and Stevens, A. (2004) 'Whose harm? Harm and the shift from health to coercion in UK drug policy', *Social Policy and Society*, 3(4): 333–42.

Jaeger, G. (2002) Letter to drug court judges on methadone. California Society of Addiction Medicine, San Francisco, CA.

Joint Committee on Human Rights (2004) *Seventh Report: Drugs Bill*. London: UK Parliament.

Kokkevi, A. and Hartgers, C. (1995) 'Europe ASI: European adaptation of a multidimensional assessment instrument for drug and alcohol dependence', *European Addiction Research*, 1(4): 208–10.

Leukefeld, C.G. and Tims, F.M. (1990) 'Compulsory treatment for drug abuse', *International Journal of the Addictions*, 25(6): 621–40.

March, J.C., Oviedo-Joekes, E. and Romero, M. (2006) 'Drugs and social exclusion in ten European cities', *European Addiction Research*, 12: 33–41.

Matrix Research & Consultancy and Nacro (2004) *Evaluation of Drug Testing in the Criminal Justice System*, Home Office Research Study 286. London: Home Office Research, Development and Statistics Directorate.

Maxwell, S.R. (2000) 'Sanction threats in court-ordered programs: examining their effects on offenders mandated into drug treatment', *Crime and Delinquency*, 46(4): 542–63.

McSweeney, T., Stevens, A., Hunt, N. and Turnbull, P. (2007) 'Twisting arms or a helping hand? Assessing the impact of "coerced" and comparable "voluntary" drug treatment options', *British Journal of Criminology*, 47(3): 470–90.

McSweeney, T., Stevens, A., Hunt, N. and Turnbull, P. (2008a) 'Drug testing and court review hearings: uses and limitations', *Probation Journal*, 55(1): 53–67.

McSweeney, T., Turnbull, P.J. and Hough, M. (2008b) *The Treatment and Supervision of Drug-Dependent Offenders*. London: UK Drug Policy Commission.

Mellor, P.A. and Shilling, C. (1997) *Re-forming the Body: Religion, Community and Modernity*. London: Sage.

Ministry of Justice (2009) *Offender Management Caseload Statistics 2008*. London: Ministry of Justice.

Mumola, C.J. and Karberg, J.C. (2006) *Drug Use and Dependence: State and Federal Prisoners, 2004. Bureau of Justice Statistics Special Report*. Washington, DC: US Department of Justice.

Mwenda, L. (2005) *Drug Offenders in England and Wales 2004*, Home Office Statistical Bulletin 23/05. London: Home Office.

Naeem, F., Bhatti, F., Pickering, R. and Kingdon, D. (2007) 'A controlled trial of the effectiveness of drug treatment and testing orders (DTTO) with standard care', *Journal of Substance Use*, 12(4): 253–65.

National Audit Office (2004) *The DTTO – Early Lessons. Report by the Comptroller and Auditor General, HC 366 Session 2003–2004*. London: National Audit Office.

National Probation Directorate (2005) *Effective Management of the Drug Rehabilitation Requirement (DRR) and Alcohol Treatment Requirement (ATR)*, Probation Circular 57/2005. London: Home Office.

NICE (2007a) *Psychosocial Management of Drug Misuse. Draft for Consultation*. London: National Institute for Health and Clinical Excellence.

NICE (2007b) *Naltrexone for the Management of Opioid Dependence*, NICE Technology Appraisal 115. London: National Institute for Health and Clinical Excellence.

NICE (2007c) *Methadone and Buprenorphine for the Management of Opioid Dependence*, NICE Technology Appraisal 114. London: National Institute for Health and Clinical Excellence.

NICE (2007d) *Opiate Detoxification for Drug Misuse. Draft for Consultation*. London: National Institute for Health and Clinical Excellence.

Nolan, J.L. (2001) *Reinventing Justice: The American Drug Court Movement*. Princeton, NJ: Princeton University Press.

Nolan, J.L. (2002) *Drug Courts: In Theory and in Practice*. New York: Aldine de Gruyter.

Phillips, J. (2007) 'The role of drug courts', speech to the ACPO Chemical Diversion Conference. Stansted: Association of Chief Police Officers.

PMSU (2003) *SU Drugs Report. Phase 2 Report: Diagnosis and Recommendations*. London: Prime Minister's Strategy Unit.

Prendergast, M.L., Podus, D., Chang, E. and Urada, D. (2002) 'The effectiveness of drug abuse treatment: a meta-analysis of comparison group studies', *Drug and Alcohol Dependence*, 67(1): 53–72.

RDS NOMS (2005) *Offender Management Caseload Statistics 2004: England and Wales*, Home Office Statistical Bulletin 17/05. London: Home Office.

RDS NOMS (2007) *Sentencing Statistics 2006*, Statistical Bulletin. London: Ministry of Justice.

Reuter, P. and Stevens, A. (2007) *An Analysis of UK Drug Policy*. London: UK Drug Policy Commission.

Reuter, P. and Stevens, A. (2008) 'Assessing UK drug policy from a crime control perspective', *Criminology and Criminal Justice*, 8(4): 461–82.

Ricketts, T., Bliss, P., Murphy, K. and Brooker, C. (2002) *The Life-Course of the DTTO: Engagement with Drug Treatment and Testing Orders*. Sheffield: School of Health and Related Research, University of Sheffield.

Robinson, E. (2003) *Failing DTTOs? Breach Cause, Partial Impact, and Follow-on Processes for Part-Completers*. Wakefield: National Probation Service, West Yorkshire.

Rollnick, S., Heather, N., Gold, R. and Hall, W. (1992) 'Development of a short "Readiness to Change" questionnaire for use in brief, opportunistic interventions among excessive drinkers', *British Journal of Addiction*, 87(5): 743–54.

Russell, J. (1994) *Substance Abuse and Crime (Some Lessons from America)*, Harkness Fellowship Report. New York: Commonwealth Fund of New York.

Saum, C.A., Scarpitti, F.R. and Robbins, C.A. (2001) 'Violent offenders in drug court', *Journal of Drug Issues*, 31(1): 107–28.

Schaub, M., Stevens, A., Berto, D., Hunt, N., Kerschl, V., McSweeney, T., Oeuvray, K., Puppo, I., Maria, A.S., Trinkl, B., Werdenich, W. and Uchtenhagen, A. (2009) 'Comparing outcomes of "voluntary" and "quasi-compulsory" treatment of substance dependence in Europe', (submitted for publication).

Sevigny, E.L. and Caulkins, J.P. (2004) 'Kingpins or mules? An analysis of drug offenders incarcerated in federal and state prisons', *Criminology and Public Policy*, 3(3): 401–34.

Simpson, D.D. and Knight, K. (1998) *TCU Data Collection Forms for Correctional Residential Treatment*. Fort Worth: Texas Christian University, Institute of Behavioral Research.

Singh Bhati, A., Roman, J. and Chalfin, A. (2007) *Going to Scale in the Treatment of Drug Involved Criminal Offenders*. Washington, DC: Urban Institute Justice Policy Center.

South, N. (1998) 'Tackling drug control in Britain: from Sir Malcolm Delevigne to the New Drugs Strategy', in R. Coomber (ed.) *The Control of Drugs and Drug Users: Reason or Reaction?* London: CRC Press.

Stevens, A. (2007) 'When two dark figures collide: evidence and discourse on drug-related crime', *Critical Social Policy*, 27(1): 77–99.

Stevens, A., Berto, D., Heckmann, W., Kerschl, V., Oeuvray, K., van Ooyen, M., Steffan, E. and Uchtenhagen, A. (2005a) 'Quasi-compulsory treatment of drug dependent offenders: an international literature review', *Substance Use and Misuse*, 40(3): 269–83.

Stevens, A., Berto, D., Frick, U., Hunt, N., Kerschl, V., McSweeney, T., Oeuvray, K., Puppo, I., Santa Maria, A., Schaaf, S., Trinkl, B., Uchtenhagen, A. and Werdenich, W. (2006a) 'The relationship between legal status, perceived pressure and motivation in treatment for drug dependence: results from a European study of quasi-compulsory treatment', *European Addiction Research*, 12(4): 197–209.

Stevens, A., Berto, D., Frick, U., Kerschl, V., McSweeney, T., Schaaf, S., Tartari, M., Turnbull, P., Trinkl, B., Uchtenhagen, A., Waidner, G. and Werdenich, W. (2007) 'The victimization of dependent drug users: findings from a European study', *European Journal of Criminology*, 4(4): 385–408.

Stevens, A., Hallam, C. and Trace, M. (2006b) *Treatment for Dependent Drug Use: A Guide For Policymakers*. Oxford: Beckley Foundation.

Stevens, A., McSweeney, T., van Ooyen, M. and Uchtenhagen, A. (2005b) 'On coercion', *International Journal of Drug Policy*, 16(4): 207–9.

Straw, J. (1996) *Breaking the Vicious Circle: Labour's Proposals to Tackle Drug Related Crime*. London: Labour Party.

Tonry, M. (2004). *Punishment and Politics: Evidence and Emulation in the Making of English Crime Control Policy*. Cullompton: Willan Publishing.

Turnbull, P.J., McSweeney, T., Webster, R., Edmunds, M. and Hough, M. (2000) *Drug Treatment and Testing Orders: Final Evaluation Report*. London: Home Office Research, Development and Statistics Directorate.

Turner, R. (2002) *Does DTTO Assessment Intensity Affect Retention? A Comparison between West Yorkshire Districts on 'Time to Drop-Out' for DTTO Offenders*. Wakefield: National Probation Service, West Yorkshire.

Turner, R. (2004) 'The impact of drug treatment and testing orders in West Yorkshire: six-month outcomes', *Probation Journal*, 51(2): 116–32.

Turning Point (2004) *Routes into Treatment: Drugs and Crime*. London: Turning Point.

United Nations (1990) *Standard Minimum Rules for Non-custodial Measures (The Tokyo Rules)*. Geneva: United Nations.

UNODC and WHO (2008) *Principles of Drug Dependence Treatment. Discussion Paper*. United Nations Office on Drugs and Crime.

Van 't Land, H., van Duijvenbooden, K., van der Plas, A. and Wolf, J. (2005) *Opgevangen onder dwang procesevaluatie strafrechtelijke opvang verslaafden*. The Hague: WODC, Ministry of Justice.

Walker, A., Kershaw, C. and Nicholas, S. (2006) *Crime in England and Wales 2005/06*. London: Home Office.

Weber, M. (1954) *On Law in Economy and Society*, ed. Max Rheinstein. New York: Simon & Schuster.

Werdenich, W., Waidner, G. and Trinkl, B. (2004) 'Quasi-compulsory treatment of drug dependent offenders – a description of existing systems', *Verhaltenstherapie und Verhaltensmedizin*, 1: 71–8.

Wild, T.C. (2006) 'Social control and coercion in addiction treatment: towards evidence-based policy and practice', *Addiction*, 101(1): 40–9.

Wild, T.C., Newton-Taylor, B., Ogborne, A.C., Mann, R., Erickson, P. and Macdonald, S. (2001) 'Attitudes toward compulsory substance abuse treatment: a comparison of the public, counselors, probationers and judges' views', *Drugs: Education Prevention and Policy*, 8(1): 33–45.

Wilson, D.B., Mitchell, O. and MacKenzie, D.L. (2006) 'A systematic review of drug court effects on recidivism', *Journal of Experimental Criminology*, 2(4): 459–87.

Winehouse, M. (2009) Oral evidence to the Home Affairs Select Committee inquiry on cocaine. 20 October 2009. http://www.parliamentlive.tv/Main/Player.aspx?meetingId=4864.

Young, J. (1971) *The Drugtakers: The Social Meaning of Drug Use*. London: Paladin.

Young, J. (1999) *The Exclusive Society*. London: Sage.

9   Drug interventions in prisons

Ian Paylor, Anthea Hucklesby and Alison Wilson

Introduction

It has become something of a truism to say that the use of drugs is related to offending (see the Introduction to this volume). Despite debates over the exact nature of the link between drugs and crime, it is evident that a large proportion of prisoners are drug users. Prisons provide an opportunity to tackle offenders' drug use and in so doing reduce levels of drug-related crime which is a key government objective. The use of drugs in prison presents further issues and tensions. The Prison Service cannot be seen to condone an illegal activity. It also has a duty of care to prisoners and is the gatekeeper to all services. Drugs have far-reaching effects on prison life, leading to violence and intimidation of prisoners largely because of levels of debt and the corruption of staff (Edgar et al., 2003; HMIP, 2008). The use of drugs also raises health concerns, particularly in relation to the spread of blood-borne viruses such as HIV and hepatitis, and leads to problems when prisoners are released (Hartfree et al., 2008).

The drug problem facing the Prison Service is twofold: firstly, there are the drug users entering the system; and secondly, there is the drug use which takes places within prison establishments. Several policy areas and government departments coalesce around these two issues. To date, policy has been driven largely by the Home Office/Ministry of Justice and has focused on the problem from a criminal justice perspective, i.e. reducing levels of drug-related offending and preventing drugs entering prisons. Many would argue that this has been at the expense of pursuing health objectives, which focus primarily on harm minimization, which is the objective of many services in the community. Consequently, they argue that a similar range of services focusing primarily on harm reduction goals should be provided in prisons and in the community. While this is a laudable objective, the particular context of the prison environment may make the simple transplantation of the range of community services into prisons impracticable or inadvisable. However, the increasing involvement of the Department of Health in the provision of health services in prisons is likely to result in a greater correspondence between community and prison drug services. This is important because significant public health issues are raised in prisons. HIV infection rates in prisons are higher than in the general population, exacerbated by overcrowding, poor nutrition, limited access to health care, continued illicit drug use and unsafe injecting practices, unprotected sex and tattooing (WHO, 2004). Rates of transmission of diseases, including tuberculosis, sexually transmitted infections, hepatitis B and C, and co-infection HIV, are also high (WHO, 2008a). The Prison Reform Trust (2005) has revealed that 9 per cent of male prisoners and 11 per cent of female prisoners have hepatitis C (twenty times higher than the rate of 0.4 per cent in the general public). The HIV rate in prison for men is 15 times higher than the rate outside at 0.3 per cent (National Aids Trust 2007).

Our intention in this chapter is to offer a short discussion of the scale of the problem of drug use in prisons in terms of the numbers of drug users entering prison and an examination of levels of prison drug use. We then provide an overview of prison drug policy with a critical discussion of the bifurcatory approach of the Prison Service/National Offender Management Drug Strategy. A critical examination of mandatory drug testing is then provided before discussing various initiatives introduced into prisons in order to tackle the problem of drug use in prisons and by ex-prisoners in the community.

Drug users in prison

The total prison population has increased significantly since the mid-1990s, rising from 61,470 in June 1997 to 83,300 in May 2009 and looks set to continue on an upward trajectory (Ministry of Justice, 2009a,b). The prison population projections for England and Wales for 2009–2015 suggest that it will increase to between 83,300 and 93,900 by 2015 (Ministry of Justice, 2009c). A significant number in the prison population are serving sentences for drug offences (under the Misuse of Drugs Act 1971 and related drug legislation) and an even greater proportion for a range of *drug-related* offences (see Stevens, Chapter 8 this volume). However, drug use both inside and outside of prison is not confined to these groups.

The number of drug users entering prison is high and the prevalence of drug users in the prison population is higher than in the general population (see, for example, Liriano and Ramsey, 2003). Studies have suggested that between one-third and three-quarters of prisoners have taken illegal drugs in the year before entering prison (Bullock, 2003; Wilkinson et al., 2003; Home Office 2006; Stewart, 2009). Studies have also uncovered significant levels of polydrug use in the period prior to imprisonment and high prevalence rates for the use of heroin, cocaine, crack and amphetamines (Bullock, 2003; Stewart, 2009). Three-quarters (74 per cent) of the sample in one study were using drugs on a daily or near-daily basis prior to entering prison (Bullock, 2003). Definitions of problematic drug use vary between studies (see Hucklesby and Wincup, Chapter 2 this volume), but studies have typically found that around 55 per cent of those received into custody are problematic drug users (Bullock, 2003). Studies also suggest that around one-third of prisoners have injected prior to imprisonment (EMCDDA, 2007). It is clear that many prisoners have significant drug-using histories as well as ongoing drug problems at the time they enter the prison system.

The prevalence of drug use among those entering prison varies between groups, and different groups of drug users have differing needs, most notably young people (Cope, 2003), older prisoners (Codd, 2008), black and minority ethnic groups (Phillips, 2005) and those with coexisting psychiatric conditions (Lyon, 2008). Arguably, the problems faced by female prisoners have become more acute because of the rapid rise in the female prison population. It has increased by nearly 300 per cent between 1993 and 2009 from an average of 1,560 women in 1993 to approximately 4,300 in May 2009 (Ministry of Justice, 2009a,b). Research suggests that a greater proportion of women than men entering prison are drug users. For example, several studies suggest that as many as eight out of ten of women entering prison have drug problems (Plugge et al., 2009). Women's drug use differs from men's and tends to fall into distinct subcultures (Fazel et al., 2006; Plugge et al., 2009). For example, white women are more likely to use opiates whereas black/mixed race women are more likely to be dependent on crack (Home Office 2003; Ramsey, 2003). The UK Drug Policy Commission recognizes that gender differences exist, especially in relation to the high level of heroin and crack usage among female prisoners prior to entering prison, and particularly in relation to younger women as opposed to young men (UKDPC, 2008). Consequently, the differing needs of men and women and other groups need to be considered when providing treatment services and throughcare within prison settings (Home Office, 2003, 2007).

The large number of prisoners entering prison who are using drugs raises considerable challenges for the Prison Service, particularly in terms of providing immediate assistance to deal with the impact of withdrawal. Additional issues are raised by the use of drugs within prisons, and the extent of the problem is discussed in the following section.

Drug use in prison

Studies of the prevalence of drug use in prison suggest that large numbers of prisoners continue to use while in prison but at a lower rate than in the community (see, for example, Bullock, 2003; Strang et al., 2006). For example, Bullock's (2003) study of male prisoners found a prevalence rate of 56 per cent. Levels of drug use have been found to vary between prisons and between different types of prisoners. However, measuring drug use in prison accurately is difficult because of the potential for under-reporting. Self-report studies are the usual method of data collection, resulting in some concerns about the accuracy of their findings which are heightened in a climate where discovery of drug use has punitive consequences (for further discussion of the issues raised by their use, see Hucklesby and Wincup, Chapter 2 this volume). Less frequent use of drugs in prisons is generally attributed to lack of availability, the price of specific substances, and a period of imprisonment underpinning the motivation to reduce or cease drug use altogether (Swann and James, 1998).

Patterns of drug use in prison differ from those in the community. Studies have consistently found that cannabis is the most widely used drug in prison, followed by heroin (Edgar and O'Donnell, 1996; Bullock, 2003). Prisoners have a preference for depressants, mainly cannabis and heroin, rather than stimulants (Boys et al., 2002; Bullock, 2003). Mandatory drug testing (MDT) results confirm this finding, with detection levels of amphetamines and cocaine being very low in contrast to the prevalence and use of depressants (Boys et al., 2002). The inclination towards the use of depressant drugs results from the prison environment and their apparent ability to help prisoners cope (Boys et al., 2002). Stimulants are less well matched to a prison setting. Bullock's (2003) research provides some insight into the motivation for the types of drugs used in prison and suggests that they were used for relaxation, escapism and relief from boredom. Measuring the prevalence of the illegal use of depressants by prisoners is difficult because it is impossible to distinguish between prescribed and unprescribed use of the drugs. Several studies have indicated the frequent use of illegally used prescribed medication such as benzodiazepines and methadone (Wilkinson et al., 1998; Plugge et al., 2009). However, the extent of the problem is largely hidden because most studies do not collect relevant data or do not report them.

Studies have consistently shown that rates of injecting in prison are low, at between one and three per cent (see, for example, Bullock, 2003). This may be linked to the stigma associated with this activity or the difficulties of acquiring and keeping injecting equipment in the prison environment. Certainly, rates of injecting prior to entering prison are much higher, at between 11 and 64 per cent resulting in the prison population being a high-risk group for blood-borne diseases (WHO, 2004). Furthermore, the consequences of injecting behaviour in prison are disproportionate to its low prevalence, with this small group sharing injecting equipment raising serious concerns about the spread of HIV, hepatitis and other infectious diseases into the community after release (Bullock, 2003; Wilkinson et al., 2003; Werb et al., 2008). A study by Wilkinson et al. (2003) found that this group was also more likely to take part in other risky behaviour in prison such as unprotected sex. Needle exchange facilities or cleaning agents are not available in prisons in England and Wales despite the introduction of needle exchanges in the community and the evidence of the potential harm caused by dirty equipment. The Prison Service has taken this stance largely because it has opted for an abstinence-based approach to drug use following concerns both about being seen to condone illegal drug use and about the safety of staff and prisoners. This is despite evidence from the UK and other EU countries (Germany, Switzerland and Spain) that a harm reduction approach in the form of sterile needles and syringes can significantly reduce, if not prevent, the transmission of blood-borne diseases and infections through drug injection (UK AIDS and Human Rights Project, 2005). Furthermore, international experience allays early fears that harm reduction services would have a negative impact on prison management, security and cause high levels of drug use (WHO, 2008b).

The continuation of drug use in prisons seems relatively commonplace, albeit at a lower prevalent rate and frequency than in the community (Bullock, 2003; Wilkinson et al., 2003). Fewer prisoners leave prison using drugs than when they entered (Bullock, 2003; Wilkinson et al., 2003; Hartfree et al., 2008). But the impact of prison on patterns of drug use is contested. In particular there is little agreement about the extent to which individual prisoners begin their drug-using careers or start using particular types of drug (most notably heroin) for the first time while in prison. Studies have produced contradictory findings. For example, Boys et al. (2002) found that approximately one-quarter of lifetime heroin users reported that their first use of heroin was in prison. Other studies have suggested that the picture is more complicated. Several studies have found that drug-using careers rarely begin in prison but that a small number of ex-users and those in treatment start using again while in prison (see, for example, Wilkinson et al., 2003; Strang et al., 2006). Similarly, studies have found little evidence that prisoners take up new drugs although some experimentation may take place. Some prisoners also recommence using drugs that they had used in their lifetime but not in the period immediately before they went to prison (Wilkinson et al., 2003; Strang et al., 2006).

Having explored the extent of the problem facing the Prison Service, the next section examines the policy response.

Prison drug policy

Until the mid-1990s the Prison Service denied that there was a drug problem within the prison estate. By the mid-1990s it was forced to acknowledge the prison drug problem and developed explicit strategies to manage it (Duke, 2003). The first Prison Service drug strategy was published in 1995 (HM Prison Service, 1995). This strategy had three main aims: to reduce the supply of drugs; to reduce the demand for drugs and rehabilitate drug misusers; and to reduce the harm caused by drugs to the health of prisoners, staff and the wider community. Despite the strategy being updated, in line with the publication in 1998 and 2008 of new government drug strategies (President of the Council, 1998; HM Government, 2008) and the National Offender Management Service (NOMS) taking over responsibility for the drug strategy of the correctional services in 2005, the main aims have remained broadly the same (Hucklesby and Wilkinson, 2001; NOMS, 2008). However, the second and current NOMS strategy explicitly includes effective throughcare as the third key element of its drug strategy in prisons rather than the more broadly defined 'community harms' (in conjunction with demand and supply) (NOMS, 2008). The Prison Service originally pursued a twin-track strategy of tackling supply and demand through an overarching abstinence-based approach. However, the first NOMS drug strategy (NOMS, 2005) acknowledged that total abstinence is not feasible, recognizing the importance of harm minimization in terms of preventing HIV, overdose and so on. Explicit reference to this issue has been dropped in the current NOMS strategy.

Subsuming the Prison Service drug strategy into the NOMS strategy has resulted in a greater alignment between the core elements of the provision of drug services in prison and in the community while also recognizing the particular issues raised by the prison setting. The strategy stresses the importance of the integration between the Drug Interventions Programme (DIP) and services in prisons in line with broader objectives of end-to-end offender management and continuity of care (NOMS, 2008). Throughcare is a central theme of the new strategy in an attempt to ensure that offenders' treatment needs are met during and after their time in custody. On past experience, the challenge will be in effective implementation.

In the past, Prison Service strategies have been criticized for concentrating too heavily on supply-side policies to the detriment of treatment provision (Hucklesby and Wilkinson, 2001). Although drug policy in prisons is arguably now more balanced (see Ramsey et al., 2005), preventing drugs getting into prison is still a key element of the drug strategy. Measures which have been used to reduce supply include a range of security measures such as adapting visiting areas, installing CCTV in visiting areas, the use of drug dogs and increased penalties for being caught bringing drugs into prison. Despite all these initatives, drugs continue to get into prisons. Mobile telephones have made communication with the outside world much easier, thereby making arrangements for drug supplies simpler and erecting additional challenges to efforts to disrupt drug supplies (Ministry of Justice, 2008a). The Blakey Report (Ministry of Justice, 2008a)

on disrupting supply of illicit drugs into prison demonstrates the priority
the government continues to place on curtailing the supply of drugs to
prisons. The report points out that drugs get into prisons in a multiplicity
of ways, including via visitors, over the wall, in post and parcels, brought
in by prisoners and through corrupt staff. It suggests that it is not feasible
simply to disrupt a single supply route because drugs will come in another
way. Instead it advocates increasing the use of mixed methods, including
more searching, the use of dogs and the law to deal with visitors and staff
who attempt to smuggle drugs into prisons, disseminating good practice
between prisons and disrupting the use of mobile phones by blocking signals. Interestingly, specialized equipment has recently been introduced
to increase surveillance of prison staff following official recognition that
some officers are involved in smuggling drugs into prison.[1] According to
the Blakey Report, reducing the supply of drugs in prison will be achieved
by a three-pronged approach: increasing the use of technology, partnership working with the police and intelligence gathering.

Drug treatment services have traditionally been the poor relation to initiatives to curtail the supply of drugs into prison. However, resources have
recently been allocated to increase drug treatment services into prisons.
The government budget for 2008/09 was £25.4 million. Cynics may argue
that this has occurred because all of the major capital projects to tackle
supply issues have been completed. However, the change in emphasis is to
be welcomed. Despite positive moves on the provision of drug treatment
in prison, a review of funding arrangements undertaken by PricewaterhouseCoopers (2008) raised a number of concerns on a strategic level.
These included a lack of a coordinated overall strategy for dealing with
prisoners between the Department of Health, Ministry of Justice and the
Home Office. It concluded that there was no agreement about whether
reoffending or health outcomes took priority. It also concluded that there
was a lack of consistent organizational arrangements for funding, commissioning and performance management and delivery of services, with
no one agency having responsibility and accountability for commissioning drug services in prisons. Instead, the report uncovered a patchwork of
services provided by a range of agencies at regional and local levels. There
was also no IT strategy, resulting in problems with information sharing.
The report made a number of recommendations, one of which was to
set up a strategy group to oversee drug treatment provision in prisons.
In response, the Prison Drug Strategy Review Group is in the early stages
of being created at the time of writing. The development of this group
seems at odds with the vision of an integrated approach to drug services for offenders in prison and in the community under the auspices
of the NOMS drug strategy. It will be interesting to see how this group
develops, especially the relationship between the Drug Interventions

Programme and the provision of end-to-end management for drug-using offenders.

Mandatory drug testing

A major plank of the drug strategy is mandatory drug testing (MDT), which was introduced as a consequence of the White Paper *Tackling Drugs Together* (Home Office, 1995) and the 1995 Prison Service Drug Strategy (HM Prison Service, 1995). MDT involves a programme of mandatory urine testing for drugs which is carried out on a random sample of the prison population at regular intervals. Testing can also take place on suspicion of drug use. It was argued that MDT would provide some measure of the extent of drug taking by prisons as well as have the potential to deter prisoners from taking drugs (Edgar and O'Donnell, 1998). A positive test for MDT is a disciplinary offence and is subject to a range of punishments, including closed visits and/or loss of privileges. According to the government, the objectives of MDT are: to increase significantly the detection of those misusing drugs and to send a message to all prisoners that the risk of being caught and punished has increased; to help prisoners resist peer pressure to become involved in drugs; to identify those who need help to tackle their drug problems; and to provide accurate information about trends and patterns of drug use (Edgar and O'Donnell, 1998).

At first sight, MDT appears to have reduced levels of drug use in prison. In 1998, 18.5 per cent of drugs tests were positive (NOMS, 2008). By 2007/08 the rate of positive tests had decreased to 9.1 per cent (NOMS, 2008). This resulted in the Prison Service suggesting that levels of drug use in prison have decreased. However, such claims are subject to considerable disagreement. It is argued that MDT is not a good indicator of drug use in prison for a number of reasons: the minimum threshold for detection is quite high; use of illegal drugs is obscured by lawful/unlawful use of prescribed drugs; some drugs are undetectable; samples can be adulterated; and testing regimes are predictable and take place infrequently at weekends (Hucklesby and Wilkinson, 2001; Djemil, 2008). In addition, a recent review of national figures for the outcome rates for MDT show that although rates have fallen the figures represent 8.8 per cent of 80,000 prisoners (approximately 6,800 prisoners) who were identified as actively consuming drugs in prisons (Ministry of Justice, 2008a). These statistics need to be treated with caution because they are likely to include predominantly prisoners who are perhaps less concerned about detection of their drug use and its associated penalties.

Outcomes statistics for voluntary drug tests (VDT) are not published (Djemil, 2008). Such tests take place in order to prove that prisoners are drug-free so that they can access a range of privileges and services such as temporary release, living on a drug free wing, working in trusted parts of prisons and so on. Publishing results for these tests would provide additional information on the prevalence of drug use in prison. For some, VDT results are considered unimportant for measuring drug use in prison because they are likely to be accessed only by prisoners not using drugs and those who have never used drugs in order to gain formal recognition of abstinence from drug use and to validate a prisoner's enhanced prison status (House of Commons Welsh Affairs Committee, 2007).

There is some evidence that MDT acts as a deterrent. Edgar and O'Donnell (1998) found that over half of their sample had changed their drug use as a result of MDT, with two-fifths reporting reductions in use. Bullock (2003) found that one-third of prisoners reported that the threat of punishment deterred them from using drugs. However, MDT appears to have more of a deterrent effect on cannabis use than on other drugs and on those prisoners who are less involved in drug use (Wilkinson et al., 2003; Singleton et al., 2005). Prisoners who claimed that they were unconcerned about the punishments reported that MDT has no impact on their drug use (Bullock, 2003). However, some commentators argue that the overall consequences of MDT have been disastrous (Gore et al., 1999; Agutter, 2002).

One concern is whether MDT has led to 'switching'. Switching occurs when prisoners choose to use heroin rather than cannabis, therefore increasing the seriousness of their drug use. It is argued that this phenomenon occurs because the chances of producing positive MDT tests are greater for cannabis than for heroin. This arises because heroin can be detected in urine for only three days whereas cannabis is detected for up to three weeks (Gore et al., 1999; MacDonald and Berto, 2002). Of equal concern is the claim that the process of MDT encourages greater use of Class A drugs because prisoners, paradoxically, have an opportunity to detox prior to MDT. This arises because prisoners can blame positive MDT results on drugs such as methadone or subutex which are used as part of the detoxification programme (Djemil, 2008). Historically, standard MDT tests did not detect the use of subutex in a prison context (it is not uncommon, particularly in the community, for buprenorphine to be prescribed as subutex for opioid dependence). Until recently, the benefits of testing for buprenorphine were alleged not to outweigh the costs. However, significant rates of buprenorphine use were revealed in a recent survey and it was acknowledged that if this drug were tested for during MDT, rates would increase (Ministry of Justice, 2007). The snorting of subutex, which occurs almost exclusively in a prison setting, demonstrates the challenges posed for detecting and controlling a changing culture of drug use (George and Moreira, 2008). Testing for buprenorphine was introduced in April 2008

(Ministry of Justice, 2008b). The illicit production of tramadol, another popular synthetic opioid, is also reportedly on the increase across Europe and is currently not tested for in UK prisons, thus its use and popularity are undetectable (EMCDDA, 2008).

A third concern about MDT relates to whether it discourages prisoners from disclosing drug problems and seeking treatment for fear of potential punishment which in the past has included added days but now is more likely to involve the loss of privileges, closed visits and so on. The fourth issue is that MDT is supposed to provide a route into treatment, with prisoners who are identified as drug users through positive tests being channelled into treatment. The accusation is that this has not occurred consistently or at all partly because of a lack of treatment services within prisons. Consequently, MDT is a purely punitive measure whereas in its original incarnation it was to be a mechanism through which prisoners would receive treatment. A fifth criticism is that MDT has become not much more than an instrument for the measurement of key performance targets relating to the extent of drug use in prison. Sixthly, there has been some concern that MDT has a disproportionate impact on prisoners from minority ethnic groups (Wilkinson et al., 1998). More specifically, black prisoners are more likely to be targeted, especially for testing on suspicion and more likely to test positive than white prisoners partly because they are heavier users of cannabis (Wilkinson et al., 1998). These arguments have led to calls for MDT to be withdrawn and more constructive alternatives to monitoring and controlling drug use put in place. For example, the Scottish Prison Service has replaced MDT with Addictions Testing. The purpose of the scheme is to support prisoners' health and assist in the recovery process and their rehabilitation. Tests are conducted for three specific reasons: for health management to support clinical prescribing; risk assessment for prisoners; and to indicate the prevalence of drug use across the prison estate (Scottish Government, 2008).

The CARAT service

The CARAT (Counselling, Assessment, Referral, Advice and Throughcare) service is the main vehicle for implementing the government's drug strategy in prisons. It was established in 1999 to offer drug treatment in every prison establishment across England and Wales. CARAT schemes have a number of functions but primarily coordinate drug treatment for individual prisoners. The multi-disciplinary teams assess prisoners, create care plans and may undertake some psychosocial work through one-to-one or group work. They also refer prisoners to other services and establish throughcare links working in conjunction with resettlement teams, the

Probation Service and the Drug Interventions Programme. In essence, they undertake a case management function. They have a pivotal role with respect to the provision of throughcare for drug-using prisoners, making the necessary contacts and arrangements for their release (HM Prison Service, 2002). In addition, CARAT workers are expected to ensure that other needs, such as accommodation and employment (referred to as wraparound issues) are addressed (HM Prison Service, 2002). Prison Service documentation relating to the CARAT service sets out a number of interventions that CARAT workers must provide to ensure that drug-users are supported in the process of leaving prison and reintegrating into the community (HM Prison Service, 2002).

There has been relatively little attempt to evaluate CARAT services, and this was highlighted as a concern in PricewaterhouseCoopers' recent report (2008). Early studies suggested that the CARAT service was overwhelmed with demand and was not providing throughcare to prisoners, with little post-release work being undertaken (HMIP, 2001; Social Exclusion Unit, 2002). Coping with demand for its services has been raised consistently ever since (see, for example, HMIP, 2009). The service provided was also found to vary considerably between prisons (HMIP, 2001; Social Exclusion Unit, 2002). Later research uncovered that little liaison took place between CARAT workers and other agencies and that assistance with prisoners' broader needs, such as housing, was rarely provided (Harman and Paylor, 2005). Prisoners' views of the service were mixed, with some prisoners reporting that CARAT had provided a useful service whereas others reported that it failed to contact them, deliver on its promises of assistance or meet their needs (Harman and Paylor, 2005). More recent research is generally more positive. The PricewaterhouseCoopers review (2008) interviewed prisoners and found that they generally valued the CARAT service. Farrell and Marsden (2005) found that where prisoners had established positive links with the CARAT service during their sentence, these links proved to be most useful in addressing some of their substance misuse issues. Many staff were found to be proactive and central to providing a continuous pathway of support and a clearer route to health care, therapeutic interventions or rehabilitation services within prisons. Moreover, Farrell and Marsden (2005) found that the standard of this service varied considerably but it was strengthened by the synchronised delivery of the Drug Interventions Programme. Some problems remain. The PricewaterhouseCoopers report (2008) found that waiting times for appointments was an issue for some prisoners. Prisoners also raised concerns about the lack of privacy when discussing issues with CARAT staff arising from a general lack of space within prison establishments, which is also a problem when running courses and programmes.

The NOMS now funds CARAT services in all prisons (NOMS, 2008). Since April 2003, responsibility for health care in prisons has passed to the Department of Health. This move was undertaken with the explicit intention of improving treatment services and maximizing their impact on a prison population. The responsibility for prison health care services has since been devolved to primary care trusts which, in this role, are responsible for commissioning drug treatment in prisons (NOMS, 2008).

Drug treatment in prison

According to official sources, a range of drug treatment services are available in prisons, including detoxification, maintenance prescribing, drug rehabilitation programmes, cognitive behavioural therapy, 12 Step abstinence-based treatment programmes provided by RAPt (Rehabilitation of Addicted Prisoners Trust) (Martin et al., 2003) and therapeutic communities (Prendergast et al., 2002; Digiusto et al., 2006; Gossop, 2006a). Shorter programmes are also available for short sentence (under 12 months) and remand prisoners. Another important component of demand-side approaches is the provision of voluntary testing which is used to demonstrate eligibility for certain procedures and services such as drug-free wings, enhanced status leading to greater access to services and facilitates within prisons, temporary leave and so on.

Not all programmes are available in every prison although the government has made a commitment to provide basic drug treatment services in every prison by 2011 (NOMS, 2008). However, such measures are threatened by current levels of overcrowding in the system, which are projected to increase still further (Ministry of Justice, 2009c). Demand for drug treatment services already outstrips supply, but overcrowding raises additional issues in relation to continuity of service and threatens individual programmes because of staff shortages, lack of space and so forth (Ministry of Justice, 2009b). A recent review of services painted a picture of patchy and uncoordinated provision of drug services in prisons and gaps in provision (PricewaterhouseCoopers, 2008). It also highlighted a lack of continuity and consistency in service provision within and between prisons, resulting in disruptions in or withdrawal of services to prisoners and a lack of effective targeting of services. A third issue was that quantity appeared to have taken precedence over quality and effectiveness largely as a result of a drive to meet targets rather than to ensure that appropriate treatments were provided.

The PricewaterhouseCoopers report (2008) raised concerns about whether the services provided in prisons were appropriate. It noted that there was a lack of evidence about the effectiveness of many of the services provided in prisons. They were particularly sceptical about the lack of evidence in relation to psychosocial interventions.[2] They suggested that resources were currently being channelled into services with little or no evidence of effectiveness, at the expense of services where there is clear evidence of success. The report stated that there was growing evidence that the 'one-size-fits-all' approach to treatment was less effective than an approach which is tailored to individual needs. Of more concern was the tendency for treatment to be based on what is available in particular prisons rather than on individual prisoners' needs (PricewaterhouseCoopers, 2008).

The PricewaterhouseCoopers review also criticized the concentration of services on dealing with one type of drug, mainly heroin. This is because most drug users use more than one drug and research suggests that better outcomes are achieved when treatment is focused on polydrug use. In reality, detoxification services are the most widespread, with 25 per cent of prisoners in the UK estimated to be receiving some form of detoxification at any one time (Farrell and Marsden, 2005). However, evidence suggests that detoxification on its own, and in particular coerced detoxification, is not an effective treatment option (Gossop, 2006b). Detoxification is more likely to succeed when it is run in conjunction with psychosocial interventions, yet this was often not the service provided. There is also some evidence that detoxification services are poorly managed, which resulted in a recent £1.35 million out-of-court settlement by the Home Office to prisoners – the case citing an appalling record of clinical negligence (Daly, 2007). A further problem with the provision of detoxification services is the lack of uniformity in the type and range of detoxification programmes available, the drugs used (methadone, dihydrocodeine (DF118), subutex and lofexidine detoxification) and the length of programme on offer to prisoners (between five and 14 days) (Farrell and Marsden, 2005).

There is evidence that maintenance prescribing (for opioid users) for offenders is effective in terms of producing positive outcomes around drug-taking behaviour and criminal activity (NTA, 2004; Holloway et al., 2005; Roberts et al., 2007). However, the provision of a methadone maintenance treatment programme is patchy, particularly for prisoners on remand or serving short sentences. According to one study the treatment was obtainable only on the presentation of evidence of prior use for this group (for example, a prescription) and was not available for prisoners wanting to achieve stability for the first time (Farrell and Marsden, 2005). Continuing a methadone maintenance programme after release was hampered by a lack of community drug treatment services in prisoners' home area. Provision of community-based substance misuse services on prisoners' release was variable, with some prisoners reporting good access whereas others faced lengthy delays and long waiting lists (Farrell and Marsden, 2005).

Drug treatment services concentrate on providing support for opiate users despite growing evidence that the popular use of other illicit substances, for instance, crack, is on the increase and contributes to a range of social problems, including crime (Jones et al., 2007). Other pharmacological interventions in prisons (for cocaine/amphetamine users) have been little utilized and there is limited evidence that these have been found to be effective but only when combined with psychosocial interventions (Roberts et al., 2007). However, the provision of psychosocial interventions generally in prison is problematic. Martin and Player's (2000) study of the intensive long duration RAPt programme offers some evidence of effectiveness (see also Martin et al., 2003), but there is little evidence that these methods, in particular the 28-day psychosocial intervention currently recommended under the CARAT service for problem drug users, is effective (see McSweeney et al., 2008, for details of the various types and numbers of prisoners undertaking all interventions within the prison estate). A further issue is that the treatment offered in prison falls short of providing support for broader issues (so-called wraparound issues) such as accommodation and employment (McSweeney et al., 2008). However, such issues often fall within the remit of other services providers such as offender managers and generic resettlement services. Indeed, research suggests that there is a lack of coordination and information exchange between drug service providers and generic resettlement services leading to overlaps and gaps in services (Hucklesby and Wincup, 2005, 2007).

Recently, the Integrated Drug Treatment System (IDTS) has been rolled out partially across the prison estate (NOMS, 2008). With the National Treatment Agency at the helm, the IDTS framework is designed to be a joint venture between the Ministry of Justice and Department of Health to improve treatment options by offering a broader range of clinical response to substance misuse, clinical management, psychosocial services, and the general volume and quality of substance use services in prison (NTA, 2008a). The implementation of IDTS is primarily in recognition of the increasing levels of illicit drug use in prisons, the vulnerability of drug-using prisoners to suicide and self-harm, and particularly of drug-related deaths upon release from custody due to opiate overdose. A key objective of IDTS is to ensure that there is sufficient integration between clinical and CARAT services, and to make certain that the pathway of care is a transparent system that incorporates 'end-to-end' care unequivocally, from the community, during imprisonment and transfer from one prison to another, and post release (NTA, 2008b). It is envisaged that this integrated service approach to treatment and support will achieve closure on the evident gaps between services and provide prisoners with a seam-less pathway of care across the criminal justice system and other related providers of care and support. It further serves to reduce the numbers of prisoners released unplanned from prison; an event which currently gives rise to the perception that some prison drug treatment services are disor-ganized and haphazard in their approach to the management of prisoner health care and related substance use issues.

The introduction of IDTS should positively impact upon the range of treatment available to prisoners, particularly methadone maintenance programmes, although teething problems with implementation have been identified (see HMIP, 2009). What is not clear is the extent to which the IDTS framework will adequately redress the balance of the current treatment bias towards opiate dependence against the evidence base for treating rapidly increasing stimulant use, particularly for crack and co-caine (Harocopos et al., 2003; EMCDDA, 2007; McSweeney et al., 2008). It also unclear whether IDTS will usher in more harm minimization mea-sures such as needle distribution provision, access to syringes and con-doms in conjunction with consistent drug-dependence treatment and substitute treatment (methadone and subutex options). In this respect, the Prison Service differs from community drugs agencies, resulting in different services being available in prisons and in the community.

Recently there has been considerable investment in prison drug treat-ment provision. However, there remains considerable scope for improving access to a much wider range of treatment options and harm reduction strategies. Initiatives to ensure greater equity and continuity of care, espe-cially to the large number of short-term prisoners processed by the Prison Service, are also required (Dolan et al., 2007; McSweeney et al., 2008). Prison provides an opportunity for prisoners to reduce their drug use and for them to be offered drug treatment. Coupled with the reduced avail-ability of drugs in prisons, it results in some prisoners desisting from drug use whereas others reduce or change their use while incarcerated. But these positive outcomes can and do easily unravel once prisoners are re-leased (Social Exclusion Unit, 2002; Hucklesby and Wincup, 2005, 2007; Hartfree et al., 2008). The following section discusses some of the issues raised when prisoners are released back into the community.

Throughcare

The importance of the transition from custody back to the community for drug users has been recognized increasingly over recent years, particularly in view of current drug policy which aims to exploit the opportunity provided by detention in custody to channel drug users into appropriate treatment interventions. Throughcare ensures that treatment provision that was started in prison continues through the prison gate and into the community. The risk is that any gains from treatment received in prison are lost after release (Kothari et al., 2002). The role of throughcare in successful outcomes has been highlighted in research findings in the UK (Hamer, 2002) and in the USA (Inciardi et al., 1997).

The transition from the highly structured environment of a prison, back into the relative freedom of community life, can be extremely difficult for individuals with a propensity to use drugs (Kothari et al., 2002; Hartfree et al., 2008). The risk of relapse or overdose on release from prison is high (ACMD, 2000). Harman and Paylor's (2004, 2005) research (utilizing follow-up interviews soon after prisoners had been released) found that for those who had achieved a period of abstinence in prison, the process of leaving prison and remaining drug free was extremely difficult. Burrows et al. (2001) report that of the 112 individuals in their research who completed a follow-up questionnaire four months after their release from prison, 86 per cent reported that they had used drugs since release, with approximately half indicating that they were using heroin on a daily basis. Similarly, all but one of the ex-prisoners followed up by Hartfree et al. (2008) who received no support with their drug use were using drugs when they were interviewed after leaving prison. A more positive picture emerged for those who had accessed drug support since leaving prison. One issue with following up prisoners in the community is that the most stable prisoners are those who are most likely to respond, skewing findings towards more successful outcomes, that is, drug free, accommodated and employed, individuals (Wincup and Hucklesby, 2007).

Evidence indicates that drug-related deaths often occur in the immediate period after release. For example, Singleton et al. (2003) investigated drug-related mortality in a sample of 12,483 newly released prisoners. They found that 79 out of 137 deaths were drug related. They concluded that prisoners were forty times more likely to die in the week immediately following release than the general population. High levels of mortality are linked to overdoses as a result of reduced levels of tolerance because of less potent drugs being available in prison, bingeing upon release and the recommencement of injecting (Seaman et al., 1998; Shewan et al., 2000). Several factors appear to increase the risk of death, including injecting, the use of alcohol and polydrug use (Gossop et al., 2002; Oliver and Keen, 2003; Ghodse et al., 2006). White males under the age of 45 are most at risk (Ghodse et al., 2006), although the Corston Report (Home Office, 2007) highlighted the high rate of accidental drug-related overdose in the first two weeks of release for women. It is probable that drug-related deaths of ex-prisoners are under-recorded because of problems with definitions, untangling the contributions of immediate (accidental, intentional or undetermined poisoning) and long-term underlying causes (including illness) and a lack of toxicology results.

Despite all the evidence pointing to its importance, throughcare services have historically been neglected. They have been called the 'Cinderella service' largely because responsibility for this issue does not fall to any single agency or post holder (Burrows et al., 2001). To fill this gap a number of statutory and voluntary agencies established throughcare initiatives, to try to bridge the gap between custody and the community. These developments were largely on an ad hoc, agency-by-agency basis rather than as part of a strategic plan (Social Exclusion Unit, 2002). The result has been a patchwork of service arrangements, with areas of overlap and gaps in service provision. The CARAT service took over responsibility for this area. The difficulties experienced by prisoners on release suggest that CARAT services are not currently bridging the gap between prison and the community (see, for example, Harman and Paylor, 2004, 2005; Hucklesby and Wincup, 2005, 2007; Hartfree et al., 2008).

A significant proportion of drug services in prison and in the community continue to be provided by non-statutory agencies (NOMS, 2008). A large number of agencies are involved in prisoners' release, leading to complicated multi-agency arrangements. Significant investment has been made in resettlement services, recently evidenced by the publication of several key government documents (for example, *National Reoffending Action Plan* (Home Office, 2004)). A number of specialist resettlement services have been set up alongside existing provisions within prisons which may include Jobcentre Plus, housing advice units and pre-release courses, in addition to support and advice from prison staff or offender managers based in prison and in the community (see Hucklesby and Hagley-Dickinson, 2007, for further discussion). Arguably, the growing patch work of services has increased the potential for overlaps and gaps in service provision and for agencies to avoid their responsibilities, as Burrows et al. (2001: 43) highlight: 'The continuing threat to drugs throughcare will be that it remains a shared responsibility, but where – in the absence of any accountability – each agency can argue "it's not my baby"'.

In this multi-agency context, effective partnership working arrangements are vital to ensure that drug users leaving prison are afforded the support they require. In reality, partnerships are difficult and are hindered by differences in organizational values and objectives and inadequate communication (Smith et al., 1993; Cross, 1997; Gibbs, 1999; Harman and Paylor, 2002). One of the key ingredients of successful partnership working is clarity in the roles of the different agencies involved, with transparent channels of responsibility and accountability (Gibbs, 2001). Harman and Paylor (2004, 2005) identified a lack of clarity among professionals about the roles and responsibilities of other individuals and services, which had created difficulties for CARAT workers and resulted in frustration with other agencies. This had also resulted in inconsistencies in throughcare provision and a highly variable service for drug users.

Difficulties also arose as a result of the divergent values and objectives of the agencies involved in throughcare provision. While CARAT workers and drug workers in community agencies are primarily concerned with responding to the needs of drug users, offender managers have a remit to assess and manage risk, and prison officers a remit to contain prisoners and maintain a secure environment. Although, in reality, agencies have multiple and overlapping functions, there is often a difference of opinion about the priority that should be accorded to each (Edmunds et al., 1999). Harman and Paylor (2004, 2005) identified that CARAT workers and workers from other community agencies sometimes cut across their statutory duties, making arrangements for a prisoner post release that they felt to be inappropriate. For instance, arranging accommodation for offenders that was too near a victim's home or which they judged to be unsuitable in view of the offender's personal history. This example illustrates the different priorities and values which drug workers and probation officers have; the former are concerned primarily with meeting the needs of drug users in order to minimize the risk of relapse, while the latter focus principally on risk management, control of the offender and protection of the public. In the absence of effective liaison between agencies, differences in organizational values and objectives can result in frustration with workers from disparate professional disciplines (Cross, 1997). Evaluations of generic resettlement initiatives have also identified that CARAT workers often work in isolation and are reluctant to share information with other statutory and voluntary organizations or to work jointly with other individuals or organizations to ease prisoners' transition back into the community (Hucklesby and Wincup, 2005, 2007). Gaps and overlaps were the result, as well as differing views about the most appropriate services to provide to prisoners.

The importance of effective liaison between partnership agencies has repeatedly been highlighted as vital to successful joint working (Cross, 1997; Rumgay and Cowan, 1998). Indeed, Gibbs (2001) identifies the need for a substantive relational basis for inter-agency work, with constant dialogue between partner agencies (not just when things go wrong), empathy with other workers' objectives and values, a willingness to address areas of conflict and genuine opportunities for multi-agency participation and consultation. Studies reveal that communication between agencies is often experienced as inadequate, resulting in feelings of non-cooperation between workers from different agencies (Harman and Paylor, 2004, 2005; Hucklesby and Wincup, 2005, 2007).

Turnbull et al. (2000) suggest that there is a need for clarity of roles and responsibilities between agencies which also enables collaboration and joint working to take place. There are, however, few identified forums for joint care planning between drug users and relevant agencies. The key mechanism for joint consultation is the sentence planning process, but this is available only to adult prisoners sentenced to 12 months or more and has itself been the subject to criticism (HMIP, 2001). Significantly this excludes large numbers of drug users, who are frequently repeat offenders serving short-term prison sentences. This gap in provision has been officially recognized in some areas, with short-term prisoners leaving custody being the primary target group of the Integrated Offender Management pioneer site in West Yorkshire (West Yorkshire Police, 2009). The problems with the existing multi-agency approach to throughcare provision for drug users are predominantly the result of ineffective partnership working arrangements between the agencies involved and have been aggravated by the creation of the CARAT service and evolving service arrangements, in the absence of an overarching strategic plan (PricewaterhouseCoopers, 2008).

As with generic resettlement services, overcrowding and transfers between prisons can disrupt work done to prepare for release (see Hucklesby and Hagley-Dickinson, 2007). Throughcare arrangements are made more difficult when prisoners are returning to areas which are not local to the prison. In such cases, CARAT workers are likely to be unfamiliar with the services available in the resettlement area, potentially resulting in additional work, links being broken or not taken up, and referrals to inappropriate services. 'Home' community drugs services may not view prisoners returning from prison as a priority, especially when waiting lists may be lengthy. The greater coordination promised between CARAT services and DIP in the latest NOMS drug strategy should assist with these logistical issues. Other problems, such as long waiting lists for treatment and the lack of service provision for certain types of drug user, are likely to remain.

Conclusion

This chapter has demonstrated the serious drug problems that many prisoners have on entering prison; that considerable numbers of prisoners continue to use drugs while incarcerated; and that many prisoners return to previous drug-using behaviour when released. Prison provides an opportunity for inventions to be put in place to assist prisoners to desist or reduce their drug use. Many prisoners also view their time in custody as a time when they can address their drug use (Hartfree et al., 2008). Reducing drug use by prisoners has many benefits. In the short term it will reduce drug-related violence and debt problems within the prison estate, making prisons safer places and easing management problems. In the long term it may reduce the level of offending and the transmission of infectious diseases between prisoners and into the wider community. It is also a crucial step in making prisoners ready to start building a crime-free life, including finding stable accommodation and employment (Hartfree et al., 2008).

The controversial issue is how one achieves the goal of reducing drug use by prisoners and ensuring that drug-using careers are not rekindled upon release. At a strategic level, criminal justice rather than health goals dominate. In line with this, the Prison Service has adopted an abstinence-based approach. It has attempted to stop drugs being used in prison by preventing them entering prison, using MDT to detect drug use and punish prisoners, and providing drug treatment services and drug-free wings. This approach is at odds with the ethos of many community-based drugs agencies which prioritize health goals, working mainly on a model of harm minimization. In doing so they accept that drug use goes on and put their efforts into reducing the harm caused by drug use through the provision of clean 'works', education and so on. Some commentators suggest that this approach should be adopted by the Prison Service (see, for example, MacDonald and Berto, 2002). But it is not clear how easily or effectively this could be done. Furthermore, it does not recognize the particular circumstances present in prisons which do not apply in the community and which may militate against a harm minimization approach being fully adopted. Some elements of the harm minimization approach, such as the provision of condoms and cleaning agents, could be implemented with relatively few consequences except perhaps a public and media outcry. Other ingredients of this approach, such as needle exchanges, are more controversial and pose logistical and ethical dilemmas for the Prison Service. The disjuncture between the ethos of the Prison Service and community drugs services raises particular challenges in relation to the provision of effective throughcare for drug-using prisoners and joint working more generally.

In common with other areas of the criminal justice system there has been considerable investment in new initiatives and drug treatment services in the prison estate. There is little evidence of their effectiveness (see, for example, Hartfree et al., 2008; PricewaterhouseCoopers, 2008). Research and evaluation of the initiatives have been largely absent. The developments do not appear to have been evidence based (see also Turnbull and Skinns, Chapter 4 this volume). What little research has been undertaken points to the considerable challenges of implementing policies to deal with drug use in prison, and these challenges are heightened by the current level of the prison population. Nevertheless, the benefits of reducing drug use by prisoners and ensuring that any gains are not lost on return to the community are considerable. For this reason it is important to continue to develop coherent, effective policies to ensure that the serious threat to the long-term health and welfare of prisoners and the wider community is minimized.

Notes

1. See http://www.justice.gov.uk/news/announcement130709b.htm.
2. There are three main types of psychosocial intervention utilized in prisons which come under the umbrella of intensive drug treatment programmes (DTPs). There are cognitive behavioural therapy, therapeutic communities and 12 Step programmes, all of which encompass a range of interventions to address drug use.

References

Advisory Council on the Misuse of Drugs (ACMD) (2000) *Reducing Drug Related Deaths*. London: The Stationery Office.

Agutter, P. (2002) 'The real cost of drug testing in prisons', *Prison Report*, 58: 26–8.

Boys, A., Farrell, M., Bebbington, P., Brugha, T., Coid, J., Jenkins, R., Lewis, G., Marsden, J., Meltzer, H., Singleton, N. and Taylor, C. (2002) 'Drug use and initiation in prison: results from a national prison survey in England and Wales', *Addiction*, 97(12): 1555–60.

Bullock, T. (2003) 'Changing levels of drug use before, during and after imprisonment', in M. Ramsay (ed.) *Prisoners' Drug Use and Treatment: Seven Research Studies*, Home Office Research Study 267. London: Home Office.

Burrows, J., Clarke, A., Davison, T., Tarling, R. and Webb, S. (2001) *The Nature and Effectiveness of Drugs Throughcare for Released Prisoners*, Research Findings 109. London, Home Office.

Codd, H. (2008) *In the Shadow of Prison: Families, Imprisonment and Criminal Justice*. Cullompton: Willan Publishing.

Cope, N. (2003) '"It's no time or high time": young offenders' experiences of time and drug use in prison', *Howard Journal of Criminal Justice*, 42(2): 158–75.

Cross, B. (1997) 'Partnership in practice: the experience of two probation services', *Howard Journal of Criminal Justice*, 36(1): 62–79.

Daly, M. (2007) 'Turkey shoot', *DrugLink*, 22(1): 3.

Digiusto, E., Shakeshaft, A.P., Ritter, A., Mattick, R.P., White, J., Lintzeris, N., Bell, J., Saunders, J.B. and NEPOD Research Group (2006) 'Effects of pharmacotherapies for opiod dependence on participants' criminal behaviour and expenditure on illicit drugs: an Australian national evaluation (NEPOD)', *Australian and New Zealand Journal of Criminology*, 39(2): 171–89.

Djemil, H. (2008) 'Revealed: how drugs trade is taking hold of British prisons', *The Observer*, Focus: Special Investigation, 8 June.

Dolan, K., Khoel, E.M., Brantari, C. and Stevens, A. (2007) *Prison and Drugs: A Global Review of Incarceration*, Drug Use and Drug Services Report 12. Oxford: Beckley Foundation.

Duke, K. (2003) *Drugs, Prison and Policy Making*. London: Palgrave Macmillan.

Edgar, K. and O'Donnell, I. (1998) *Mandatory Drug Testing in Prisons: The Relationship between MDT and the Level and Nature of Drug Misuse*, Home Office Research Study 189. London: Home Office.

Edgar, K., O'Donnell, I. and Martin, C. (2003) *Prison Violence: The Dynamics of Conflict, Fear and Power*. Cullompton: Willan Publishing.

Edmunds, M., Hough, M., Turnbull, P.J. and May, T. (1999) *Doing Justice to Treatment: Referring Offenders to Drug Services*, DPAS Paper 2. London: Home Office.

European Monitoring Centre for Drugs and Drug Addiction (EMCDDA) (2007) *Annual Report on the State of the Drugs Problem in Europe*. Lisbon: EMCDDA. http://www.emcdda.europa.eu/.

European Monitoring Centre for Drugs and Drug Addiction (EMCDDA) (2008) *Annual Report 2008: Opioids still at Heart of Europe's Drug Phenomenon*. Lisbon: EMCDDA. http://www.emcdda.europa.eu/.

Farrell, M. and Marsden, J. (2005) *Drug-Related Mortality among Newly Released Offenders 1998–2000*, Home Office Online Report 40/05. London: Home Office.

Fazel, S., Bains, P. and Doll, H. (2006) 'Systematic review of substance abuse and dependence in prisoners', *Addiction*, 101(2): 181–91.

George, S. and Moreira, K. (2008) 'Subutex snorters: a case series', *Journal of Substance Use*, 13(2): 131–7.

Ghodse, H., Corkery, J., Oyefeso, A., Schifano, F., Tonia, T. and Annan, J. (2006) *Drug Related Deaths in the UK: Annual Report 2006*. London: International Centre for Drug Policy.

Gibbs, A. (1999) 'The forgotten voice: Probation Service users and partnerships', *Howard Journal of Criminal Justice*, 38(3): 283–99.

Gibbs, A. (2001) 'Partnerships between the Probation Service and voluntary sector organizations', *British Journal of Criminology*, 31(1): 15–18.

Gore, S.M., Bird, A.G. and Cassidy, J. (1999) 'Prisoner's views about the drugs problem in prisons, and the new Prison Service drug strategy', *Communicable Diseases and Public Health*, 2(3): 196–7.

Gossop M. (2006a) 'Methadone: is it enough?' *Heroin Addiction and Related Clinical Problems*, 8(4): 53–64.

Gossop, M. (2006b) *Treating Drug Misuse Problems: Evidence of Effectiveness*. London: National Treatment Agency.

Gossop, M., Stewart, D., Treacy, S. and Marsden, J. (2002) 'A prospective study of mortality among drug misusers during a 4-year period after seeking treatment', *Addiction*, 97(1): 39–47.

Hamer, S. (2002) 'It takes two to tango', *Criminal Justice Matters*, 47: 14–15.

Harman, K. and Paylor, I. (2002) 'A shift in strategy', *Criminal Justice Matters*, 47: 8–9.

Harman, K. and Paylor, I. (2004) '"Throughcare" for drug-using prisoners in Britain: a clinical report', *Journal of Offender Rehabilitation*, 40(1/2): 61–83.

Harman, K. and Paylor, I. (2005) 'An evaluation of the CARAT initiative', *Howard Journal of Criminal Justice*, 44(4): 357–73.

Harocopos, A., Dennis, D., Turnbull, P.J., Parsons, J. and Hough, M. (2003) *On the Rocks: A Follow-up Study of Crack Users in London*. London: South Bank University.

Hartfree, Y., Dearden, C. and Pound, E. (2008) *High Hopes: Supporting Ex-prisoners in their Lives after Prison*, Research Report 509. London: Dept of Work and Pensions.

Her Majesty's Chief Inspector of Prisons and Probation (HMIP) (2001) *Through the Prison Gate: A Joint Thematic Review*. London: Home Office.

Her Majesty's Chief Inspector of Prisons and Probation (HMIP) (2008) *Annual Report 2007–8*. London: House of Commons.

Her Majesty's Chief Inspector of Prisons and Probation (HMIP) (2009) *Annual Report 2008–9*. London: House of Commons.

HM Government (2008) *Drugs: Protecting Families and Communities. The 2008 Drug Strategy*. London: Home Office.

HM Prison Service (1995) *Drug Misuse in Prison*. London: HMSO.

HM Prison Service (1998) *Tackling Drugs in Prison: The Prison Service Drug Strategy*; London: HMSO.

HM Prison Service (2002) *Counselling, Assessment, Referral, Advice and Throughcare Services*, Prison Service Order 3630. London: HM Prison Service.

HM Prison Service (2007) *Annual Report and Accounts 2006–2007*. London: The Stationery Office.

Holloway, K., Bennett, T. and Farringdon, D. (2005) *The Effectiveness of Criminal Justice and Treatment Services in Reducing Drug-Related Crime: A Systematic Review*, Home Office Online Report 26/05. London: Home Office.

Home Office (1995) *Tackling Drugs Together: A Strategy for England 1995–1998*, Cmd 2846. London: HMSO.

Home Office (2003) *The Substance Misuse Treatment Needs of Minority Prisoner Groups: Women, Young Offenders and Ethnic Minorities*, Development and Practice Report 8. London: Home Office

Home Office (2004) *National Reducing Reoffending Action Plan*. London: Home Office.

Home Office (2006) Home Office FOI Release 4631, 6 December 2006.

Home Office (2007) *A Review of Women with Particular Vulnerabilities in the Criminal Justice System* (Corston Report). London: Home office.

House of Commons Welsh Affairs Committee (2007) *Welsh Prisoners in the Prison Estate*, Third Report of Session 2006–07. London: HMSO.

Hucklesby, A. and Hagley-Dickinson, L. (eds) (2007) *Prisoner Resettlement: Policy and Practice*. Cullompton: Willan Publishing.

Hucklesby, A. and Wilkinson, C. (2001) 'Drug misuse in prison: some comments on the Prison Service drug strategy', *Howard Journal of Criminal Justice*, 40(4): 347–63.

Hucklesby, A. and Wincup, E. (2005) *Connect: An Evaluation of a Resettlement Initiative: Report to National Probation Service* (West Mercia Probation Area) (unpublished).

Hucklesby, A and Wincup, E. (2007) *The Pyramid Project: Final Report to Depaul Trust and Nacro* (unpublished).

Inciardi, J., Martin, S., Butzin, C., Hooper, R. and Harrison, L. (1997) 'An effective model of prison-based treatment for drug-involved offenders', *Journal of Drug Issues*, 27(2): 261–78.

Jones, A., Weston, S., Moody, A., Millar, T., Dollin, L., Anderson, T. and Donmall, M. (2007) *The Drug Treatment Outcomes Research Study (DTORS): Baseline Report*. Home Office Research Report 3. London: Home Office.

Kothari, G., Marsden, J. and Strang, J. (2002) 'Opportunities and obstacles for effective treatment of drug misusers in the criminal justice system in England and Wales', *British Journal of Criminology*, 42(2): 412–32.

Liriano, S. and Ramsay, M. (2003) 'Prisoners' drug use before prison and the links with crime', in M. Ramsay (ed.) *Prisoners' Drug Use and Treatment: Seven Research Studies*, Home Office Research Study 267. London: Home Office.

Lyon, J. (2008) 'State of mind', *Prison Report*, 72 (Winter): 9–10.

MacDonald, M. and Berto, D. (2002) 'Harm reduction in Italian and UK prisons: the gap between policy and implementation for HIV and Drugs'. Paper presented at the 13th Annual Conference on the Reduction of Drug Related Harm, Ljubljana, Slovenia, 3–7 March.

Martin, C. and Player, E. (2000) *Drug Treatment in Prison: An Evaluation of the RAPt Treatment Programme*. Winchester: Waterside Press.

Martin, C. Player, E. and Liriano, S. (2003) 'Results of evaluations of the RAPt drug treatment programme', in M. Ramsay (ed.) *Prisoners' Drug Use and Treatment: Seven Research Studies*, Home Office Research Study 267. London: Home Office.

McSweeney, T., Turnbull, P.J. and Hough, M. (2008) *The Treatment and Supervision of Drug Dependent Offenders: A Review of the Literature prepared for the UK Drug Policy Commission*. London: UK Drug Policy Commission.

Ministry of Justice, (2007) *A Survey of Buprenorphine Misuse in Prisons*. London: Ministry of Justice, Prisons Drug Strategy Team Interventions and Substance Abuse Unit.

Ministry of Justice (2008a) *Disrupting the Supply of Illicit Drugs into Prisons. A Report for the Director General of National Offender Management Service* (Blakey Report). London: Ministry of Justice.

Ministry of Justice (2008b) 'Minister announces latest move in the fight against drugs in prisons', News Release, 13 March. http://www.justice.gov.uk/news/newsrelease130308a.htm (accessed 9 January 2009).

Ministry of Justice (2009a) *Population in Custody: Monthly Tables May 2009 England and Wales.* http://www.justice.gov.uk/publications/docs/population-in-custody-05-2009.pdf.

Ministry of Justice (2009b) *Offender Management Caseload Statistics England and Wales 2008.* London: Ministry of Justice.

Ministry of Justice (2009c) *Prison Population Projections 2009–2015.* http://www.justice.gov.uk/publications/docs/stats-prison-population-projections-2009-2015.pdf.

National Aids Trust (2007) *HIV and Hepatitis in UK Prisons: Addressing Prisoners' Healthcare Needs. A Report by the Prison Reform Trust and the National AIDS Trust.* http://www.nat.org.uk/document/105 (accessed 1 November 2007).

National Offender Management Service (NOMS) (2005) *Strategy for the Management and Treatment of Problematic Drug Users with the Correctional Services.* London: Home Office.

National Offender Management Service (NOMS) (2008) *The National Offender Management Service Drug Strategy 2008–2011.* London: Ministry of Justice.

National Treatment Agency (NTA) (2004) *More than just Methadone: Enhancing Outcomes of MMT with Counselling and other Psychosocial and Ancillary Services.* London: NTA.

National Treatment Agency (NTA) (2008a) *Integrated Drug Treatment System in Prisons (IDTS).* http://www.nta.nhs.uk/areas/criminal_justice/integrated_drug_treatment_system_in_prisons(IDTS).aspx (accessed 7 January 2009).

National Treatment Agency (NTA) (2008b) *IDTS Commissioning Guidance: Sample Clinical Service Specification for Clinical Management of Drug Dependence in the Adult Prison Setting.* http://areas/criminal_justice/docs/idts/IDTS_sample_clinical_service_specification_v6.doc (accessed 8 January 2009).

Oliver, P. and Keen, J. (2003) 'Concomitant drugs of misuse and drug using behaviours associated with fatal opiate-related poisonings in Sheffield, UK, 1997–2000', *Addictions*, 98(2): 191–7.

Phillips, T. (2005) Guest editorial, *Prison Report*, 67: 3–4.

Plugge, E., Yudkin, P. and Douglas, N. (2009) 'Changes in women's use of illicit drugs following imprisonment', *Addiction*, 104(2): 215–22.

Prendergast, M.L., Podus, D., Chang, E. and Urada, D. (2002) 'The effectiveness of drug abuse treatment: a meta-analysis of comparison group studies', *Drug and Alcohol Dependence*, 67(1): 53–72.

President of the Council (1998) *Building a Better Britain: The Government's Ten-Year Strategy for Tackling Drug's Misuse*, Cm 3945. London: HMSO.

PricewaterhouseCoopers (2008) *Review of Prison-Based Drug Treatment Funding. Report to the Department of Health and Ministry of Justice.* London: Ministry of Justice.

Prison Reform Trust (2005) *Prison Failing on HIV and Hepatitis C.* London: Prison Reform Trust.

Ramsay, M. (ed.) (2003) *Prisoner' Drug Use and Treatment: Seven Research Studies*, Home Office Research Study 267. London: Home Office.

Ramsay, M., Bullock, T. and Niven, S. (2005) 'The Prison Service Drug Strategy: the extent to which prisoners need and receive treatment', *Howard Journal of Criminal Justice*, 44(3): 269–85.

Roberts, A., Hayes, A., Carlisle, J. and Shaw, J. (2007) *Review of Drug and Alcohol Treatments in Prison and Community Settings: A Systematic Review Conducted on Behalf of the Prison Health Research Network*. Manchester: University of Manchester.

Rumgay, J. and Cowan, S. (1998), 'Pitfalls and prospects in partnership: probation programmes for substance misusing offenders', *Howard Journal of Criminal Justice*, 37(2): 124–36.

Scottish Government (2008) *Drug Misuse Statistics Scotland*. Edinburgh: Scottish Government. http://www.drugmisuse.isdscotland.org/publications/abstracts/isdbull.htm.

Seaman, S., Brettle, R. and Gore, S. (1998) 'Mortality from overdose among injecting drug users recently released from prison: database linkage study', *British Medical Journal*, 316(7156): 426–8.

Shewan, D., Hammersley, R., Oliver, J. and Macpherson, S. (2000) 'Fatal drug overdose after liberation from prison: a retrospective study of female ex-prisoners from Strathclyde region (Scotland)', *Addiction Research*, 8(3): 267–78.

Singleton, N., Pendry, E., Simpson, T., Goddard, E., Farrell, M., Marsden, J. and Taylor, C. (2003) *Drug-Related Mortality amongst Newly Released Offenders*, Research Findings 187. London: Home Office.

Singleton, N., Pendry, E., Simpson, T., Goddard, E., Farrell, M., Marsden, J. and Taylor, C. (2005) *The Impact of Mandatory Drug Testing in Prisons*, Home Office Online Report 03/05. London: Home Office.

Smith, D., Paylor, I. and Mitchell, P. (1993) 'Partnerships between the independent sector and the Probation Service', *Howard Journal of Criminal Justice*, 32(1): 25–39.

Social Exclusion Unit (2002) *Reducing Re-offending by Ex-prisoners*. London: Social Exclusion Unit.

Stewart, D. (2009) 'Drug use and perceived treatment need among newly sentenced prisoners in England and Wales', *Addiction*, 104(2): 243–7.

Strang, J., Gossop, M., Heuston, J., Green, J., Whitely, C. and Maden, A. (2006) 'Persistence of drug use during imprisonment: relationship of drug type, recency of use and severity of dependence to use of heroin, cocaine and amphetamine in prison', *Addiction*, 101(8): 1125–32.

Swann, R. and James, P. (1998) 'The effect of the prison environment upon inmate drug taking behaviour', *Howard Journal of Criminal Justice*, 37(3): 252–65.

Turnbull, P.J., McSweeney, T., Webster, R., Edmunds, M. and Hough, M. (2000) *Drug Treatment and Testing Orders: Final Evaluation Report*, Home Office Research Study 212. London: Home Office.

UK AIDS and Human Rights Project (2005) *Prisoner's Rights and HIV: HIV Prevention in UK Prisons – Needle Exchange Programmes*, Fact File 4.2. http://www.aidsrightsproject.org.uk/pdfs/FactFile4.2NEPs.pdf.

UK Drug Policy Commission (UKDPC) (2008) *Reducing Drug Use, Reducing Reoffending: Are Programmes for Problem Drug-Using Offenders in the UK supported by the Evidence*. London: UKDPC.

Werb, D., Kerr, T., Small, W., Li, K., Montaner, J. and Wood, E. (2008) 'HIV risks associated with incarceration among injection drug users: implications for prison-based public health strategies', *Journal of Public Health*, 30(2): 126–32.

West Yorkshire Police (2009) *Drugs and Offender Management Unit*. http://www.westyorkshire.police.uk/section-item.asp?sid=6&iid=4378 (accessed 10 September 2009).

Wilkinson, C., Hucklesby, A., Pearson, Y., Butler, E., Hill, A. and Hodkinson, S. (1998) 'A needs analysis of drug misuse in three Leicestershire prisons'. Unpublished report to HM Prison Service.

Wilkinson, C., Hucklesby, A., Pearson, Y., Butler, E., Hill, A. and Hodkinson, S. (2003) 'Management of drug-using prisoners in Leicestershire', in M. Ramsay (ed.) *Prisoners' Drug Use and Treatment: Seven Research Studies*, Home Office Research Study 267. London: Home Office.

Wincup, E. and Hucklesby, A. (2007) 'Researching and evaluating resettlement', in A. Hucklesby and L. Hagley-Dickinson (eds) *Prisoner Resettlement: Policy and Practice*. Cullompton: Willan Publishing.

World Health Organization (WHO) (2004) *World Health Organization, UNAIDS, UNODC Policy Brief: Reduction of HIV Transmission in Prisons*. Geneva: WHO. http://www.who.int/hiv/pub/advocacy/idupolicybriefs/en/.

World Health Organization (WHO) (2008a) *Policy Guidelines for Collaborative TB and HIV Services for Injecting and other Drug Users: An Integrated Approach*. Geneva: WHO.

World Health Organization (WHO) (2008b) *Status Paper on Prisons, Drugs and Harm Reduction*. Geneva: WHO. http://www.euro.who.int/document/e85877.pdf (accessed 24 October 2008).

Drug interventions in criminal justice: guide to further resources

This guide provides readers with suggestions for resources, many of which are available online. They present opportunities to find out more about specific issues identified in the preceding chapters and to keep abreast of new developments in policy and practice, emerging research findings and the latest statistics.

Government departments, agencies and advisory bodies

- **The Advisory Council on the Misuse of Drugs (ACMD)**
  http://drugs.homeoffice.gov.uk/drugs-laws/acmd/
  - The ACMD is an independent expert body that advises government on drug-related issues in the UK.
  - The Advisory Council makes recommendations to government on the control of dangerous or otherwise harmful drugs, including classification and scheduling under the Misuse of Drugs Act 1971 and its regulations. It considers any substance which is being or appears to be misused and which is having or appears to be capable of having harmful effects sufficient to cause a social problem.
  - It also carries out in-depth enquiries into aspects of drug use that are causing particular concern in the UK, with the aim of producing considered reports that will be helpful to policy-makers and practitioners.

- **Crown Prosecution Service** www.cps.gov.uk
  - Detailed guidance for Crown Prosecutors on the implementation of the government's Drug Interventions Programme, including the provisions of the Drugs Act 2005, testing on arrest, assessment and Restriction on Bail.
  - See in particular:
    - www.cps.gov.uk/legal/d_to_g/drug_intervention_programme
    - www.cps.gov.uk/legal/a_to_c/bail/#Toc170036744

- **Department of Health** www.dh.gov.uk
  - The website provides information on Offender Health, a partnership between the Ministry of Justice and the Department of Health working to improve the standard of health care for offenders. It

provides links to a variety of information and publications, including the implementation of the Integrated Drug Treatment System for Prisons.

o Under the 'Public Health' section of the website there is a subsection called 'Health Improvement' which contains a further link to a variety of resources relating to drug use, including:

■ facts and figures on drug treatment
■ the implementation of the treatment aspects of the drug strategy (2008–2018)
■ campaigns
■ treatment services and advice
■ prison and offender drug treatment
■ treatment guidelines and funding
■ official statistics and publications.

- **Home Office** www.drugs.homeoffice.gov.uk
  o A comprehensive guide to the government's drug strategy, including the Drug Interventions Programme (DIP) which aims to reduce crime and provide treatment and support to drug-using offenders. Also includes links to Home Office and other relevant publications on the progress of the DIP, operational guidance and relevant legislation.

- **Ministry of Justice** www.justice.gov.uk
  o Various policy documents, legislation and guidance relating to illegal drug use and the measures put in place to deal with drug use in the criminal justice process.
  o Includes links to numerous relevant publications, including reports by the Chief Inspector of Probation regarding the delivery of the Drug Interventions Programme.
  o Also includes the annual reports of the Correctional Services Accreditation Panel, whose main work is to accredit programmes for offenders which are designed to reduce reoffending, including programmes specifically for drug-using offenders.

- **National Offender Management Service (NOMS)** www.noms. homeoffice.gov.uk
  o Information and guidance on the management of offenders and reducing reoffending.
  o The 'Latest News' section of the website includes weekly new digests from the Criminal Justice Group within the Ministry of Justice of which NOMS forms part.
  o Drugs and Alcohol is one of the seven pathways within the *National Reducing Re-offending Action Plan* introduced by NOMS in 2004. Specific information about this pathway can be found at http://noms.

justice.gov.uk/managing-offenders/reducing_re-offending/
reducing_re-offending_pathways/drugs-alcohol.

- **National Treatment Agency for Substance Misuse (NTA)**
  www.nta.nhs.uk
  - ○ The NTA is a special health authority established by government
    in 2001 to improve the availability, capacity and effectiveness of
    treatment for drug misuse in England. It is responsible for moni-
    toring the performance of the drug treatment system in England.
    The website contains a wealth of information on the individual
    work areas of the NTA, with links to relevant information in Scot-
    land, Wales and Northern Ireland. It also contains statistical re-
    ports compiled by the National Drug Treatment Monitoring Sys-
    tem (NDTMS) and the National Drug Evidence Centre, both based
    at the University of Manchester (www.medicine.manchester.ac.uk/
    healthmethodology).

- **Police Service**
  - ○ Most individual police forces have developed their own drug strate-
    gies which include the implementation of the government's DIP
    in their particular geographical area. Further information can be
    found on force websites. For example, the Metropolitan Police Ser-
    vice drugs strategy (2007–2010) can be found at www.met.police.
    uk/drugs/publications/drugsstrategy.pdf.

- **HM Prison Service** www.hmprisonservice.gov.uk
  - ○ Contains a link to the Ministry of Justice website where the annual
    report of the National Offender Management Service can be found.
  - ○ A section aimed at families and friends of prisoners contains links
    to a number of addiction support groups including Addaction, Ad-
    fam, Lauren's Link, Narcotics Anonymous and Phoenix Futures. It
    also contains a link to the Prison Drug Treatment Strategy Review
    Group.
  - ○ The website also contains a 'Resource Centre' section which has
    links to a number of Prison Service reports and publications, in-
    cluding the *Prison Service Journal* and information on how to apply
    for Prison Service approval to conduct research within prisons.

- **Probation Service** www.probation.homeoffice.gov.uk
  - ○ Information and guidance for professionals and offenders regard-
    ing the Drug Rehabilitation Requirement of community orders and
    suspended sentences.

- **Youth Justice Board** www.yjb.gov.uk
  - ○ The Youth Justice Board for England and Wales (YJB) is an executive
    non-departmental public body which oversees the youth justice

system in England and Wales. It works to prevent offending and reoffending by children and young people under the age of 18.

- ○ The website contains information about the work of the YJB in providing drug workers to individual Youth Offending Teams and their Resettlement and Aftercare programme which provides ongoing treatment and support for substance use after young offenders are released. There is also information about an early intervention scheme run by the YJB which aims to prevent offending by focusing at an early stage on risk factors such as drug use.
- ○ It contains information about the Youth Rehabilitation Order which may include a drug treatment requirement.
- ○ The website also contains a 'Research' section which details the YJB's strategy and contains links to recent publications, including joint research projects with the National Offender Management Service.

- **UK Drug Policy Commission** www.ukdpc.org.uk
  - ○ An independent body providing objective analysis of UK drug policy since April 2007 with the aim of encouraging a wider and better-informed debate on drug policy.
  - ○ The website contains a link to the independent report published on the launch of the organization: *An Analysis of UK Drug Policy*. This is only one of a number of published reports that are available to download from the website, the latest of which is *Refocusing Drug-Related Law Enforcement to Address Harms* (2009).

- **Local Information**
  - ○ Information about local drug treatment, advice and support services can be found via local authority and city council websites. Information on the way in which national drug policies are being implemented at a local level via Crime Reduction/Crime and Disorder Partnerships is also available on their websites.

Policies and legislation

- ***Drugs: Protecting Families and Communities*** (HM Government, 2008)
  - ○ The government's most recent ten-year strategy for tackling drug use in England is available at www.drugs.homeoffice.gov.uk/publication-search/drug-strategy/drug-strategy-2008.
  - ○ Previous strategies, including the preceding ten-year strategy *Tackling Drugs to Build a Better Britain* (1998) are available at www.archive.official-documents.co.uk.

- *National Offender Management Service Drug Strategy 2008–2011*
  - This drug strategy provides staff, delivery partners, service providers and other stakeholders with an overview of the role of NOMS in addressing the link between drug use and crime.
  - The strategy and accompanying action plan are available via the Ministry of Justice website at www.justice.gov.uk/publications/noms-drug-strategy-2008-2011.htm.

- *The Road to Recovery: A New Approach to Tackling Scotland's Drug Problem* (2008)
  - The Scottish Government's national drug strategy focuses on recovery but also looks at prevention, treatment and rehabilitation, education, enforcement and protection of children. It is available at www.scotland.gov.uk/Publications/2008.

- *Working Together to Reduce Harm: The Substance Misuse Strategy for Wales 2008–2018*
  - The Welsh Assembly Government's ten-year substance misuse strategy which aims to set out a clear national agenda for tackling and reducing the harms associated with substance misuse in Wales is available at www.wales.gov.uk/topics/housingandcommunity/safety/publications.

- *New Strategic Direction for Alcohol and Drugs 2006–2011*
  - The Northern Ireland Executive published a five-year strategy in 2006 bringing together, for the first time, strategic thinking about alcohol and drugs. It is available at www.dhsspsni.gov.uk/nsdad-finalversion-may06.pdf.

- **Legislation**
  - Legislation such as the Misuse of Drugs Act 1971 and the Drugs Act 2005 can be found at www.opsi.gov.uk.

Statistics

- **Ministry of Justice** www.justice.gov.uk
  - Statistics, research papers and policy reports can be found in the 'Publications' section of the website.
  - The Ministry of Justice publishes a range of statistics on aspects of criminal justice policy, and on other areas of responsibility, including those designated as National Statistics (NS).

- **Home Office** www.homeoffice.gov.uk
  - ○ Responsibility for statistics on offending has transferred to the Ministry of Justice. However, the website for the Research Development and Statistics Directorate (RDS), a branch of the Home Office, contains a range of published research and statistics relating to drugs and offending and can be reached via the Home Office website or at www.homeoffice.gov.uk/rds. A full list of the types of research and statistics available can be found in the 'Publications' section of the website.

- **Department of Health** www.dh.gov.uk
  - ○ Under the 'Public Health' section of the website there is a subsection called 'Health Improvement' which contains a further link to a variety of resources relating to drug use, including UK Focal Point on drugs (www.ukfocalpoint.org.uk) which is based at the Department of Health and the North West Public Health Observatory at the Centre for Public Health, Liverpool John Moores University. The Focal Point collates data and information on the drug situation in the UK and reports it to the European Monitoring Centre on Drugs and Drug Addiction based in Lisbon. Further information is available on the UK Focal Point website.

- **National Drug Treatment Monitoring System (NDTMS)** www.ndtms.net/
  - ○ The NDTMS has nine regional centres across England, each of which is commissioned to collect, validate and process data.
  - ○ The NDTMS website provides links to data on:
    - ■ treatment waiting times (since 2006)
    - ■ monthly statistical reports based on data provided by the National Drug Evidence Centre based at the University of Manchester. The monthly reports include:
      - □ information on the number of clients in contact with drug treatment services
      - □ the proportion of clients retained in treatment for 12 weeks or more
      - □ compliance with national targets
    - ■ annual statistical bulletins and a detailed annual report of drug treatment activity in England. Data can be accessed through the Department of Health website at www.dh.gov.uk
    - ■ information on the current level of the drug treatment sector workforce and comparisons to historical information
    - ■ prevalence estimates (provided by the Home Office) of opiate use and/or crack cocaine use at regional and Drug Action Team area level.

Research

Research findings related to drug use are published in a wide range of journals covering different disciplines and on various websites, reflecting the multi-disciplinary base of drugs research as well as the dispersal of strategic and management responsibilities among government departments and agencies. Below is an indicative list of places where research and statistics related to drug use is often published: it is not exhaustive.

Journals
Addiction
Addiction Abstracts
Addiction Research and Theory
British Journal of Criminology
Criminal Justice Matters
Criminology and Criminal Justice
Drug and Alcohol Review
Drugs: Education, Prevention and Policy.
Harm Reduction Journal
Howard Journal of Criminal Justice
International Journal of Drug Policy
Journal of Alcohol and Drug Education
Journal of Criminal Law and Criminology
Journal of Drug Issues
Journal of Drug Policy Analysis
Journal of Public Health
Journal of Substance Misuse
Probation Journal

Websites
Relevant research publications and statistics can be found at the following:

- Centre of Drug Misuse Research (University of Glasgow): www.gla.ac.uk
- Centre for Research on Drugs and Health Behaviour based at the London School of Hygiene and Tropical Medicine: www.lshtm.ac.uk/crdhb
- Department of Health: www.dh.gov.uk
- Home Office Research and Statistics Directorate: www.homeoffice.gov.uk/rds
- Joseph Rowntree Foundation: www.jrf.org.uk
- Ministry of Justice: www.justice.gov.uk/publications/research
- National Treatment Agency for Substance Misuse (NTA): www.nta.nhs.uk
- Public Health Agency: www.healthpromotionagency.org.uk

Charities and voluntary organizations

- **Addaction** www.addaction.org.uk
  - The UK's largest drug and alcohol treatment charity. It provides free and confidential advice, information and support.

- **Compass** www.compass-uk.org/home/
  - Compass is a non-profit, non-government organization that provides services to people concerned with the health and social impact of illicit drug use. It is one of the leading providers of drug treatment services in the UK. The website contains information and advice on its services and case studies of those it has successfully helped.

- **Drugscope** www.drugscope.org.uk
  - The UK's leading independent centre of expertise on drugs. The aim of Drugscope is to inform policy development and reduce drug-related harms to individuals, families and communities. The website includes a database of drug services and a drugs encyclopaedia. A number of posters, help manuals and other publications can be purchased through the website, including a subscription to its own bi-monthly magazine *Druglink*. The website also includes a comprehensive resources section.

- **Nacro** www.nacro.org.uk
  - A crime reduction charity that focuses on providing services that assist ex-offenders to resettle into the community. The website does not refer specifically to drug-related programmes, but by searching the site using relevant terms a number of pertinent briefing papers relating to the link between drug use and offending can be found, particularly in relation to youth offending. Nacro has also published a policy report entitled *Drugs and Crime: From Warfare to Welfare* which can be purchased via the website.

- **Release** www.release.org.uk
  - The national centre of expertise on drugs and drugs law. It provides free and confidential specialist advice to both the public and professionals. It campaigns for changes to drug policy and focuses on reducing the suffering caused by drugs, advising the socially excluded, and promoting debate based on research, health and human rights.
  - Services include a legal and drugs telephone/email helpline and comprehensive information regarding relevant drugs legislation.

- **Transform Drug Policy Foundation** www.tdpf.org.uk
  - ○ A charitable organization that campaigns for the control and regulation of drugs rather than their prohibition.
  - ○ The website has a large amount of material relating to the work of Transform, including a number of its own published reports and a section on relevant parliamentary debates, policies and key publications. It also has links to a wide variety of other relevant organizations, including European and other international drugs organizations and human rights/civil liberties organizations.

- **Turning Point** www.turning-point.co.uk
  - ○ The UK's leading social care organization which provides specialist services for those affected by various problems including drug misuse. The website contains a variety of information on the services it provides.

- **UK Harm Reduction Alliance (UKHRA)** www.ukhra.org/
  - ○ A campaigning coalition of drug users, health and social care workers, criminal justice workers and educationalists that aims to put public health and human rights at the centre of drug treatment and service provision for drug users.
  - ○ The website provides a number of discussion forums for those interested in harm reduction policy and practice, including forums dedicated to women, needle exchange and young people.

- **Drug treatment**
  - ○ A directory of drug rehabilitation and treatments centres can be found at www.uk-rehab.com.

Training

- **Society for the Study of Addiction** www.addiction-ssa.org
  - ○ The aim of the society is to promote the scientific understanding of addiction and the problems associated with it and to inform policy and practice. The website includes a list of accredited training courses relating to addiction and counselling and links to its own journal *Addiction* published by Blackwells.

International websites

International websites are too numerous for us to provide details here. However, two websites of particular relevance to the contents of the book are:

- **Drug Courts in the USA** www.whitehousedrugpolicy.gov
  - This website is for the US Office of National Drug Control Policy and includes links to publications regarding the effectiveness of drug courts and other 'problem solving courts' in the USA.

- **The QCT Europe Project** www.kent.ac.uk/eiss/projects/qcteurope/index.html
  - Coordinated by the European Institute of Social Services, University of Kent, England.
  - The project aimed to create a European evidence base on quasi-compulsory and compulsory approaches to drug treatment for drug-dependent offenders.
  - The website provides detailed information about the study and its outcomes, including links to papers and publications arising from the study.

Further reading

There is a growing literature on drugs. The following texts are particularly recommended. All are published in the UK.

On drugs generally

Barton, A. (2003) *Illicit Drugs: Use and Control*. London: Routledge. The book illuminates the complexity and diversity of illicit drug use through tracing the historical development of the drug 'problem'.

South, N. (ed.) (1999) *Drugs: Cultures, Control and Everyday Life*. London: Sage. This interdisciplinary compilation of essays aims to offer a foundation for a new approach to drugs and drug use for the twenty-first century.

On drugs and crime

Bean, P. (2008) *Drugs and Crime*. Cullompton: Willan Publishing. Now in its third edition, this book aspires to provide an authoritative overview of the range of issues associated with drugs and crime, with a particular focus on reducing supply.

Bennett, T. and Holloway, K. (2005) *Understanding Drugs, Alcohol and Crime*. Buckingham: Open University Press. This textbook provides a succinct overview of current theory and research on the links between drugs, alcohol and crime.

Bennett, T. and Holloway, K. (2007) *Drug–Crime Connections*. Cambridge: Cambridge University Press. Drawing upon extensive research with arrestees, this volume argues against the assumption that there is a widespread association between drug use and crime and identifies a number of highly specific connections.

Hammersley, R. (2008) *Drugs and Crime*. Cambridge: Polity Press. Challenging simplistic and misguided thinking about drugs and crime, this text argues that the relationship between drugs and crime needs to be examined in its complex social and psychological context.

On responses to the drug 'problem'

Holloway, K., Bennett, T. and Farrington, D. (2005) *The Effectiveness of Criminal Justice and Treatment Programmes in Reducing Drug-Related Crime: A Systematic Review*, Home Office Online Report 26/05. London: Home Office. http://www.homeoffice.gov.uk/rds/pdfs05/rdsolr2605.pdf. This review comprises a summary of the research literature on the effectiveness of interventions aimed at reducing criminal behaviour among drug users

Hough. M. (1996) *Drug Misuse and the Criminal Justice System*, Drug Prevention Initiative Paper 15. London: Home Office. This oft-cited literature review explores the links between drug use and crime and ways within the criminal justice system to reduce the demand for illegal drugs among dependent drug users and others who fund their drug use through crime.

Simpson, M., Shildrick, T. and MacDonald, R. (eds) (2007) *Drugs in Britain: Supply, Consumption and Control*. Basingstoke: Palgrave Macmillan. This edited collection explores the distribution and consumption of illicit drugs and debates surrounding the policing of drugs and the care and control of drug users.

On drug treatment

Bean, P. and Nemitz, T. (eds) (2004) *Drug Treatment: What Works?* London: Routledge. Edited by two criminologists, this book provides a series of chapters written by academics, policy makers and practitioners, all concerned with the effectiveness of drug treatment.

MacGregor, S. (ed.) (2009) *Responding to Drug Misuse: Research and Policy Priorities in Health and Social Care*. London: Routledge. The edited volume brings together the findings from research on the progress of the government's strategic thinking about drugs and places them in the context of policy, practice and service development.

Index